TWO EGGS ON MY PLATE

This edition, issued in 1954, is for members of the Companion Book Club, 29-30 Bedford Street, London, W.C.2, from which address particulars of membership may be obtained. The book is published by arrangement with the original publishers, George Allen and Unwin Ltd.

"A blessed companion is a book"—JERROLD

TWO EGGS ON MY PLATE

*

OLUF REED OLSEN

TRANSLATED
FROM THE NORWEGIAN
BY
F. H. LYON

THE COMPANION BOOK CLUB
LONDON

TO
CARL SIGURD ELLIGERS

Made and printed in Great Britain
for The Companion Book Club (Odhams Press Ltd.)
by Odhams (Watford) Limited,
Watford, Herts.
T.254.ZQ.

CONTENTS

ILLUSTRATIONS

MAPS

ILLUSTRATIONS

CHAPTER I

APRIL 1940

THIS story begins soon after April 9, 1940. The German invasion of Norway was in full swing. Oslo, Kristiansand, Stavanger, Bergen and Trondheim were all occupied by the enemy, while fighting was still going on in the interior of the country. The greater part of the population of Norway were still paralysed with amazement at what was happening outside their own door.

I, too, undoubtedly belonged to the large percentage who were completely bewildered, and as a lad of twenty-one with no previous military training I did not at all understand the seriousness of what was taking place. But I was not alone. With a good friend of mine, Kaare Moe from Bestum, I tried to get a clearer idea of what we ought to do, and where (if we decided to do so) we could report for duty. We asked an officer cadet in the Army whom we met on the morning of the 9th down at the East Station, but like hundreds of others received a negative answer: 'Just go home, resistance is useless!'

The rebuff we had received from a military officer had undoubtedly been influenced by enemy instructions, and the same evening we laid our plans for a fairly long trip to the north. These plans, however, were not carried out, for other friends gave us an account of conditions at Hvalsmoen, where we had thought of reporting. The whole region was being bombed by the Germans, and evidently the same confusion prevailed there as at most other places fairly far south. Moreover, we came into contact with a British captain who was then working for the secret British intelligence system in Oslo. After more intimate conversations with 'the captain' we were requested not to carry out the plans we had made for a journey to northern Norway through Sweden, but to report for service with him instead.

Our first jobs were small ones, but nevertheless our greatest wish was fulfilled—to be able to do our duty as Norwegians.

Photographing and sketching German airfields, and mapping them; the same for German defence works and military positions and installations; also, finding out about German troop movements, what kind of troops were concerned, to what units the German troops who passed through Oslo belonged, where they came from and where they were going—this was work which often led to exciting minor incidents which suited our then fairly modest demands. But at that time our more or less impressive achievements were inspired by a thirst for adventure; the whole business was a manifestation of sporting enthusiasm.

It was while fighting was going on a little way outside Oslo that we were given our first sabotage job. Small parties of Norwegian volunteers were fighting a hard battle against German motorized detachments; the enemy was far superior in both numbers and material. One of these small parties sent out a runner on skis through the German positions. He arrived early one morning with the following information: the Norwegian forces about Skaret and the road along the Tyri Fjord could not hold out much longer. At all costs supplies for the German forces along the roads from Oslo, and along the Drammen road via Lysaker and Sandvika, must be cut off so that the Norwegian troops could prepare fresh positions to the northward, along the road via Sundvollen. Four bridges were to be blown up—one on the road from Drammen to Hönefoss via Skaret, both bridges at Sandvika and the bridge over the Lysaker river at Lysaker. The last bridge was our job. All were to be blown up at four next morning precisely, so there was not much time.

Neither Kaare nor I had the least idea of how a bridge should be blown up. Certainly the man from whom we got our orders knew that we had handled dynamite before, when clearing the ground where our scout hut stood. We knew how a charge was fired with fuse, percussion cap and ordinary dynamite, but from that point to the successful blowing up of a bridge was a long step. How much dynamite was wanted and how should it be placed? Clearly we had not the smallest qualification for undertaking the job. But there was no time for talking; the job must be done, whether we got others to carry out the actual blowing up or had to do the best we could by ourselves.

As it was, we knew no one else who could be warned in so short a time. We must do the blowing up ourselves, and our plans were laid. I had a stock of dynamite, stolen two days before from different establishments in the neighbourhood with the object of making hand grenades.

Another man must be got, however, and it was not difficult to find people who would be glad to have a hand in it. But the difficulty at that time was to find a man who could hold his tongue, who could control the desire which, especially in those days, was a common failing of practically the whole Norwegian population—the desire to make oneself popular with others after having oneself taken part in some exciting incident.

There was another factor, too, to be considered. Among the friends we consorted with daily nearly all were eager to make a contribution to the fight in progress. Discussion and fantastic plans were first on the daily programme. The greatest mistake here was that every action was planned on private initiative, which could as easily hurt our own side as the Germans: often, indeed, more. We therefore made it our guiding principle from the very beginning that no one but ourselves should know that we were working for a particular organization, irrespective of how many helpers we were obliged to recruit for the various tasks.

Kaare's brother Leif became our third man for this special job. The afternoon was used for a short reconnaissance of Lysaker bridge and its surroundings. The bridge was probably being watched, but no regular sentry was to be seen. For ten minutes we stood hanging over the parapet, while a quantity of motorized material passed over the bridge in long convoys. To our great disappointment we perceived that the middle pier, which we had thought of 'moving' a bit, was enclosed in timber from below the surface of the water up to the top, where the three main beams of the bridge rested. This was a serious check to our plans, as it was obvious that we could not begin to strip off a board covering in the middle of the night to reach the most effective places between the large stones of which the pier was built. It would make too much noise. Round the pier of the bridge, however, down close to the water's edge, there was a wide projection, probably intended for reinforcement. By means of a ladder about twelve feet long, let down on a rope and leaning against the pier itself, it would be possible to get down under the bridge in relatively few seconds. When we had got so far, the possibility of blowing it up fairly effectively would have to be more closely investigated.

The evening was spent in further preparations. The dynamite was packed in four separate parcels, sixteen pounds in each; each parcel was fitted with a double fuse twenty feet long and a powerful charge with two percussion caps on the end of each fuse. A twenty-foot fuse would give us about a quarter of an hour to get away in according to the calculations we had made with the material we had in stock—if everything went according to plan.

At one o'clock that morning a rather curious silent procession went down the Vekkerö road, and turned off towards Lysaker bridge: Leif with a light ten-foot ladder over his shoulder, Kaare with a pack containing thirty-four pounds of dynamite, and myself with a similar parcel containing dynamite, fuses and percussion caps.

There were not many people out so late, but every time someone approached us we had to fling ourselves into the ditch for a few minutes and lie quite still till he had passed.

About a hundred yards from the bridge we stopped, took off our loads and went on under cover of some bushes and trees. Some fifteen yards from our goal we lay still, watching the silhouette of the bridge. Now and again a German car passed, but otherwise the neighbourhood seemed quite deserted. We lay there for a good half-hour. Then the now familiar sound of a pair of iron-tipped boots rang through the silence of the night. The steps came from the Drammen road itself, from Oslo towards the bridge. We lay as silent as mice; stared till our eyes nearly left their sockets, and listened. The light shone on two helmets—two German sentries stood out in silhouette against the night sky as they passed over the bridge. I stole cautiously after them in rubber shoes, only to ascertain in the next five minutes that the Germans had a larger area to patrol than the immediate neighbourhood of the bridge—they went on up through Lysaker itself.

Minutes passed while we lay waiting for the sentries to come back, so that we could roughly time their round and get an idea of for how long at a time we should be able to work in peace.

The plan was repeated in whispers for the last time: every man knew exactly what was to happen—and every man knew exactly what a mistake meant both for our task and himself. The bridge must be blown up at all costs. Leif's task was to keep a look-out from a place fixed in advance, while Kaare and I did the work under the bridge. If the sentries discovered anything while we were arranging the fireworks display, it would be up to Lief to make us knock off. At sixteen minutes to four Lief was to leave his post and go home as quickly as he could by a roundabout route.

Time passed. The sentries crossed the bridge; five minutes past three! Forty minutes to do it in! A pressure of Lief's hand, a last check-up of the revolvers, and Kaare and I crept noiselessly towards the bridge with the dynamite on our backs and the ladder between us. At that moment the sound of a car engine broke the silence of the night and forced us to lie flat in the ditch for a few seconds. A German lorry passed with troops on board, and the road was clear again. We reached the middle of the bridge, the ladder was cautiously lowered over the parapet, and the rope which held it was made fast with a slippery hitch. Kaare climbed over and down on to the pier of the bridge; I followed, and the rope was jerked loose from the parapet. We stood side by side under the bridge and listened—all was still.

Kaare whispered a joke in my ear—which none but he could have done at such a moment! 'Shut up!' I whispered back, 'or I'll set a match to the dynamite when you've got it!' Even though the dark made the smile on Kaare's lips invisible, I could distinctly feel it. I was to learn in the following months that Kaare's special sense of humour came to the fore at just such moments.

We continued our preparations in silence. The ladder was moved under the bridge and set up against the centre of the pier. Kaare held it while I climbed up to find the best places to put the charges. It soon became clear that it was impossible to use four different places. Instead of blowing the whole pier to bits, as we had originally intended to do, we should have to content ourselves with shattering the roadway and hoping for as much other damage as possible.

Our reflections were suddenly interrupted. Steps! The two German sentries. We remained motionless. Kaare hung on to the ladder with both hands while I clung to the top of it. Two pairs of iron-tipped boots resounded on the road above us, grew louder—and died away again.

We had twenty minutes left when something happened which almost took our breath away. A car came from the Lysaker side, drew nearer and stopped in the middle of the bridge right over our heads! Orders and loud talk reached us, standing on tenterhooks below. I felt a slight trembling of the ladder, perhaps from my own trembling legs, perhaps from Kaare's convulsive grip. It was a German car!

We did not understand all that was said, but so much was clear: someone had been discovered trying to blow up the Sandvika bridges farther out along the Drammen road, and now orders had been given to reinforce the guard at the Lysaker bridge by two men! An extra close watch must be kept! ... The car started again and disappeared in the direction of Oslo.

Now there were four men on the bridge. They talked together in low voices as they went over towards one parapet. For a few breathless seconds they stood discussing the possibility of the bridge being effectively blown up; then they moved on again, and this time their steps died away towards Lysaker. It did not sound as if they took their task too seriously, nor the attempt to blow up the Sandvika bridges. But what were their plans?

I glanced at the illuminated face of my wrist-watch: a quarter to four! The sweat ran down me as I worked feverishly; the whole charge under the central beam, the fuse down—and I after it. We had not a second to lose: the Germans might be expected back at any moment! An old raincoat served as a screen while I lighted the fuses. Meanwhile Kaare had set up the ladder against the outside of the pier, and it took him a fraction of a second to clamber up, stick his head over the edge and report that all was clear. A moment later we were both on the bridge; we left the ladder where it was and made off as quickly as we could up towards the Vekkerö road. For the first hundred yards we went in silence, but after that the only consideration was speed.

Fourteen minutes later we stopped, panting, and listened. Not a sound! Fifteen minutes—still as quiet as the grave! Kaare turned quickly to me and said: 'You don't say we've got to do it again?'

I could not even open my mouth to reply before the roar from Lysaker shattered the air round us! One handshake and Kaare disappeared up towards the Baerum road, I homewards towards Montebello.

We had our knuckles rapped next morning in the Oslo wireless news bulletin. Quisling, in those days the pillar of the law, peace and order, made a speech of 'admonition' to the Norwegian people! He said among other things that in the course of the night there had been a regrettable case of sabotage and attempts at sabotage elsewhere. Fortunately these attempts had been frustrated at the last moment, and the malefactors had been caught and taken into custody by the German police. On the other hand, a bridge in the Oslo area had been partly destroyed, but the police were hot on the track and expected an arrest in the course of the day.

At nine o'clock the telephone rang. It was Kaare. Had I heard the fearful explosion in the night and did I know that someone had tried to blow up the Lysaker bridge? . . . No, I hadn't heard anything—I was a sound sleeper. . . . Yes, his brother Lief had just heard it from another friend who had been down and had a look at the bridge, so there must be something in it!

At ten o'clock I was up at Kaare's and we two and Lief

joined the many curious Sunday walkers who had collected round Lysaker. The bridge itself was closed to all traffic, but unfortunately, as far as we could see, it was not completely destroyed. Still, the damage was enough to stop the transport which was to leave Oslo the same morning with reinforcements for the troops which were engaged in the country round Skaret-Hönefoss, and to delay it for a day and half, so that the pressure on our Norwegian troops in those parts would be considerably reduced.

How the police (according to Quisling) had got on the track remained for the present an unsolved problem to us and to the other walkers. Their house-to-house searches, which were still going on while we were looking at the bridge, were without result; so were a number of random arrests. As far as we were concerned, it was only regrettable that the plan had not been carried out in its entirety, as the breaking of a single link was thus rendered less valuable. On Sunday afternoon, when we reported to 'the captain,' we learned of the German proposal to shoot twenty Norwegians as a reprisal for what had happened. But happily this was not carried out.

The German higher command soon took over the few anti-aircraft positions the Norwegian army had had around Oslo, and developed them on a large scale. Among these positions was Björnebo, near Smestad, about two miles west of Oslo. The most modern anti-aircraft guns and heavy machine-guns, listening apparatus and searchlights now replaced our old anti-aircraft machine-guns. Björnebo now became, in the earliest period, the strongest anti-aircraft battery near Oslo, and it was of great importance during the British bombing attacks on Fornebu airfield that summer.

After a short time a new German heavy machine-gun was brought into action at Björnebo, and among our many tasks we were asked one day if we could obtain detailed information about it, with photographs or sketches.

British bombers had for three nights plastered Fornebu airfield with good results, and the German crews of the various batteries in the inner Oslo fjord had had a pretty hard time. The gun positions at Björnebo had at that time no barbed-wire obstacles of any size, so it was possible for a Norwegian civilian to get quite near the guns in daytime. The heavy machine-gun in question had been sited a little way from the main battery, and stood alone on a small hillock. After a close reconnaissance of the place I went up to the gun at a time when all the guards but two had gone down to the camp for dinner. When I came loafing up to the position, one of the guards was busy greasing the machine-gun, while the other was packing ammunition boxes and evidently getting everything ready for the next night's visit. I sauntered up to the gun as indifferently as I could, saluted the guard with one hand raised to my hat and opened a conversation by asking for a match. At the same time I offered the German a cigarette. He was a man of about thirty, small and thickset with rough hands, presumably a peasant or workman. At first he seemed little inclined to talk, but when he had accepted the cigarette and lighted it, his tongue began to wag. We talked about the weather; I told him that I was a land-worker, that my sympathies were entirely pro-German, that I hated the English and was much impressed by the invincible German war machine. He talked about himself, his wife and three children on a small farm outside Bremen, his faith in Hitler and the coming New Order in Europe, etc. etc.

After a while I sat down beside the gun. He cleaned, greased and chatted, and I looked on and now and then interjected some intelligent remark. We had been using the second person singular for a long time, and after a bare half-hour we were talking as if we had been old school friends. The conversation gradually shifted to some unflattering observations on our common enemy, the English tyrants, then to the bombing raids of the last three days, and now I had the chance of getting in a few remarks about the working of 'the fantastic German air defence with its magnificent guns!' 'But how in the world can a machine-gun like that fire with such tremendous velocity?' I put the question with blind admiration, and it was with pride that the guard described and showed me every single detail—working, measurements and improvements effected on his wonderful weapon. Repeatedly during the demonstration I raised my hat and rubbed my forehead with the back of my hand, coughed and put my hat on again. Inside the hat, fixed firmly in the lining, was a small camera, a strip of film, focused at six feet six inches, a little adapter for longer distances, an automatic winder, and the lens just visible through a small hole in the crown of the hat. The coughing coincided with the taking of each photograph, to prevent the proud demonstrator from hearing suspicious noises.

An exact description and a series of splendid photographs of the heavy machine-gun under discussion, thanks to a chance German private. We parted as eternal friends, with a cordial '*Auf Wiedersehen,*' and with a German cigarette in the corner of my mouth I sauntered home to write my report and develop the photographs.

CHAPTER II

A VISIT TO FORNEBU

BUT our tasks could not always be executed in so simple and painless a manner.

One night at the beginning of July, Kaare Moe and I were lying on our stomachs in a patch of wood at the edge of the north-western corner of Fornebu airfield. At that time it was surrounded by a fence nearly ten feet high, with four rows of barbed wire on the top, and at regular intervals along this fence hung placards: 'Photographing most strictly forbidden!' Sentries patrolling the fence all round the airfield made it difficult to get in, but it was still a relatively easy matter to take general views of the airfield from outside.

The task which was to be carried out that night was, in short, as follows: to photograph the site of the ammunition and bomb dump, and sketch it with explanatory details. The plan was to be executed as follows: Almost every night British planes bombed the airfield, and, we had learned by reconnaissance, most of the German sentries and all the other personnel disappeared from their posts and sat in safety in the shelters for the duration of the attack, allowing free access to anyone who could get over or under the fence.

There was just one small detail to which any normal person would undoubtedly react—the bombs which the British planes dropped! But that was a chance which had to be taken. Our plan was to get under the fence, get as near the bomb and ammunition dump as possible, find a suitable place to lie till daylight came, make our sketches, take the photographs and then get out as best we could.

Our operation must begin at the same time as the British bombing.

For the last time every detail was gone through in whispers. But each time the German sentry passed we lay quite still, noting the time he took on his round. It was eight minutes on an average, which would give us about five minutes in which to do our work, once daylight came.

At seven minutes to twelve the raid warning was sounded. From where we lay we could hear high-pitched orders at the hangars, while the shadows of two sentries hurriedly disappeared along the fence towards the shelters a little way off in the wood. At the same moment there came from the north-west the steadily increasing drone of bombers.

The moment for action was near. The anti-aircraft defences had long ago opened their deafening concert; heavy anti-aircraft guns, heavy and light machine-guns in a few seconds transformed the clear starry night sky into a sparkling fireworks display, and the ground literally trembled where we lay. The aircraft were now almost overhead; then down came the first parachute flares. Next moment the whole airfield was flooded with light. An ear-splitting crash; we were flung head over heels: another—and yet another! The earth trembled and shook beneath us, and earth and stones began to rain down upon us where we lay under some bushes with our hands over our heads.

The first attack was over, and to judge from the sound the planes were now turning in towards Oslo. The moment had come!

Two Junker 52's had caught fire close to the longest runway, and a few Germans were already on their way to try to put the fire out. *'Now!'* We made at top speed for the chosen point in the fence. A ditch had been dug from the ammunition dump through a light copse which concealed it, over an open space and out under the fence. The ditch was half full of water, and our cameras came near getting wet when with a splash we finished up in it side by side.

We were under cover now, and our way on from this point was relatively simple. It did not take us long to cut through the barbed wire in the ditch under the fence, allowing for the risk of there being an alarm system. Once through the hole, we arranged the wire as best we could, and went on along the ditch towards the ammunition dump, half-creeping, half-walking.

Meanwhile the bombers had come round again for a new attack. To judge from the sound there were four of them. They had now evidently changed their tactics, for one plane, presumably that which had dropped its bombs first, had gone up to a good height, flown into the beam of light from one of the searchlights (about twenty) in operation, and, directly it was spotted, attracted everyone's attention. Everything that could shoot was in action and the noise was ear-splitting. But the aircraft obviously was not troubled; it suddenly made a turn to starboard and was gone. The searchlights worked feverishly, till suddenly a light flashing a series of V's could be seen against the black night sky a little way off. Again all the searchlights were turned on the one plane, and wild firing continued.

All this time we squatted, watching the lavish spectacle. Then all of a sudden came a terrific crash; plane, searchlights, guns, all were gone from me, drowned by a furious ringing and roaring inside my head. I felt myself flung against something—then everything went black.

I cannot say with certainty whether I was unconscious for seconds or minutes. I came to myself with a curious feeling that something wet was running steadily down my face. Cautiously I opened my eyes. I was lying with my head half under water at the bottom of the ditch, with something heavy and wet half-way across me. I thought at first that I was dreaming, and shut my eyes to get back to reality. But no, it was no dream! The heavy wet object which lay across me in a twisted posture began to stir gradually: it was Kaare. 'The devils!' were the first words he spat from his mouth, along with earth and stones. 'If they have to drop bombs just where we're doing a job, they don't positively need to aim at us!' I agreed entirely; but was too busy feeling to see if I was still intact, and if the camera was dry, to be able to give an acceptable answer.

We cautiously stuck our heads over the edge of the ditch. There, barely twenty-five yards from where we lay, and about forty yards from the ammunition dump, were six gaping craters more or less in a straight line over towards the hangars!

We had now come so close to the ammunition dump that according to our plan we were to separate. One of us was to remain in the ditch, to take photographs of the dump which would clearly show its position in relation to the larger part of the airfield. The other was to try to reach a point south-west of the dump and take photographs of it at 315 degrees true, so that the position of the dump in relation to the central building and the hangars was clearly shown. In this way crossbearings on the ammunition dump would be obtained, and it could subsequently be pin-pointed on the map. We had tossed up in advance to decide who should carry out the last part of the task, which was undoubtedly the worst because the distance back was nearly twice as far. The lot had fallen on Kaare.

Our watches were now synchronized for the last time: a handshake, a glance over the edge to see if all was clear, and Kaare vanished into the darkness. The illuminated face of my wrist-watch showed four minutes past one.

Hardly three minutes after Kaare had disappeared the British bombers came in for a new attack. This time I laid myself flat against the edge of the ditch with both arms well over my head and my jacket pulled well up. Four more deafening crashes, but this time not nearly so loud as in the previous attack. Almost at the same time came a series of lesser reports, and when, after a moment to steady my nerves, I peeped cautiously over the edge of the ditch, I could not prevent myself from exclaiming 'Good work!' If no one else heard it, it was an expression of silent admiration for the crews of the aircraft high up in the night sky. The four bombs had made hits right across the longest runway and, what was still better, a stick of incendiary bombs had set on fire a whole row of aircraft in the northern corner of the airfield! It was like broad daylight over there, and yelling Germans were busy trying to put the fires out. A brilliant spectacle—so brilliant that for a few minutes I quite forgot our own rather dangerous position.

This was the last attack that night. The anti-aircraft fire died away, and the planes disappeared in a south-westerly direction. The minutes crept away, and all was relatively quiet again. Only shouted orders and loud cursing from the Germans who were putting out the fires, and occasional explosions from the burning planes, reached the spot where I lay. The sentry guarding the fence had resumed his patrol, and about every eighth minute he passed the hole we had made in the wire.

The first hour went fairly quickly; so long as the planes were burning there was entertainment. I had got pretty wet from the rather rough treatment we had received during the attack, and my legs, which had to be under water all the time, had gone to sleep long before. The minutes crept past. I had to stop looking at my watch; it seemed to want oiling very badly—I had never thought a watch could go so slowly. I began instead to calculate the time by the regular passing of the sentry. At last he too seemed to have fallen asleep, and I thought for a moment of following his example. It was nearly three, and the sky in the east had long begun to assume a rather lighter hue; day was about to break. But it was chilly, and I was horribly cold. For the hundredth and I don't know how many times, I pulled my sleeve up a little and looked at my watch. Five past three! Still fifty-five long minutes to wait before we could go into action!

The sentry had just passed the hole, and as usual I raised

myself high enough above the edge of the ditch to be able to have a look round and see that all was in order. . . . There! I remained motionless and held my breath! Two tractors with bomb trailers behind them, and with nine men in all, came driving towards the ammunition dump! I hardly dared breathe; cold and numbed feet were forgotten in a second. Which entrance would they use? The south, where Kaare lay, or the north, where I lay? Yard by yard they approached the fork where the road divided to go to the two entrances. North! I sank back into the ditch when the first tractor swung towards me, pulling the fresh leafy twigs we had brought for camouflage well over my head. The tractors passed the spot where I lay at a distance of about four yards. The conversation between the four men on one tractor and the five on the other could be heard plainly; they were talking about the night's bombing. It was with some relief that I heard them stop in front of the entrance to the ammunition dump. So far everything had gone well. But this was a thing we had overlooked in our otherwise so meticulous plans—that planes should be loaded up with bombs so soon after the night's attack.

How long would the Germans stay in the dump? Would all nine Germans leave the place as soon as they had done the necessary loading up, or was this the start of a prolonged spell of work? Had Kaare seen them come, and had he counted how many men there were, so that he could, as arranged, return to the ditch where I lay when his photographing was finished, without being detected by some straggler? A string of questions raced at high speed through my brain. Only time would answer them. I lay listening, still motionless. The northern entrance to the ammunition dump was just opposite, and the slightest movement would be enough. If earlier minutes had seemed like hours, seconds now became still longer. I lay with my arm in front of me so that I could follow the course of the minute-hand on the dial. A quarter past three—half past three—twenty-five minutes to four—twenty minutes to four—eighteen minutes to four, and then! First one tractor, and close behind it the other, came slowly towards me. Past! I lifted my head inch by inch with my eyes fixed on the northern descent to the ammunition dump. Not a soul to be seen!

As carefully I raised my head, covered with foliage, just above the edge of the ditch. One—two—three—yes, nine Germans in all were on the two tractors which had disappeared with their cargoes of explosives towards the upper part of the airfield.

The way was now clear for the time being—only the regular passing of the sentry demanded attention. The time was very nearly four. Day had come, and in the east the sky was flaming red. Fires were still burning among the aircraft over by the runway, and dense smoke was still pouring up.

Six minutes to four; the sentry passed for the last time before being relieved. The moment for action had come at last. I rose cautiously and examined my surroundings with care. Not a German to be seen nearer than the hangars, only the back of the sentry who was slowly moving off and disappearing behind some trees. One—two—three photographs, all with different exposures to get as good a result as possible. Then I crawled on my stomach over the edge of the ditch into the grass, with my compass in my hand and the camera in the other. I was to take a few photographs of the dump at 225 degrees true, just as I had done with the greater part of the south-western section of the airfield. The direction coincided most fortunately with a big raspberry bush, and in the shelter of this the remaining photographs were taken. Back on my stomach to the ditch, and this part of the job was completed without misadventure as far as I was concerned. It was now three minutes past four. I cautiously took up the same position as before, with leaves and twigs over my head, and did some sketching.

But how was Kaare getting on? It had been agreed that he should take photographs at the same time, assuming the coast was clear, and then wait twenty minutes at the spot where he was lying. We calculated that the new sentry who began his patrol a little after four would keep a specially sharp look-out, particularly on his first two rounds, and then slack off a bit after having confirmed that there was nothing suspicious within his area. I remained lying quite still and looking at my watch. The sentry came—and passed. Exactly seven minutes past four. I followed the minute-hand, anxious to see how long he was taking. Nine minutes—there he came again, and passed. Sixteen minutes past four. Four minutes more, and Kaare would begin to crawl. . . . Twenty past four! Kaare had started on his difficult journey back to the ditch. . . . The sentry passed again; this time he had taken ten minutes. Good fellow, the new sentry! Again he passed, this time on his way down towards the place where Kaare was toiling up to the ditch. Tense minutes followed, and I listened with strained ears. Suddenly a cracking noise broke the silence—a sound like the breaking of a dry twig. The sound undoubtedly came from the direction in which Kaare now ought to be. I grew hot where I lay. The sentry should have passed long since on his upward journey; a quarter of an hour had gone since he last came by. Had he heard what I heard, become suspicious and gone into the scrub to investigate? I was just going to rise to have a closer look, when the heavy dragging step of a sleepy sentry broke the silence. Thank God—not this time!

The sentry passed. Four minutes later Kaare slid cautiously down the side of the ditch, smiling all over his face, but as black as a sweep! A silent pressure of the hand, and we both sank down motionless, with the foliage over our heads. The sentry passed—and now for the way out under the fence. About ten minutes to do it in. We moved along in the ditch cautiously on our hands and knees; the barbed wire was pushed aside—through—barbed wire replaced as far as possible—on in the ditch across the open area and into the woods.

After nine minutes we stopped. The sentry must not hear anything suspicious now that the worst of the job was over. We waited for five minutes, and then continued into thicker wood and across the main road into Oslo, where our bicycles were hidden. There I heard Kaare's story of his hours of waiting and the journey back on his stomach. It was in the last stage things had nearly gone wrong. Kaare had without noticing it laid his arm on a dry twig, which snapped when the sentry was on his way down and close by. The man had undoubtedly heard the noise of the breaking twig; he had stopped and stood for a few seconds staring in through the fence.

CHAPTER III

A NEW JOB AT FORNEBU

THE following days were devoted to the less eventful work of watching German troop movements through Oslo and the surrounding district, and it must have been a week before another job made us renew our acquaintance with Fornebu airfield.

A Heinkel 111 had the same day turned a somersault down the slope of the north-south landing runway. It was the interior of the aircraft that was of interest—the direction-finding apparatus and its fittings, a new type of wireless compass with which the Heinkel was believed to be equipped, and the lay-out of the pilot's cockpit in general. This—with the taking of several more photographs of the airfield—was the occasion for a fresh visit, which unfortunately did not have the happy ending our first had enjoyed.

The idea of utilizing the chaos caused by a possible British bombing raid on the airfield was this time rejected. The chances of our being killed were too great in proportion to the result which could be achieved. Moreover, the possibility of an attack that night was very small, as the weather was very bad and a strong wind was blowing.

In daylight the same afternoon I made a little survey of the area round the coming field of operations. The survey was made quite simply and openly along the road which ran close to the fence on this side of the airfield, on a Sarolea 500 cc. motor-cycle with a plate marked 'Oslo police' in front of the lamp. At the beginning of my work for the secret British intelligence service I had discovered that with a motor-cycle such as I then possessed I could get about pretty quickly, especially if a plate marked 'Oslo police' was attached to the machine. I answered a newspaper appeal to the civilian population to join the civilian fire and A.R.P. service, the motor-cycle was registered and given a police plate stamped by the German police office. I received a special pass and was appointed section leader at Furulund Fire Station, and now had the opportunity of driving about freely, both inside and outside a series of military barriers. The limitations of the position were gradually extended according to my needs. Petrol came from my own store, stolen from Wideröes aircraft base on the Bogstad lake after it had been seized by the Germans.

Our plan was made the same evening. Under cover of darkness we were to climb over the fence at the northern corner of the airfield, where the road ran close by and the woods extended right down to the road, reach the Heinkel as best we could—it was lying about fifty yards inside the fence—try to remove the direction-finding apparatus, carry it into safety in the wood, return to the Heinkel and remain in it under cover till about six a.m. Our equipment consisted of two white mechanics' overalls, cloth trays to pack stolen instruments in, cameras, writing pads and pencils.

At six a.m., dressed in the overalls, we were openly to start an external and internal 'inspection' of the damaged plane, making notes of what repairs the aircraft required. In this way we should make the German guards, who were the most likely people to detect the bluff, think that we were two of the assistant mechanics belonging to the airfield, who could be seen about all day in their white overalls when aircraft were being repaired. Cheek took one a long way in those days, but we both realized that for the successful execution of this plan we needed luck as well. There was very little possibility of retreat, but time would show what was practicable.

The first part of the plan went without a hitch. We reached the northern corner of the airfield at about midnight. We lay here for about three-quarters of an hour and, from an excellent hiding-place up on the edge of the wood, noted the times at which the sentry passed. It soon became clear that from this side we had little to fear for the present. It was pretty dark, and the sentry took a good time over each round —on an average a quarter of an hour between each passing.

We went over the plan again, synchronized our watches, and at ten minutes to one we started. Half-creeping we reached the fence, which on a closer inspection proved not to be fitted with an alarm system at this point either. Our plan of climbing over the fence was abandoned at once when we found a hole under it filled up with movable stones. In spite of the strong wind it would be possible for the noise made in climbing over the fence to be heard by one of the sentries, in which case our chances would undeniably be small. The possibility that the sentry, when daylight came, would detect the hole we had made under the fence had also to be taken into consideration. But the advantages of the hole were decisive.

No great exertion was required to get through. The open ground between the fences and the Heinkel was also crossed without trouble. The half-open 'door' under the fuselage of the plane was cautiously opened, and Kaare climbed in. I myself sat quite still under the plane, for it was time for the sentry to pass. I had been sitting for about two minutes when steps were audible from the direction of the fence. The shadow of the sentry slowly approached the place where we had crept through, passed and disappeared. No, he had neither heard nor seen anything, and all was quiet again; only the howling of the wind could be heard. Over in one of the hangars a light was burning: it was badly screened, the door stood ajar and now and again shadows of Germans passed across.

I carefully wriggled myself up into the plane where Kaare lay. It was pitch dark, but in a little while we had felt our way forward to the entrance to the pilot's cockpit, where the radar apparatus should be. On the previous day, when I had received orders for the job from 'the captain,' he had shown me a rough sketch of the interior of a Heinkel 111, and showed me the place where he supposed the direction-finding apparatus to be.

We used a small electric torch, thoroughly shaded and screened and with a weak blue bulb. If Kaare knelt with his back to the windscreen and turned on the light under his jacket, he could regulate the light so that only a glimmer fell upon the interior of the aircraft. It was a big risk to run, but without light we were utterly helpless. It was turned on only for a moment at a time, until we had found what we were looking for. The main apparatus was built into the end of the wireless table and a small regulating apparatus screwed fast to the bulkhead was combined with it.

I worked for a good half-hour with a rubber-covered pair of cutters and screw-driver I had brought with me, with my white mechanic's overall over my head, before I succeeded in getting the main apparatus loose. Every little click seemed a crash to our strained auricular nerves; we thought the guard must have heard. While the direction-finding apparatus was being dismounted, Kaare sat on the ground under the aircraft, to give me warning as soon as anything suspicious happened. Each time the sentry approached he pulled twice on a stout linen thread which, running through the opening under the plane, was made fast to my leg. When the sentry had passed he pulled three times, and if there was imminent danger he was to pull several times.

Every time the sentry passed, I hid the torch under the white overall and stood quite still till the three tugs came. Then at last both the main apparatus and its regulator were loose, and with the two parts wrapped up separately under my arm, I felt my way cautiously to the opening and out to Kaare. The sentry had just passed, and it was now Kaare's job to get both parts out by the same way he had come in, and up to the dry hiding-place we had prepared under a rock in the woods.

It had gradually grown lighter and we had not much time. Kaare vanished like a shadow in the direction of the fence. The minutes slipped away. Here came the damned sentry again! Had Kaare managed to get out? Yes, the sentry passed at the same slow pace. Then a shadow approached the plane in which I sat. It was Kaare coming back. 'Everying O.K.' A faint whisper announced the result. An important part of our task was done, and *so far* all had gone well. But the most difficult part still remained. What would happen when six o'clock came and the Germans began their usual work on the airfield?

We crept cautiously into the plane again and lay down on the floor. We might as well try to sleep for the time which remained before we could continue our work. One man would keep watch while the other tried to sleep. But precious little sleep we got! Our brains were working at high pressure. How should we get away when the job was completed? One plan after another was made and abandoned. A great deal depended upon chance, and only time would show what the end would be. The minutes slipped away.

Rather more than an hour had passed, and it was my turn to try and sleep. It was not long before Kaare shook me. 'There's someone coming!' At the same time I heard steps approaching. To judge by the sound there were two men. The steps came right up to the plane, then stopped for a moment; there was German conversation in subdued voices, so faint that only isolated words could be distinguished. 'Be repaired — twelve o'clock — be quick'— and the two Germans went on. We had remained lying on the deck of the aircraft without moving a muscle, almost without breathing. If the plane was to be repaired, perhaps taken away to the hangar, at twelve o'clock, we had plenty of time; or had twelve o'clock been mentioned in some other connection, and were the repairs to be started as soon as possible? In the latter case it would be only a question of minutes before we were discovered, and what then? We dared not pursue the thought! . . . But nothing happened. The minutes passed and became hours.

Half-past four! We could start our preparations for photographing. It was quite light in the pilot's cockpit now, but at the same time the danger of our presence being detected through the windscreen and the turret was greatly increased. The photographs must be taken by time exposure, as it was not light enough for snapshots, and the cameras were set up on the tripods we had brought with us. But it was no easy task to place the cameras; there was little space, and a series of photographs would have to be taken to cover everything. All the time I was working, Kaare stood on guard. Several times we had to break off our work and retreat to the fuselage while German soldiers passed the aircraft. A few breathless seconds followed, but for the time being all went well.

At last the necessary photographs were taken; there remained only two of the outside direction-finding gear and several general views of the airfield.

The used film was now taken out of the camera and transferred in a light-proof cloth bag which we had brought with us to a small light-proof hermetically sealed cylinder. I then stored the cylinder in a place which was hardly likely to be discovered during a preliminary search of my person—my own anus!—a hiding-place which was known and well used in international espionage in the first world war, but which in existing conditions would hardly be thought of in a possible examination.

At ten minutes past six we put on the mechanics' overalls, and with note-pads and pencils in our hands, and cameras ready for action hanging on our chests under the overalls, we stepped out of the aircraft as two dignified skilled mechanics, apparently engaged in a close discussion of the possibility of quickly repairing it. Our thoughts and eyes, however, were turned in quite a different direction. What interested us was the immediate neighbourhood of the plane, and whether we had been observed.

A sentry sauntered towards the plane, glanced at us as we went round it busily making notes with our blocks and pencils, passed about ten yards away and went on, evidently without suspecting anything!

The photographs of the direction-finding gear were taken at the beginning of a new film. This was done quite simply as follows: the overall was slightly pushed aside, the direction taken more or less at random, and the photograph taken at a moment when no 'unauthorized person' had his eyes fixed on the Heinkel.

It was when we were about to take our last photographs, general views from a little rise in the ground about five yards from the aircraft, that the overture to the catastrophe began. In the very direction in which the first photograph was to be taken a white-clad man, a real mechanic, appeared, walking towards the Heinkel with two German officers! It was as though every muscle in one's body had for a moment ceased to function. Their intention could not be misunderstood; they were coming to make a survey of the damage the Heinkel had suffered in its unfortunate landing.

In a moment we were back at the aircraft; we tore off the white overalls in the lee of the Heinkel, pushed them in through a broken window, and sauntered with apparent nonchalance—I repeat 'apparent'—across to the fence round the airfield, towards the spot where we had come in during the night.

I do not think anyone had noticed the rather curious behaviour of the two 'mechanics,' and all would certainly have gone well if the damned sentry had not been just on his way back and only a few yards from the hole through which we had meant to slip out. We slackened speed when he noticed us, and when he stopped right by the hole and stood watching us, we slowly changed direction and walked along the fence, chatting together as if nothing was the matter. Then, when we were feigning composure and both had some hope, but still did not believe that we should 'get away with it,' a shout of 'Halt!' rang in our ears like the report of a gun. We stopped; I gave Kaare a long look and we turned round with the most innocent expressions imaginable.

'Wie, bitte?' There seemed to be something in my throat which prevented me from getting my words out as firmly as I meant to.

'Come here, please!' and rather more severely, 'What are you doing here?'—these two sentences followed one another quickly, while the tommy-gun in the sentry's hands was pointed at us as if to emphasize each question. Our explanation, the gist of which was that we were out for a morning walk and had strayed inside the fence through a hole under it out sheer curiosity, was obviously not taken as seriously as we had hoped. An imperious 'Come out and follow me!' concluded the not very amicable conversation, and there was nothing else to be done—for the time being.

We crept out through the hole in the fence, and then a melancholy march began towards the main building and, more particularly, the commandant of Fornebu airfield. Kaare and I walked side by side and the sentry with his tommy-gun formed the rearguard. We were thinking furiously. If we could only get rid of the cameras it would be all right, and we might get off with a warning. But how were we to do it? Every time we tried to talk in Norwegian, one of us was prodded in the back with the muzzle of the sentry's gun, a gesture which spoke for itself and did not encourage conversation of any length. If we both suddenly became interested in 'something,' for example, up in the woods to our left, attracted the sentry's attention to it, and managed to throw a camera away on the other side, he would undoubtedly hear the noise of its fall. In that case we should have signed our own death-warrants, there was no doubt of that, and the plan was rejected. Could we strike the sentry down by a sudden attack and then escape into the woods? I threw one glance back, and that was enough. The sentry was walking with his finger on the trigger, and a shot, even if it hit neither of us, would be enough to bring all the airfield guards on to their legs, and our chances would be hardly better. No, we should have to follow quietly and await events, hoping for a chance later.

The first place we became intimately acquainted with was the guard-room. Here a string of impudent questions and accusations was flung at the two morning walkers, our answers twisted into an admission of the charges, a report written by the sergeant on duty, and a telephone call put through to some senior officer. I endeavoured to raise further objections to those charges which I considered to be beneath our dignity, but without any result worth mentioning.

We now proceeded from the guard-room to the main building in company with two surly armed guards, and here, after a short wait, we were introduced to no less a person than the commandant of Fornebu airfield. Here what we had hoped to escape for as long as possible took place—a personal search. The cameras were laid on the table before the commandant; nothing more was found, but that was enough to increase the suspicion we had incurred. The valuable film lay well concealed in its hiding place, and I did not think it probable that after having found the films which were then in the cameras they would suspect we were hiding any more.

We now had to wait, locked into what had been a cloakroom, with a sentry outside, till the films were developed and the results laid before the commandant. Here the Germans committed a serious tactical error; the task of guarding us was given to one of the ordinary guards of the building, and he, having presumably other things to attend to, was obliged to stand *outside* the shut door. Not that we could by any means have escaped from our temporary cell; but it was now possible for us to talk together, agree upon the explanation we were to give the commandant, and frame a possible plan for escape during the transport from Fornebu into Oslo which would undoubtedly come sooner or later.

Time passed, and what really tormented us most was hunger and thirst. Neither of us had eaten anything since the evening before, nor drunk anything either, so we felt just a little empty. Twice I vainly attempted to attract the sentry's attention by hammering on the locked door. Three is a lucky number, an old proverb says, and it proved to be true this time too, though in rather a different way from what we had hoped. Scarcely had I begun to attack the door with my clenched fists and a few vigorous kicks before it opened. I had hardly opened my mouth to convey our common wish for a cup of water before the answer came in the form of a punch which in the next few seconds revealed to me a series of new constellations in a rather misty sky!

'Whosoever shall smite thee on thy right cheek, turn to him the other also!' It was Kaare who, with these ironical words and a commiserating smile, brought me back to earth after my rather dubious tour of the stratosphere, and I found myself lying stretched on the stone floor. 'This shall be paid back with interest!' I muttered, but kept the rest of the curse to myself.

It was nearly one when the door opened again. My friend the sentry came in and pointed at me with an imperious: 'You! Come here!' I did not over-exert myself as regards speed when I rose from the sitting position we had taken up on the floor, but it was soon clear that the tempo did not satisfy the sentry. A hard kick behind, followed by a long rigmarole of orders, emphasized his opinion.

We now went back to the commandant's office through the same doors as before; I ahead and the sentry behind, with the tommy-gun pointed at my back all the time. The gleam in his malignant, half-sneering little pig's eyes showed that the blows and kicks he had had a chance of giving me had highly gratified his sadistic instincts!

There was no amiable 'Sit down, please!' when the commandant at last looked up from the reports laid before him and surveyed me with flashing eyes. There was a rapid hail of questions: name, occupation, date of birth, year, place, domicile, parents, their names, occupation, etc. etc. Obviously a check to see if what we had both said in the guard-room was false. Meanwhile I had suddenly forgotten how to speak German, and had still more difficulty in understanding it, so these repeated polite formal questions saved a possible slip of the tongue. For example, of course I had no telephone at home in my humble position as a workman, but it was very unfortunate that an inquiry by telephone to check the information I had given could not be made, as there was certainly someone at home where I lived!

That the commandant took my answers as genuine is hardly likely. That an ordinary casual labourer was in possession of a Retina Kodak obviously seemed rather doubtful, and my fairy tale of the many years it had taken me to save up for this treasure did not noticeably improve the impression I was making. Nor did my story of the two keen amateur photographers, who in their search for suitable subjects had had the ill-luck to creep under a fence and into a forbidden area, seem to fall on good soil.

For about three-quarters of an hour there was a hail of questions which had to be answered. The whole thing went off fairly satisfactorily until suddenly a mechanic appeared in the doorway with a bundle of white cloth under his arm, went up to the commandant, saluted him, laid down the white bundle with an open bag containing a few rubber-handled tools, and reported that the direction-finding apparatus in the damaged Heinkel 111 at the northern end of the airfield had been stolen in the course of the night! Our 'mechanics' overalls'—our tools!

I felt myself grow rigid where I stood, and half-turned away so that no one might detect my somewhat changed colour.

'Do you know these? What have you done with the stolen apparatus?'

'I don't know anything about the parts,' I replied, 'and for that matter have never seen a direction-finding apparatus or whatever you call it. On the contrary, I demand that my explanation of our conduct be accepted.' At the same time I tried to show a growing indignation at the 'impudent' and 'groundless' accusations by underlying my 'demand' with an angry stamp on the floor.

The commandant rose from his chair scarlet with rage and crossed the floor in four long strides.

'You've no right to demand anything. Remember that!' Three stinging blows on the ears nearly made me lose my balance. I lifted a clenched fist to hit back, but lowered it instantly despite the rage which was boiling within me, for I saw that a blow aimed at the commandant would be the last I aimed in this world! The two tommy-guns which were pointed at me all the time would make short work of me. . . .

There was a further hail of questions, but now I found it best to keep silent. He dealt me three more blows, this time with his clenched fist, before he reeled off his last words:

'We've got other methods of making thick-skinned Norwegians answer! Out with you!'

A good two hours of by no means 'friendly conversation' had passed, and when a kick sent me head first into the cloak-room to Kaare, it was a welcome change. There was, however, no opportunity to tell Kaare of the somewhat unexpected development that had occurred. He was hauled out, as inhospitably as I had been kicked in, to make the closer acquaintance of the commandant.

I lay for a time cursing our predicament. It was now clear that the suspicion the Germans had had from the beginning had been strengthened by the finding of the mechanics' overalls and the discovery that the direction-finding apparatus was missing. Our only possible course was to play for time. Perhaps a chance of escape would come later.

The time passed terribly slowly. I tried to get a little sleep, but the stone floor seemed to me rather hard to lie on; moreover, I could not help thinking of Kaare. Every time steps approached the door my hopes rose, only to disappear with the steps next moment. But at last the key was thrust into the lock from outside and turned, and in came Kaare in the same way as I had made my entry an hour and a half before. For a few seconds he lay on the floor, breathing heavily. There was no need to ask about the treatment he had received. Blood was trickling from a wound at one corner of his mouth, his upper lip was swollen and his cheeks flaming red.

'You look as if you'd followed your own advice to me about a blow on the left cheek!' I tried to make a joke, but the joke evidently fell on very bad soil, and I saw, as soon as the words had slipped out of my mouth, that it was no time for any jokes. In a hushed voice Kaare told me what had happened, what questions he had been asked and what answers he had given. Fortunately we had followed the same line under examination; all that I had said had simply been confirmed by Kaare. The devils had tried to force the truth out of us in the same brutal manner. The photographs from our cameras, which had now been developed, had betrayed little; perhaps they had rather confirmed our joint statement about a search for good subjects. On the other hand, the photograph of the Heinkel from which the direction-finding apparatus had been stolen worked the other way: on the whole, advantages and disadvantages cancelled each other out.

The hours crept by. It was a little after half-past six when the steps of several iron-tipped boots approached the locked door. We lay quite still on the floor, pretending to be quite dead beat, and took not the least notice of what was about to happen. The key was thrust into the lock, the door opened, and in came three Germans. They had helmets, tommy-guns and full equipment. We were hauled to our feet with loud words of command. We both tottered as if we had difficulty in standing. Kaare was lame, too, and could evidently hardly stand on his left leg. It was noticeable that we were both about a head taller than our respective guards.

Our tactics were now completely changed; it was two broken-down, submissive creatures who were half-dragged out of the building to a lorry which was parked outside the entrance, and replied 'yes' to every order that was given. Only a tarpaulin on iron hoops covered the whole deck of the lorry; the entrance was behind, closed with straps. This was the first thing I noted with pleasure as we shambled over to the lorry, apparently quite uninterested, and were ordered in. The places allotted to us were on two long empty boxes facing one another, and we collapsed. I took care to get one of my feet close beside Kaare's.

Our now seemingly humble and submissive appearance had obviously had its effect on the senior of our three guards, a German corporal with a high, squeaky voice. In fact, he ordered the two others into the lorry with us and seated himself beside the driver in the separate driver's cabin. I noted with pleasure that the guard nearest me was the one who had so kindly knocked us about in the cloakroom. 'Just wait!' I thought, as I sat huddled up on the box with half-closed eyes.

The lorry started and went bumping along the bad road out of Fornebu airfield. The fateful journey had begun! Out of one corner of my eye I took the measure of the two guards as they sat coolly chatting together. I saw that Kaare was watching them too. The distance between us and the guards was about six feet; they sat between us and the tail of the lorry, each with his back to an iron hoop. Their tommy-guns lay across their knees with the muzzles pointed at us. Now and again they gave us a look, but each time they turned we were just sitting with our eyes shut, half asleep.

The journey into town went slowly; there was heavy traffic on the road from the airfield, and it became still heavier when we at last came out on to the Drammen road. Through the flapping strips of tarpaulin over the exit at the tail, we could see how far we had come.

We were approaching Lysaker, the place which offered the only real chance! The traffic into town had to slow down here, first because of cross-traffic through Lysaker itself, and then because of the narrow, dynamited bridge over the Lysaker river with cross-traffic on the other side. We had already taken a good grip of the iron hoop between us and the guards, as if for support, and, a fraction of an inch at a time, we moved nearer the guards and the exit. We now followed all their slightest movements. They now both looked as if they were tired of the job, had stopped talking and were sitting staring out through the gap in the flapping tarpaulin, without a thought of trouble to come.

The lorry slowed down. Lysaker! Now or never! I gave Kaare's shoe a touch with my foot, let out with my own leg and caught my guard in the midriff! Kaare's leg hit its target a fraction of a second later—a combined gasp from the two Germans and they tumbled in a heap on the deck of the lorry. In the same second we were on our legs, scored direct hits on the Germans' jaws with swings of our right arms, snatched up their tommy-guns, tore back the cloth, opened it and cast a lightning glance round before jumping out. We were in the middle of the Lysaker bridge and the lorry was not moving quickly. Evidently neither of the men in the driver's cabin had so far noticed anything. The whole thing had take a few seconds. First Kaare, then I—out on to the bridge, the distance to the parapet covered in three long strides, and then we took our more or less graceful headers almost side by side.

We had both, in leaping over the parapet, taken a bearing on the Lysaker Coal Company's wharf about fifty yards downstream. A long under-water swim would take us down under the wharf itself, among the piles. I felt a pleasant cooling of the brain as the water closed over my head. But the water was black—both an advantage and a disadvantage. It prevented those who had seen our curious proceedings from finding out what had become of us, but it prevented us from seeing much as we swam side by side under water. There was a strong current with us, and there was no doubt that we should get there. All the way we were following one slope of the bank, passing at regular intervals the stern-posts of the boats which lay moored along the bank. . . . There was the first pile of the wharf! We had still plenty of breath left and continued in underneath the wharf, as far in as we could get, and then up! Every movement was made with the utmost caution, and now we lay side by side, gasping for breath as we hung on to the cross-beams between the piles. I thought with gratitude of the many years during which we had practised swimming under water!

But we were far from safe, even if the worst was now over. Loud shouts were heard from the bridge, and from what we could see it was clear that a large crowd of people had stopped and were hanging over the parapet, pointing and gesticulating. We remained for a while where we had come to the surface. It was queer how quickly all became quiet up on the bridge; only a boat with three Norwegians in it began to row about where we had dived into the river. Had some sensible person grasped the situation and got the rest away, so as not to attract the attention of passing German cars, or had just one or two people seen us dive into the river and, when nothing more was seen of us, been disbelieved by those who listened to them? But we had no time to get a certain answer to the question.

We now proceeded carefully downstream from pile to pile, keeping well under cover of the wharf all the time. On the south side of this lay the stairs we knew so well, and these we reached after about forty minutes in the water. The possibility of waiting at the stairs till dark was considered but rejected. Our two 'friends' on the deck of the lorry had quite certainly recovered consciousness and given the alarm long ago.

We went on through the coal company's premises, under cover of the great heaps of coal and afterwards of sheds. Not a soul was to be seen, as the working day was long over. But we thought with a certain regret of the two tommy-guns we had got out of the lorry, but had had to abandon when we entered the water. It was now to be hoped that we should not find ourselves in a situation in which such things were necessary. Kaare remained where he was while I went on over a fence or two to the back of the Lysaker Co-operative Society's building. From here I proceeded openly, half-sauntering, out to the paling along the Drammen road, over this and into private grounds on the other side. Two minutes later Kaare arrived in the same way. We continued over fences and through hedges, across roads and through copses, trying all the time to avoid meeting people at close quarters. Oevrevoll Stadium was passed; we crossed the dam of the Lysaker river at Röa, went through Ullern wood and at last reached Montebello. We were safe! Luckily no one was at home.

An hour later we were sitting each in an armchair before a flaming log fire with a steaming hot rum toddy. The last twenty-four hours had been a long time. The plan had not gone just as it should, but nevertheless, we had had luck with us at the end, and—what was most important—the job had been done in its entirety. The valuable film had been taken from its hiding-place and everything transferred to a secret chamber.

Next day the film was developed, and five days afterwards, by a successful night expedition, the direction-finding apparatus with its accessory gear was fetched from the place where it was hidden near the northern corner of the airfield.

CHAPTER IV

'WIR FAHREN GEGEN ENGLAND'

EARLIER in this story I have just touched upon the great importance we were obliged to attach to holding our tongues. We Norwegians of the present generation, in the April days of 1940 and the time that followed, had great difficulty in understanding the importance of completely obeying this paragraph in the orders of the day. Of course, it was not exclusively a Norwegian weakness during the first year of the war, and in our case the reason may have been that there had been no war in our country for about 125 years.

Loquacity was our great difficulty, even in the earliest days, when intelligence work and espionage were by later standards relatively simple matters. It was hard to get fellow-workers who could resist the temptation to tell their friends and relations what they were doing. This was the reason why in the course of the summer of 1940, as the result of a series of incidents, we had to get away from Oslo and up to parts where we were not known.

On one of these trips we paid a short visit to Gardermoen airfield with orders to get photographs of the airfield itself, with the hangars and repair shop and also the ammunition dump. Gardermoen, which is about twenty miles north of Oslo, had before the invasion been used by the Norwegian Army as a training-ground, and parts of it as a reserve airfield. The training-ground and its surroundings were admirably suited for the laying out of airfields on a large scale; their strategic position for military operations was excellent and so was their geographical position, which made an effective defence possible.

The German guard work at Gardermoen was at that time exceedingly bad, and it soon appeared that there was no need even to have 'legitimate' work at the airfield to obtain the necessary photographs. With our cameras on our chests inside our shirts, or in some cases built into a tool-box with a hole in the side for the lens and a release string under the handle, we pottered about the airfield in working clothes among the other workmen and took the photographs which were later used in England as a basis for intelligence work and espionage at Gardermoen.

Neither of us, however, felt entire personal satisfaction with the work we were doing. Neither of us had had any training for it at all, and the result depended more on lucky chance than on efficient and methodical execution. In consequence of this the great question was how long those who then directed our operations would be able to keep things going without being caught.

As concerned myself the position was almost clear. The Norwegian Government, which was now established in London along with our King, had ordered all airmen to leave Norway as quickly as possible in order to join a new Norwegian Air Force which was being formed in England and

Canada. Many had already succeeded in getting out of Norway by boat across the North Sea to the Shetlands or Scotland, and throughout the autumn of 1940 the same idea became more strongly and deeply rooted in our minds. And by degrees, as we became engaged in various undertakings which did not always end as we meant them to, this growing desire to pack up and clear out became a compelling necessity.

We encountered many difficulties. The three chief things which had to be secured were a crew, a boat, and equipment, and these three things in themselves were problems at that time. The first, a crew, proved to be a question that gave rise to arguments one would not have thought possible under the prevailing conditions. But the fact remained that there were very few indeed of our circle who at that time could consider the possibility of leaving all they had, completely breaking off their daily life, and going over to England to fight. 'The war might be over before one got so far!' was the usual argument. This was unfortunately the general way of thinking among a large part of the male population of Oslo in the autumn of 1940. We still found it very hard to understand that the struggle now in progress between the Great Powers of Europe was also a struggle for the existence of our own little country and people.

In my own case it may then have been a longing for adventure as much as anything, combined with the real idealistic motive, that made me put the plan into execution. Kaare Moe was the only one of my many friends who really saw things as I did and was willing to risk everything in the great undertaking. His calculation was that even if he had not the necessary qualifications to become an airman, he could, with his education and experience, make himself useful in many other ways; there was, moreover, the possibility that he might be accepted as a pupil at the flying school and get his training in Canada.

Never, either before or later, have I met a man who threw himself into a task so whole-heartedly as Kaare Moe. He meant more to his family, perhaps, than most others; when still quite a lad he had had to take over the care of them when his father died, and yet had always something to spare for his friends. No one else I have had the pleasure of knowing was so punctual in the discharge of his duty to his mother and his two brothers and his duty to society. Kaare Moe was also a Scout, second in command of No. 3 Bestum troop, and the promise he had given with his hand on the flag was always his highest ideal. We had worked together in the Scout movement for some years, and I never met anyone who lived up to this promise in the same degree as Kaare.

The plan for a voyage to Britain, however, was to prove rather more complicated than we had at first thought. It was no simple matter to obtain a serviceable boat. The Germans had long ago become alive to the increase in the traffic from the west coast of Norway over to Britain; fishing boats were always disappearing, and the British wireless reported the arrival of many refugees from Norway. An immediate consequence of this was increased activity on the part of the German police; the guards along the coast and in the larger towns of the west and south were strengthened considerably; every boat moving along or outside the skerries must have a special permit from the German harbour police, and every sale and purchase of a boat of any size must be sanctioned by the same body. For the Oslo Fjord the sailing regulations were rather simpler, probably because the Germans could not imagine the possibility of any Norwegian trying to sail the distance from Oslo to Britain. All traffic in the Oslo basin was free, apart from a few military penalties, but no one might sail through or outside the Dröbakk sound without permission from the German harbour police in Oslo.

The regulations as to German sanction for the purchase and sale of boats of any size made it very difficult to get a fishing smack of about forty to fifty feet. We found that people were afraid to sell to strangers; and the few who were willing to sell behind the backs of the German authorities demanded prices far beyond our economic capacity. Another thing was that if in those days one had been able to go to a man, whether one knew him personally or not, and lay one's cards on the table, the whole thing would have appeared in a different light.

We ourselves had a pretty good idea of what we wanted for sailing in the skerries, as we had both sailed in comparatively small boats since we were boys. But sailing in the open sea, we were told, was something quite different, and we realized later that the experience we had had together was to be put to a pretty severe test. The North Sea on a quiet summer day was one thing—the North Sea after the autumn gales had begun was another!

The plan gradually took shape in the late hours of the night. Charts and maps were obtained from various private quarters, as these were not for sale in the shops, having been confiscated by the Germans, and our route down the coast was planned. Other necessary equipment for the voyage was slowly but surely collected from different sources. But here, too, we met with difficulties. Those who were partially initiated into the plan, and whose support for the enterprise we had reckoned on absolutely, still went about wearing a faintly ironical smile. Wherever we applied, we felt that the words 'a boyish prank' were whispered behind our backs each time we left, with a more or less negative result, one of those in whom we had put our trust. But there were others who, although rather sceptical as to the result, were willing to put a few shillings on our horse. Among these was an Oslo dentist who, in partnership with a friend, owned the lifeboats *Bergen* and *Stavanger*.

I did not know him personally, but got into touch with him through a friend. We hoped at first to charter or buy one of these boats, and possibly get the dentist to make the trip with us. But none of these things could be done. The Germans had for a long time past had their eye on the *Stavanger,* which was lying in Oslo, and the dentist's friend had the other one, the *Bergen,* down at Sandefjord. As for getting the dentist to make the trip, this was out of the question, as his wife was ill and his family must come first with him. In other ways the dentist was of very great help to us. He had sailed across the North Sea himself in summer in a small boat and had otherwise done a good deal of sea sailing as a hobby. Consequently he could tell us what we might get up against and what precautions we ought to take to come safely through possible bad weather. He also gave us much good advice about equipment which later was invaluable.

One item in the programme still remained open—a boat, one that could really stand a dusting. One possibility after another was gradually considered—and rejected, till one day we came across an eighteen-foot smack-built half-decker, which had for some time been lying for sale at Nesset, at the southern end of the Bundefjord. The boat was inspected and accepted one afternoon in the middle of August. Certainly, eighteen feet were nothing to boast about, but as she lay drawn up on the slip she did not look by any means so bad by our standards. After we had paid, the owner told us that the bottom dated from 1909, but the three upper strakes plus the deck he had built himself about a year ago; the mast was fairly new and the sails not too bad. The boat had an old Bolinder motor with a hot bulb, but this the owner could not guarantee. As far as he knew it had not been used much in the last ten years!

The purchase money, 1,000 crowns, was obtained by the sale of my motor-cycle. To avoid 'public control' of the sale, the motor-cycle was sold to an elderly engineer in Oslo, a man who had never sat on a motor-cycle in his life and in all probability would never attempt to do so. But he was one of the few who in those days had 1,000 crowns in ready money, not under control in a frozen bank account, and like the good Norwegian he was he put his money into an enterprise in which he would more than gladly have participated himself.

A few days later the boat was sailed in from the Bundefjord to Bestumkilen, outside Oslo, in a fresh northerly wind; a maiden trip which already was to raise doubts in our minds as to the result of the 'great voyage' and the boat's true qualifications. Every fairly strong gust of wind that came made the boat heel till her rail was under water. I sailed and—Kaare baled! The water simply squirted in through cracks in the new bulwarks! We thought for ourselves as we sat, and in our thoughts we formed a picture of the same boat in a gale out in the North Sea. 'There'll probably be a leak or so in the bulwarks, as she hasn't been sailed for some years,' were the seller's last words, and we kept them fresh in our memory during the following six weeks. . . .

Not many words passed between us as we went into town. We both hoped that this most important matter would improve when the wood had swelled for a few days; of course there was nothing new about leaks in a boat which had been laid up for rather a long time. As for her noticeable wetness, a couple of hundred pounds of ballast, in addition to what was in her now, would do wonders. In the meantime, one thing must be said in favour of the seller and his boat: she was a very good sailer!

Early next morning I met Kaare down on the quay. 'She's a bit lower in the water today than when we left her yesterday!' Kaare pointed to our newly acquired treasure. I just nodded. What a sight! When we came alongside the marvellous craft, our martial spirit sank to below zero. The water on board stood a good foot and a half above the cabin floor: mattresses and other gear from the tiny cabin were floating about. Words were unnecessary, but England seemed at that moment something remote and historic! Here something had to be done, and that 'something' done quickly. Every day that passed brought us nearer to autumn and its gales.

The boat was now hauled up on to the slip at Bestumkilen and the state of affairs explained to the owner of the slip, who was an old acquaintance. We further hinted to him that there was a possibility of our starting a new firm, the North Sea Shipping Company. We left the rest to him, and he promised to do his best. 'She'll never be watertight,' he said; 'the bottom's too rotten, and the new upper part with the deck too inaccurately built. These things apart, I should advise most strongly against any participation in the North Sea Shipping Company with this craft!' This was the boatbuilder's last word.

Apart from all the difficulties I have mentioned we had two things to contend with: time and money. But we *must* do it, and we *would* do it! Another thing was: would two men be enough on the voyage across? In fine weather, yes; in a gale, in all probability not. But it would be impossible to get hold of a third man. There was only one who was willing, and that was Kaare's brother. Certainly he was only a boy, but nevertheless capable of working turn and turn about with us. But the facts of the situation made his coming impossible. The chances of getting to England across the North Sea in autumn in an 'unsuitable' eighteen-foot boat were about even, and that was the answer as far as Leif was concerned. It would be more than enough if one member of the same family were to take this chance.

While the boat was undergoing a thorough overhaul, we proceeded to one of the last items on the programme—getting a sailing permit from the German authorities. For this purpose a series of false papers were produced, papers which showed that we were both employed as travellers by a large wholesale provision firm, whose head office was in Oslo with branches in Bergen and Trondheim. As the use of private cars or motor-cycles had long ceased and the possibility of travel by land was thus limited, the only and best solution was the use of a boat—to wit, an eighteen-foot smack-built half-decker with a cabin. By this means we could get into contact with the very smallest country shop along the coast which shared our firm's interests. Provisions were most important to the maintenance of life, and that our German 'liberators' of course appreciated.

We now proceeded with the necessary false references to the office of the German naval *Hafenkapitän,* and after a little conversation the matter was arranged and three special travelling passes and sailing permits issued: Oslo–Mandal, Mandal–Bergen and Bergen–Trondheim.

Here, in the meantime, another little episode occurred which is worth a few words. During the negotiations with a German clerk with the rank of corporal, the clock reached 12.30, and we noticed that the entire personnel except the man we were talking to left the room and went down to lunch. We had been told by the corporal's immediate senior that when we went into Bergen we should have to go through a German minefield outside the entrance to Bergen harbour. We should therefore get the exact positions of the channel through this, and the necessity of following these for the sake of our own skins was strongly impressed upon us. The corporal now went over to a big filing cabinet in one corner of the room, pulled out the third drawer from the top and took out the first file in the fourth compartment. With the file in his hand he went back to his desk, opened the desk and took out a photographed chart of South Norway including Trondheim. With it were two lists of positions for the open channels through the minefields. Our eyes nearly popped out of our heads! But at the same time we let the corporal get a definite impression that this part of our travel plans did not greatly interest us; we talked together in a low voice, and the subject was the sales prospects for provisions in the various districts. The corporal, who sat with his back to us, did not seem to be interested in anything but being ready for his lunch as quickly as possible. He first looked up the list, noted five different positions, checked these with the chart and then turned to us with a detailed explanation. The conversation was in German, and by this time we had become quite good friends. We took our leave after having given a satisfactory answer to the corporal's question where he could find 'a good hot Norwegian *Fräulein*!'

Next day we were back at the office of the *Hafenkapitän* five minutes before lunch-time. There was something about our papers we did not quite understand; would the corporal be so kind as to inquire of his chief? 'Yes, with pleasure,' and the corporal disappeared into the next room. There was no one else in the room. Like a streak of lightning Kaare was over by the door into the passage and I at the filing cabinet —third drawer from the top, fourth compartment, first file, photographed chart and lists under my shirt, drawer and cupboard shut and back to my place outside the barrier! We were talking about foodstuffs again when the corporal came back a moment later with the answer to the question we had put. One or two questions and answers about the 'good hot Norwegian girl' and we withdrew. . . .

It was pretty obvious that it would not be long before the half-empty file was discovered, but in all probability it would be longer before the corporal reported the matter, as he would in the first place be held responsible for his own stupidity. Moreover, so many people, both German and Norwegian civilians, were going in and out of that office every day that suspicion would hardly fall in the first instance on two innocent commercial travellers. But again the chances were half and half, and this small but important event was a further stimulus to speedy departure.

The photographed chart proved on closer examination to show in detail the German minefields laid from the Swedish frontier to Frostahavet (outside Trondheim) in the period from April 8 to August 31, 1940. The two lists showed exactly the open channels for coastal traffic through these minefields.

I reported for the last time to my English friend 'the captain,' and asked him if he thought I was justified in taking the chart and lists with me on the impending voyage across the North Sea together with our photographs—rather more than a thousand—of German defence works. The final result was that the chart and lists were micro-photographed at our own photographic workshop in Oslo. The originals were handed back to us and were now placed in a secret chamber on board the boat, while the copies were to be sent to England via Sweden at the first opportunity. Thus one set would get there in any case.

At the same time we received our last orders from 'the captain.' As many photographs of the German defence works as possible were to be taken on the voyage down the coast. Special attention should be paid to Kristiansand with Kjevik and Mandal airfields, and we should also try to find out something about the big new airfield which was projected at Lista, on the south-west coast of Norway.

The final preparations for the 'great journey' were now continued with increased speed. Our calculations were: fourteen days for the voyage down the coast, at best five days across the North Sea to Scotland, at the worst ten days. Food for twenty-four days must be obtained, and this in itself was not an altogether simple matter. Food rationing had come into force a long time back, and there was far from being a superfluity. But contributions from various private individuals' hoards saved the situation comparatively easily.

Among our provisions a keg of mountain butter must be mentioned—nearly seven pounds—which my mother procured on a trip into Telemarken and which, despite vigorous protests, she insisted on our taking with us. I mention this because these seven pounds of mountain butter played a decisive part later on.

I told my mother about the plan a week before we left. I must say that I had expected strong protests, as my mother was only human and I was her son. When we were sitting on the veranda at home one afternoon I said:

'A week from to-day Kaare Moe and I are going to England together to report for duty.'

At first my mother did not say a word. She only gave me a long look. Then, slowly: 'What clothes do you want me to get ready for you, my boy?' . . .

I shall never forget that afternoon, nor the understanding and support she gave to a plan which in all probability would take the life she herself had brought into the world and toiled for through twenty-one long years. She only expressed one wish: she wanted to see the boat in which we were going to sail. The same evening we three were sitting together in the little cabin on board, and over a cup of good coffee with home-baked cakes we heard her verdict: 'A bit small if it came on to blow really hard from the north-west—but with God's help it'll go all right.' This opinion was not one to be despised—on the contrary. Not for nothing was she the daughter of one of Norway's greatest sailing captains, and she herself had seen both the North Sea and the Atlantic in storm and calm.

That evening, August 30th, the boat received its name, *Haabet* (*Hope*). She was named after the last sailing ship my mother's father had sailed across the North Sea from England in the autumn of 1905. This time, too, there were many who said that voyage was madness. The barque *Haabet* leaked like a sieve! But the old skipper was not a man to shrink from adversity and danger, and with his most loyal crew he 'pumped' *Haabet* into a Norwegian port through one of the worst storms in the memory of man. *Haabet's* flag accompanied him through three shipwrecks in the world war of 1914-1918, hanging as a souvenir in his cabin, and it was always among the few possessions he managed to save. The flag which Kaare and I hoisted a few days later on our *Haabet's* mast consisted of scraps of one old flag sewn together. This time, too, it was to prove that it could bring its crew through safely, though *Haabet* today lies 150 fathoms deeps in the North Sea.

Everything was ready. *Haabet* had been made as water-tight as she possibly could be. But she still leaked very appreciably, and our only chance was that her timbers would swell on the voyage down the coast. Our friend the dentist's advice had been taken and the fore halyard replaced by a new quarter-inch wire in case of a gale. In addition to this the forestay was arranged so that the foresail could also be used as a storm-sail. A wireless receiver was installed on board, working on a six-volt accumulator, so that we should be able to keep ourselves informed of any new German ordinances, which at that time were a regular daily feature. The cabin was fitted with two small bunks, one on each side of a narrow strip down the middle. Special importance was attached to an adequate supply of fresh water. Two wine kegs of approximately one and two gallons respectively and a round glass vessel holding three and a quarter gallons were obtained and filled. If the voyage across, in the worst event, should take more than ten days, each man would have a ration of two and a half pints a day, which, allowing for the making of coffee and tea, should be ample.

September 1st opened with a fresh northerly breeze and overcast, just the weather we wanted for the sail from Oslo to Dröbakk. Our departure was fixed for 11 a.m. from Bestumkilen, and after a short leave-taking from our respective families Kaare and I went on board. But Friday has always been a bad day to start on, according to an old sailors' superstition, and this proved to be so this time, too. The wind died down, and at eleven o'clock it was a dead calm with light rain.

Next day, September 2nd, 1940, the weather had improved. A fresh northerly wind and fairly clear. A fresh good-bye, and this time a real one! On the stroke of eleven we cast off from the buoy and *Haabet* stood out from Bestumkilen under full sail, running before a fresh breeze. The great 'voyage' had begun.

But *Haabet* was not the only craft which stood out under full sail from Bestumkilen that morning! Almost at the same time a 32 sq. m. racing yacht cast off from her buoy, and on board her were five German naval officers. It was not till they came up alongside us that we realized what kind of company we had got, and for a time we felt uncomfortable. But the Germans did not appear to have any serious intentions; what they wanted seemed to be a race. Of course we promptly took up the challenge, and the two boats went like smoke side by side, southward down the fjord. At first we led, but the Germans gradually overhauled us. All the time a lively conversation passed between the two crews. Of course, the Germans were sailing a boat which, frankly, they had confiscated, a fact which did not seem to trouble their consciences for a moment, to judge from their behaviour. Their sportsmanlike spirit seemed to reach its climax when, after having sailed past us twice, they came up alongside and threw a box of German cigarettes across to us—a box containing precisely *one* cigarette.

Our suspicions of the Germans, however, proved to be unjustified when they, with a bellowed *'Auf Wiedersehen,'* altered course 180 degrees and began to cruise back to Bestumkilen. Soon afterwards we, too, altered course and sailed at full speed towards Dröbakk.

What we had been dreaming of for weeks had now become a reality, and even if this was only the beginning of the great adventure, it was none the less a good start. We both, indeed, felt the weight of the question-mark which hung over the whole enterprise—not only the actual voyage across the North Sea, but what the future had in store over on the other side. But at the same time we were too proud to say anything about this to one another; we were naturally afraid of robbing ourselves of the enthusiastic illusions we had built up in our own minds in the past months.

At 8 p.m. we lay to at Dröbakk. Sailing after 9 p.m. was forbidden by the Germans, and we had no grounds for taking any chances at that time. But all the same it was not long before we got into difficulties. Half an hour after our arrival Kaare and I were sitting down in the little cabin eating our supper, when a German voice hailed us from the wharf. We both started, took a rapid look round over what was lying in view, and while Kaare remained sitting below I went up to hear what it was all about. It was a German harbour policeman who wanted to see our papers. I grew hot all over. Had the chart and lists affair been discovered already? No, there was certainly no reason to worry unnecessarily. But evidently something was not quite right, for I had the pleasure of spending a good hour and a half up at the German harbour office while the policeman responsible checked up our papers with Oslo. It happened, the local policeman told us, that Oslo were looking for a couple of men, but finally he was able to inform us that these two were not identical with us! I can only say that I felt more than relieved when this message came by telephone and I was able to return to *Haabet*. But I received another message that evening which neither Kaare nor I understood. We were told that we could not leave Dröbakk next day, but must wait for further orders.

Neither of us slept much that first night on board. We were both tormented by the question whether to take our chance next morning and clear off as soon as it was light, or to take our chance by 'awaiting further orders' from the Germans. We agreed to wait.

Three days passed and we grew tired of waiting. I went up to the German police officers and put forward our arguments, based on the agreements which as commercial travellers we had made with our customers along the coast to southward. The police rang up Oslo again, and we got permission to proceed instantly without further ceremony.

We had made most diligent use of the three days we lay at Dröbakk, and we sailed away with a quantity of good photographs of the various German defence works in the neighbourhood.

The time which followed was unforgettable. Everything went as smoothly as possible, and mile after mile disappeared in our wake; day after day, brilliant weather and a steady fresh breeze. We kept as a rule outside the actual skerries, except when time and our photographic interests demanded a little short cut or detour. When evening came and the wind died down, we gladly turned into one of the thousand small creeks, cast anchor and took life easily. Wherever we went the skerries of South Norway lay open and smiling, islet after islet, rock after rock, clad in the loveliest autumn colours. On some days the sailing could be fairly hard, and we had an opportunity of testing *Haabet's* various merits and defects. There were many things which must be put right, many things on board which must be altered and improved.

One day, when we were beating up against a strong south-westerly wind, we got the baptism *Haabet* needed. We were on a long run southwards in the open sea off Svenör light, with close-reefed mainsail and foresail. The wind had been increasing steadily during the day, and the seas were breaking white. Both Kaare and I were sitting in the open steering cockpit, clad in oilskins from head to foot and dripping wet from the seas which at regular intervals poured in over the deck. A squall literally flung itself over the boat; we heeled over and the water poured in. At the same moment there was a crack like a pistol shot, and the next thing we knew was that the close-reefed foresail had torn itself away from the sheet. *Haabet* swung up into the wind and rose again half-full of water, while the mainsail and foresail thrashed wildly. It was the iron shackle between the forestay and the sheet which had given way! . . . Three hours later we were in the shelter of islets and rocks again, and richer by an invaluable experience, but with a considerably more sceptical view of *Haabet's* chances on a stormy night in the North Sea. We kept our opinions to ourselves, however. . . .

The whaling port of Sandefjord had already been ruled out for us before we started from Oslo; this was because I was myself very well known among the inhabitants there. We therefore agreed to keep well outside and under no circumstances to come under any control which would bring us into port there. Early one morning we sailed past the entrance and the island of Rauer just outside; it was hazy and bad weather, so that we could hardly make out any features, and not a soul was to be seen.

The curious thing was—I learnt this two years later in Iceland—that on that very day our friend the dentist's partner, with the lifeboat *Bergen,* lay waiting for us in Sandefjord harbour with provisions for three months on board. The dentist had written from Oslo when he first heard of our plans, and asked his partner for assistance. The letter had been censored by a man who at that time called himself a good Norwegian, and who took the letter to the addressee in person with a stern warning that letters of that kind ought not to be sent by post. No reply, therefore, came from Sandefjord. Instead, the dentist's partner had got the lifeboat ready and asked the lighthouse keeper at the Rauer lighthouse to hail us when we approached and keep us there till a message could be sent in to him at Sandefjord. He would then set sail at once and meet us at Rauer. This was the plan. But on the morning we passed Rauer the haze made it impossible for the lighthouse-keeper to see us, and it must have looked as if we had sailed past our biggest and best chance.

But the destiny of the lifeboat *Bergen* was not what the owner had pictured. The man who brought the fateful letter from Oslo was no good Norwegian. He proved later to be one of the best snoopers the German police at Sandefjord had in so-called Norwegian circles, and the result was that from the moment the letter arrived the owner of the lifeboat was shadowed wherever he went. When he heard from Rauer that in all probability *Haabet* had sailed past, he set sail at once with the intention of taking the boat to England alone. His movements, however, were reported to the German harbour police, and next day he was arrested off Jomfruland and the lifeboat *Bergen* confiscated. After being released from several months' detention in the Grini concentration camp, this man made another attempt with the lifeboat *Stavanger,* which also was detected, and after having escaped from German control he at last succeeded in getting into Sweden and from there straight to England, where he joined the Norwegian forces.

There were crowds of Germans everywhere we went along

the coast, both in large and in small towns. But everywhere too there were people who were ready to give a helping hand when any kind of assistance was needed. People asked as a rule where we meant to go, and the reply to this was always 'West!' Of course 'west' could mean anything, and we left it to people's intelligence to form an opinion of the real meaning of the word.

Our voyage had reached a harbour outside Kristiansand without any difficulties worth mentioning. In the last few days we had had pretty bad weather with a strong southwester, and this meant continual beating up against the wind. *Haabet* was still as leaky as on the day we left Bestumkilen, but we had grown accustomed to it and baled at regular intervals without paying any great attention to it. One question worried us, however: how would things go when we were compelled to sail both night and day? Would two men stand the exertions alone if it blew a gale for any length of time? This question could not be answered for the present. We should have to wait and see.

Kristiansand was the Germans' great naval harbour, and, in conjuction with Kjevik airfield, the place was of great interest. One day when I was up on the second floor of a building whence there was an excellent view over the harbour and naval station, our great plans for reaching England nearly received their quietus. I had taken a number of photographs, and was just about to thrust the camera under my shirt, when I noticed a German sentry on the opposite pavement, staring keenly up at the place where I stood. It did not take me many seconds to reach the first floor, but the German was as quick. We positively collided in the corridor, and for a few seconds I stood in confusion, searching for polite German phrases. Had I been taking photographs? Did I not know that it was strictly forbidden to take photographs of German military positions and material? Had I not heard the announcement that spies would be sentenced to death immediately if caught in the act? No, I had not the slightest idea of it. I came from a farm far away in the countryside, was engaged in timber-felling for the Germans, knew little of the regulations in force in a 'big town.' The only thing I was interested in was to get a souvenir of this time and of the splendid German Navy, the pearl of the German services!

The conversation went on for a good quarter of an hour, with the result that when we parted we were the best friends in the world. I had invited the German to drink a glass of beer at six the same evening and—I might keep the film on condition that I promised to hide it till after the war (which, of course, the Germans were going to win) and not tell a soul that I had taken any photographs at all.

There is no need to say more than that the appointment with the German sentry was not kept by me.

The same afternoon, as Kaare and I were sitting down in the cabin eating our dinner, we heard over the wireless the following announcement by the German higher command: 'Any boat which from to-day onwards attempts to escape from Norway, and crosses the boundaries laid down for coastal traffic by the German higher command, will be attacked by every means and sunk without warning!'

We were startled. Of course it was just what we had expected, but at the same time it was a rather blunt reminder which invited reflection. It was this—combined with the events of the day as far as I was concerned—that made us decide to try to get away from Kristiansand the following night, abandon our proposed visits to Mandal and Farsund, and set our course direct for England. But what about our papers and equipment as commercial travellers in case we were hailed or caught outside the permitted boundary? Something had to be done about this, and that 'something' was a rapid alteration of our equipment and papers in the hours that followed. For this we owe our thanks to a quite simple, ordinary tobacconist, 'Abrahamsen on the Quay,' a man with whom we had quite casually come into contact earlier. It did not take him long to obtain a complete fishing outfit, second-hand, and fishermen's passes which were filled in with the identification marks of *Haabet*. 'Abrahamsen on the Quay' also obtained an American and a German flag which he thought would come in useful. We ourselves had a British flag, sewn into the mattress on board.

At 1 a.m. *Haabet* stood out from Kristiansand through Vestergabet, with a light night breeze from the north. The sky was overcast and it was dark, but not too dark for us to see clearly the outlines of islets and rocks. We passed out slowly between the various German fortifications. To us who sat there working and did not even dare whisper to each other, our pace seemed still slower. We ran a risk by keeping to the middle of the waterway, as neither of us knew the various submerged rocks in the channel and could not use too much light in consulting the chart. But all went well. We did not hear a sound from anywhere, and after about two hours we left behind the last rocks of the skerries.

But fate this time willed it otherwise. The wind dropped —and dropped quickly. How far out we had got it was difficult to judge while it was dark. We had an answer a few hours later. When it grew light the coastline appeared on the horizon; we had not come as far out as we had hoped. The sails hung flapping, and the boom swung in time with the boat's movements in the swell. Not a breath of wind! Kaare and I looked at each other and said nothing. It was a long way to England. . . .

Then Kaare started up, stared and pointed. 'Look there!' I turned round, weary and worn after twenty-four hours without sleep. But what we both saw had more effect on a sleepy man than a bucket of ice-cold water! A German destroyer! We heaved ourselves into our kit: out with the fishing-lines! There was no doubt about the destroyer's intention she was making straight for us at full speed. Next moment two shots rang out in quick succession, followed by two explosions in the water straight ahead of us.

The destroyer was slowing down. In the meantime Kaare and I continued to haul on lines as if nothing had happened. A man shouted to us in German from the destroyer's bridge and ordered us to prepare for boarding. We continued to haul on lines. A boat was launched with three men in it, and in a short time we had the three on board. They were a lieutenant and two ratings. There were no polite phrases this time! The lieutenant ordered curtly that *Haabet* should be thoroughly searched, and then turned to Kaare and me.

We both feared the worst. First papers. Then an explanation as to why we were so far out. We who had fishermen's passes ought to know quite well that we might not go farther than one sea mile from the coast, etc.

It took us a long time to explain that we had started the evening before, that a dead calm and strong southward current had driven us far beyond where we had originally meant to fish, and that our engine had broken down. Curiously enough, the lieutenant certainly believed our explanation, and when one of the two ratings reported the finding of a whisky bottle, three parts full, there seemed to be no doubt in the lieutenant's mind. Till then we had been in great anxiety lest the Germans should discover the secret place in the tie-beam which supported the cabin roof. But the whisky bottle seemed to have saved the situation! I utilized the interest momentarily aroused to ask the lieutenant if we could have a tow in towards the coast again, to which he very amiably agreed. He ordered the two ratings back to the destroyer, which throughout the visit had stood with two machine-guns trained on us.

The episode which followed was too comic to be ever forgotten. We went coastwards in tow of the destroyer so fast that the water spurted up at our bows. On board *Haabet* sat the lieutenant, Kaare and I swallowing one grog after another—we made sure that the lieutenant's glass was full all the time. The bottle was soon nearly empty. Kaare and I pretended to be drunk, and the lieutenant actually was as drunk as a lord! And the best part of it was an admirable musical contribution by three voices: *Denn wir fahren gegen England*!

Off Mövika, three and a half miles from Kristiansand, the destroyer stopped, a boat came over to fetch the intoxicated lieutenant, wishes for a good voyage were exchanged, and we set sail again and began to cruise westward with a freshening breeze. Evidently the destroyer had not acted on any information from the German naval headquarters at Kristiansand; the whole incident was simply a routine apprehension of fishermen breaking the regulations.

We now took the risk of proceeding to Mandal, where our

next task was Mandal airfield and the surrounding area.

There was one thing we noticed when we lay to at one of the wharves up in the Mandal river—a rather dark, thickset fellow who stood leaning against a telegraph post, following us with his eyes, keenly interested. We were now accustomed to expect almost anything, and Kaare called my attention to this fellow. At regular intervals in the course of the following three days this man stood on the same spot and watched every one of our movements. When, on the third day, we began to set sail, he came up to the boat and introduced himself as Rolf Gabrielsen, bank clerk, living in Mandal. We chatted about one thing and another, till he suddenly asked if we wanted a third hand.

'A third hand? What for?' Kaare asked.

Well, he thought he could say with certainty where we meant to go, after the preparations we had been making on board the boat, and in view of our age and our behaviour! Without waiting for an answer he went on to tell us that he had tried once before to get on to a boat which was going to England, but that time the boat was overcrowded. Now it looked as if we wanted a hand, and it was his greatest wish to get over to the other side and report for duty. He gave us a number of references in Mandal, without our asking for any; among them was a leader of one of the former Mandal Scout troops, whom I had met a few years before. Of course neither Kaare nor I gave him an inkling of our real thoughts. We insisted most strongly that there was no question of a voyage to England. We were professional fishermen and meant to go to Bergen. Gabrielsen fully accepted our statement, but remarked, before leaving us, that if there was anything with which he could help he was willing to do all that was in his power. Then Gabrielsen departed.

A long and thorough discussion took place that afternoon in *Haabet's* cabin. We wanted a third hand; there was no chance of our being able to hold out for several days on end if there was a gale on the way over. Certainly there was not room for three in the cabin at once, but that question would not arise when the voyage really started.

Among the many people whom Gabrielsen had given us as

references were two who we knew were good Norwegians—and safe. The same evening I went up to see one of them and cleared up the question of Gabrielson's identity. He was a first-class man and knew at any rate *something* about sailing.

This was enough. Rolf Gabrielsen started with us next day and moved on board *Haabet* as the third member of the crew. At five in the afternoon all was ready, the necessary photographs had been taken so far as time allowed, a final overhaul of *Haabet* had taken place, the fore-hatch covered with canvas and securely battened down, and a thick tarpaulin drawn on solid trestles over the greater part of the open cockpit, leaving only a small hole open for the steersman. In case of severe weather it was our hope that any water which might wash over the deck would be prevented from getting into the boat. This was the theory! A fresh water supply was taken on board, and for safety's sake we asked Gabrielsen to get fifteen bottles of seltzer as an extra supply.

It was still blowing hard from the south-west when we set our course that evening for Lindesnes, the most southerly point of Norway on the mainland. The same wind which had hindered our progress down the coast all the time. South-west was just the direction in which we should sail to get across to England, and the wind was dead against us. We agreed, therefore, to drop anchor in a sheltered little creek between Mandal and Lindesnes, which Rolf knew from earlier times, wait there for the night and proceed next day.

We dropped anchor at eleven p.m. A little Sörland paradise in itself, well hidden amid a ring of wooded islets. All was still; only occasional gusts from a gentle night breeze reached us. It was mild and rather muggy, and for over an hour we lay on deck talking over prospects.

We sailed again early next morning. The same wretched weather; south-west wind and rough sea. The wind rose during the day and when we rounded Lindesnes it was blowing hard, and we were obliged to shorten sail. Earlier that morning we had discussed the question of sailing straight from Lindesnes with England as our next stop, but the weather conditions put an end to that. As the wind grew stronger the sea rose, *Haabet* was tossed up and down like a nutshell, and we all three had our first taste of sea-sickness. . . . There were no protests when I announced the final decision to put into Farsund as quickly as possible.

The next day was Friday, September 13. It is unnecessary to explain why the question of departure was not raised on such a day. Besides, we had plenty to do in investigating the new airfield which was projected at Lista; and through some connections of Rolf we had obtained a considerable quantity of material.

Saturday, September 14, 1940, broke with just the weather we wanted. Easterly wind, overcast, fresh breeze. It could not have been better if it had been ordered! It did not take us long before all was ready, and then 'Cast off!'

The sail which followed I shall never forget. We went like smoke down the fjord from Farsund. It was not long before we decided to run close-reefed. The wind had increased to a strong breeze and we shot out in a wild dash towards the open sea. This was what we had all been waiting for. A wind which would blow us in the right direction either under or above the surface!

One of the Lifeboat Society's well-known smacks emerged from among some islands to starboard, also close-reefed. The water foamed about the proud vessel's bow as she swung up towards us. If only we had had a craft like that! We all had the same thought as we stood in the steering cockpit dripping wet from the spray which swept in over us. The lifeboat came up alongside, set the same course as ourselves, and now began a race the like of which none of us had taken part in before. *Haabet* was in her element. In this kind of sailing there were not many boats that could beat her. A man on board the lifeboat hung in the rigging with a megaphone to his lips: 'All under control?' 'Couldn't be better!' I shouted back at the top of my voice to overcome the noise of the rushing sea and howling wind. Then the man yelled back through his megaphone: 'Good luck and wish them all the best on the other side!'

We stood for a few moments without saying a word. It was queer how well-informed the fellow seemed to be. But a moment later our suspicion disappeared; the lifeboat was dipping the Norwegian flag to us. Kaare crept forward along the deck to the mast and dipped our Norwegian flag in return.

This was the greatest and most stirring moment of the passage. The great voyage had begun! The lifeboat altered course inshore again, and it was not long before we were alone on the rough sea, a nutshell abandoned to the will and decree of the forces of nature.

'All under control?' That was a question we were to ask ourselves many times that day. With a 30-knot wind on her beam *Haabet* showed herself at her best. The water poured incessantly over the deck, and the man whose turn at the helm it was had a hard job to keep the boat on an even keel. We sailed and pumped, pumped and sailed; gradually and surely the coastline astern of us grew fainter and fainter.

Kaare was at the helm, Rolf pumping, and I sitting in the cabin and doing my best to light the Primus stove. We were all hungry, and it was time to get a bite of food. This, however, was easier said than done. Inside the cabin there was already chaos, ship's stores and personal belongings flung about between the bulkheads. *Haabet* pitched and rolled in the big seas, and I had to sit down to keep a tight hold on both Primus and cooking pot.

'You'd better come out if you want to say good-bye to old Mother Norway; the coastline's just disappearing below the horizon!' Kaare shouted through the cabin door. Rolf and I let go what we had in our hands and crawled out to the steersman's post. The jagged mountains of Norway were just vanishing below the horizon. Nothing was said. Each of us had his own thoughts. Was it for the last time? How long would it be before we saw that land which we loved so much?

Suddenly Kaare yelled 'Look!' We followed the direction of his outstretched hand. A plane—two planes! We all three stood staring for a few seconds. They were coming towards us—they had seen us! 'Out with the lines! back the sail!'

Before I could get the order carried out Kaare was on his way into the cabin, and came out again a moment later dragging the smallest of our two fishing lines. Over the side went the line, and a minute later, when the planes reached

Rolf Gabrielsen
in the cockpit after four days at sea.

After an eight days' gale off the Danish Coast.

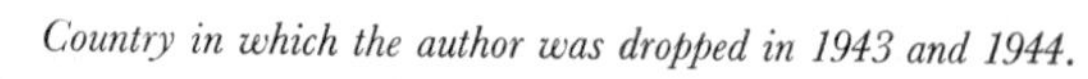

Country in which the author was dropped in 1943 and 1944.

us, we were busy hauling on it. They were two German Heinkel 115's. For a few breathless minutes they circled round *Haabet*, which was now flying the German swastika flag together with the Norwegian. We continued to work at our lines, but found time to wave to the airmen with a white cloth, while *Haabet* heaved up and down all the time in the rough sea with backed sails. The planes grazed the masthead three times, then circled round and finally dropped two red flares outside us. To emphasize their meaning one of the planes came in on a last run and fired a salvo of machine-gun bullets hardly ten yards from us—between us and England. They bore away again while we stood literally gasping for breath.

Was that all? Or was it only the beginning? It seemed, however, that they were satisfied. Soon after, they both disappeared landwards and were lost in a heavy shower of rain which was approaching from the eastward. 'In with the lines!' And our mad career continued.

Now the great question was whether these two aircraft would report our position and if we could expect a visit from a German coast patrol. If this happened the result was clear. We were far outside the permitted zone. But fate was kind to us. Soon afterwards an unbroken cover of mist and rain moved in towards the coast, and we ourselves could not see for more than a few yards. Only rough sea and low rain-filled storm-clouds.

Darkness came on slowly, and with it the wind increased. I shall never forget that first night on board an eighteen-foot sailing boat in the North Sea. There was no question of any of us getting any sleep; instead we had ceaseless toil to keep the little craft afloat. The wind increased steadily and surely, and our impression was that *Haabet* was more under than above water. Every other hour the cabin floor was under water, and it was not long before practically everything inside the little cabin was soaking wet. With every movement caused by the heavy sea the water on board was flung up above the bulkheads, spurted over everything that was not covered up and ran down into the bottom again. While I took the wheel during the first half of the night, Kaare managed to cook quite a decent meal over the Primus. Rolf had a full-time job pumping, and, when this was not necessary, tidying up all the things which had been flung about the cabin by the boat's violent motion.

At 11.20 that night the mainsail split across, along one of the seams by the third reef. The noise was like a pistol-shot, and for a good half-hour Kaare and I lay out on the cabin roof, lashed ourselves fast and tried to fix things up provisionally. But finally we had to give this up. The wind was too strong, and it appeared that running before it under the foresail alone was enough that night. Gradually but surely, one defect after another was discovered—things which ought to have been put right before we started. Now it was too late, and the only thing to do was to make the best of the situation. Our martial spirit, which had been to the fore earlier in the day, had long disappeared. All three of us had the same thought; if only I had known better and not come on this trip in a boat like this! Instead we all tried to make a joke of the serious situation, tried to convince one another that these matters were all trifles. But none of us would bite on that hook; we all three realized that things were serious. . . . Never before have the hours and minutes of a night been so long. Everything was dark. We could only hear the rushing of the wind and the roaring of the seas that broke incessantly over the little craft. But in spite of everything we sent up our fervent thanks to Him who had arranged this weather. What should we have done if the same wind had come from the west?

At last the day of September 15 dawned. We were all three dead tired after the physical and mental strain of the darkness. What a night! And this was only the first!

During the three days and nights that followed there was no need to repair the mainsail. We ran westward with our foresail filled. Our speed was irreproachable and the direction of the wind perfect. Slowly and surely we became accustomed to the life on board; slowly and surely we learnt what sea sailing was with a small leaky boat. What we at first thought was a gale was doubtless only a fresh breeze, but nevertheless it was enough for both *Haabet* and ourselves.

Now and then, in the course of the daylight hours, each man in turn had an opportunity of getting a half-hour's nap on one of the bunks in the cabin; of proper sleep there was no question, the boat's sudden movements were too violent for that. But we kept afloat, and mile after mile vanished in our wake. Our direction? We had at last set up a kind of compass in gimbals on the engine casing, an old compass Kaare had got hold of before we left Oslo. Curiously enough this compass served us well on the voyage across, without any regard being paid to deviation or other metallic influence on the magnetic needle. The direction was west-south-west, and this was pretty well kept.

On the third day, however, something happened which caused us a bit of a problem. A heavy sea suddenly flung the boat over on one side. The motion was so violent that it caused the watertight bottle containing matches and tinder, which had its regular place upon one of the shelves, to be flung against the bulkhead on the lee side, and it was smashed into a thousand pieces. The contents were thrown about the cabin and the greater part ended up in the water, which at that moment was over the deck. Strong language was of little use. For over two hours Kaare and Rolf were busy drying matches in the frying-pan over the Primus, a system which was applied more than once later on.

We had been at sea for four days and nights when, on the morning of September 18, the weather began to change. The wind dropped steadily, and at twelve o'clock it was practically speaking quiet. What next? We had, for that matter, so much to do in the way of repairs that we did not think about this for many minutes. All the clothes on board, and every stitch we had on us, had been wet through for the last two days, and this opportunity of drying clothes was more than welcome. Moreover, the weather at last gave us a chance of getting a little rest. We were all dead tired after our exertions and anxiety, and while one man was on watch, two others were able to get a few hours' sleep. Stockings, underclothes, top clothes and sleeping-bags were hung up wherever there was room, and for the next few hours *Haabet* looked like an untidy fishing smack. I myself set about repairing the mainsail, and it was not long before *Haabet* was under full sail again.

But that did not help us much. The sails hung and swung round the rigging, and at last we were obliged to lash the mainsail boom because it looked like knocking us overboard. The swell was still running high, and a queer thing was that now for the first time since Farsund the earliest symptoms of sea-sickness appeared. First Rolf, then I, and lastly Kaare. The reason for this not having happened before was probably the state of tension in which we had all lived, so that none of us had had time for that sort of thing. We all felt wretched for the whole day.

It was Kaare who at half-past four that afternoon roused me from a nightmare I was having while trying to get a nap in the cabin. I was dreaming of waves higher than a house and a little nutshell of a boat when the cry 'Plane!' rang in my ears. I heaved myself out of my sleeping-bag, crawled out on deck and there, in the direction indicated by Kaare's outstretched arm, was a little black dot against a deep-blue sky. 'Get hold of the British flag that's sewn up in the mattress!' I yelled the order, and Kaare disappeared into the cabin like a streak of lightning and returned a moment later with the Union Jack in his hand. We yelled, hooted, waved with everything we had. The dot against the sky in the west grew larger and larger. Yes, it looked as if the plane had seen us, but—what kind of a plane was it—friend or enemy? We stared and stared at the dot, stared till our eyes almost popped out of our heads—why, what was he doing? Had he not seen us? We stopped our wild gestures and movements and stood gaping open-mouthed. The plane swung westward, grew smaller and smaller—and disappeared.

I will freely confess that I was not far from weeping as I looked at the faces of the other two. Not that my own was any better. For a few unforgettable moments toil and fear were totally forgotten—in a hope which for a moment seemed on the verge of fulfilment. It must have been a British plane so far out. We could not be far from the Scottish or English coast after the last four days' sailing. But it was no good whining; it was a good sign and we could only hope for better luck next time. But what annoyed us more than I can say was that not till it was all over did we remember the three rockets which had been stolen from a German dump before we left Oslo and which I had intended for use in just such a case.

Rolf was now put on watch while Kaare and I tried to sleep. What lay before us no one knew. There was no doubt that the worst could still happen.

Again we were both awakened by a shout from Rolf: 'Ship!' Again we popped out, and there, above the horizon in the west, rose a little cloud of smoke. There was no doubt, it must be a ship! Again we worked ourselves up into a mood of triumph; again we had to accept defeat in the shape of a negative result. For a good hour the column of smoke continued to rise above the horizon from the 'something' which we all hoped so desperately would appear. At last there was no longer any smoke, and with the smoke vanished our hope.

It was now past six, and the sails still hung flapping round the rigging. Not a breath of wind! The sun had gone down in the west and we had taken the opportunity to check the compass. We were all three sitting on deck; we had almost forgotten what had happened in the last few hours, and were watching the brilliant spectacle in the western sky, where the sun had sunk into the sea, leaving behind it a river of red. I myself was thinking of what awaited us behind that horizon, what the future would bring to us all, what the future would bring to the world.

Then it was my turn to start. A sound—a distant buzz. 'Plane!' I yelled. And there—in the midst of the blood-red river the sunset had left was a tiny dot which steadily increased in size! We were all a little more reasonable this time, took it rather more quietly, and were all pretty sceptical as to the result. The Union Jack was spread over the cabin roof, which was white and so formed a good background for the bright colours in the flag. Two flares were got ready; if they did not succeed this time it was a good thing to have one in reserve for later. . . . Again we stood and stared. . . . Yes, the dot in the west grew gradually and surely; we begun to distinguish details—it was a double-engined plane. Nearer—

nearer—it *must* see us, it *must*! I let off one of the rockets; it shot up into the air, burst high up and three red lights drifted slowly down towards us. We stared and stared at the plane. Yes—it *had* seen us! We cheered, danced about the deck, waved back with every strip of cloth and flag we had.

The plane, a double-engined Avro Anson, came roaring over *Haabet*. What a sight! Twice it swept past us on a level with the masthead, so near that we could see the crew on board, could see them waving. Then they began to fly in a narrow circle round *Haabet* and to send a message by signal lamp. None of us were at first capable of receiving any message. It did not matter so long as they had seen us! But they repeated their signals, and at last we got a receiving station organized; Kaare took down whilst I dictated dots and dashes. At the speed at which they sent I could make out only a few of the letters; the rest we should have to find out afterwards. I clung tight to the rigging with a signal flag in each hand:

'Will report your position and arrange for rescue!'

I sent back three times: 'Have escaped from Norway using call sign D for David thank you!'

For more than twenty minutes the plane continued to fly round us in now wider, now narrower circles, and as a last farewell it came roaring down over *Haabet* at full speed. Our jubilation can be imagined! All weariness was gone, the toil and struggle with the elements of the previous nights were forgotten; there was only one thing that counted—we should be picked up by a British ship perhaps that same evening, or in any case early next morning!

It was almost incredible! The inward doubt which had pursued each one of us since the day we sailed from Oslo and which had grown stronger with each day, each night that passed, was now suddenly removed. It was reality; we had been seen by a British plane and it had reported us! Our sea-sickness was gone, and before the plane had disappeared on the horizon it had been unanimously decided that the occasion must be celebrated. We had not much in the way of extras, but soon after we were all three sitting on deck, eating bread soaked in salt water, thickly spread with butter and sardines!

At 7.30 that evening we quite suddenly noticed wind in the sails. As we lay at our ease on deck with our pipes in our mouths, chatting of the great possibilities which had now so suddenly become almost reality, we saw thick, dark cloud-banks in the west. *Haabet* heaved regularly and steadily in the swell, which now seemed to be coming in from all sides. We sat and stared. The faint breeze which now began to fill the sails came from the *westward*! The black cloud-banks approached us slowly but surely. We looked at each other—and said nothing. All three of us felt the menace those clouds held.

The wind increased. We began to beat up against it. The best course *Haabet* managed to keep was south-west by south. We agreed to sail for exactly half an hour on each tack, courses south-west by south and north-west by west.

The wind increased; the seas began to drive in from the west, growing gradually bigger as the hours passed. But there was still only a light breeze and we assured one another that it was nothing to worry about; we had a sea anchor and this change of wind would certainly not continue for long.

At 9 p.m. the wind had increased to a fresh breeze. It was fairly dark now. We had the choice between taking in sail in case the weather grew rough during the night or lying to with a sea anchor. We chose the latter. It was pretty certain that the aircraft had reported us, and even if we drifted a short distance in the course of the night, a vessel of any size would be quite sure to find us. The sea anchor was a sort of large funnel, made of solid canvas with quite a small hole in the end of it, and mounted on a frame of thin steel. An old corked paraffin can served as a buoy to hold this up, at a fixed depth below the surface. The whole sea anchor was attached to a 100-foot chain, and as it had originally been made for a lifeboat (being a present from our friend the dentist) there was no doubt that it would hold us through the night in more or less the same place.

Rolf took the first watch, while Kaare and I turned in to try to get a little sleep. We had by now grown accustomed to the steady heaving and it was not long before we both fell asleep.

At 11.30 we were awakened by a shout from Rolf: 'The wind's getting higher! The sea's beginning to go white!' We had hardly got out of our sleeping-bags when the next warning shout came: 'The anchor chain's broken!' At the same moment we were both flung against one of the bulkheads: things were getting serious!

Without a word we crept out through the cabin opening. It was pitch dark and impossible to see a thing. We felt our way forward to where Rolf was standing and hauling in a loose, broken chain. We had to act quickly. We must set sail, close-reefed, and try to beat up against the wind or try to lie to, head to wind.

Anyone who has tried to set sail on a boat with no steerage way on her on a pitch-dark night out in the North Sea will be able to understand the labour and difficulties this involves. For over half an hour we struggled desperately with sails and halyards, reefs and rope ends, before we were able to get the sails set satisfactorily. The attempt to get *Haabet* to lie head to wind soon proved hopeless. We had no sooner got her steady than a heavy sea poured over us and drove us off our course, with the result that we got the wind right on our beam and came near being forced under. There was nothing else to be done but to try to beat up *against* the wind.

What sailing! *Haabet,* with close-reefed sails, lay quite flat with half the deck continually under water. It was impossible to see forward to the bow, much less ahead of it, so as to be able to try and avoid the worst breaking seas. Two of us hung on to the tiller and tried to keep the boat's head to the wind. Spray flew over us, and the noise of the seething, boiling seas, mingled with the howling of the wind, seemed to grow stronger and stronger. Sea after sea poured over the tiny nutshell and threatened every time to capsize *Haabet* altogether; we were shaken and thrown up and down, to and fro, like a restless leaf in a storm.

'We'll go to the bottom if it goes on like this!' I yelled across to Kaare. 'We'll have to take in the mainsail!'

I had not finished the sentence before Nature gave the answer. With a noise like a pistol shot, we heard the mainsail go; in seconds it was split right across, a reef higher than the time before! 'Take the tiller!' I shouted to Rolf. With Kaare I slithered along to the mast, clung tightly to it at the very moment when a fresh sea poured over us, took a gulp of sea water and for a moment lay gasping for breath. Yes, Kaare was still on board; he had clung tightly to the cabin roof. The mainsail was thrashing in the wind and it was no easy task to recover the strips. But we managed it; we got the remains lashed fast to the mainsail boom and finally lashed up the boom properly. Meanwhile Rolf did a fine piece of work keeping *Haabet* hove to under her backed foresail.

For a good half an hour we kept going, beating up against the wind under the close-reefed foresail. But *Haabet* would not sail in this manner under the prevailing conditions, as she had shown herself capable of doing earlier in a gentle breeze outside the skerries. It was impossible to get up any speed, for as soon as she began to slide down into the trough of the waves and to get a little way on her, the sea from the next wave-top came pouring over her and put a stop to each attempt. It was hopeless.

Something new came to light, *Haabet* was now leaking about twice as fast as she had done earlier. Rolf tried to find the new leak with an electric torch and soon reported that the water was literally spurting in through new cracks which had formed along the tabernacle in the bottom of the boat.

While Rolf was caulking the leaks, a fresh sea came rushing over us. Kaare and I, where we hung on to the tiller, could hear its approaching roar. Before we were sure of its direction it had reached us, and for a few seconds everything was submerged in a seething mass of water. We were within an ace of capsizing. But that was not enough; when the boat rose again and Kaare and I had spat out enough sea-water to be able to call to one another, we both discovered that we were clinging to a smashed tiller. There was nothing to be done about it. Another sea like that, and we were done for.

'Get up the spare tiller on the starboard side!' I yelled to Rolf under the tarpaulin. Meanwhile Kaare hung over the stern of the boat and vainly tried to maintain steering way with the little stump that was left. And now, about turn! There was no choice; we must run before the wind. I shouted the order in full consciousness of what it meant for us all: back the same way we had come!

As the night gradually wore on, there was no doubt that the weather had worsened and that the wind must certainly have reached what in meteorological language is called 'a moderate gale.' We had rigged up a little storm-sail from the foresail, set crossways on the forecastle, and astern we had hung out a 'warp' about sixty feet long made of the remains of the anchor chain and some thick rope we had brought with us for use if required. Altogether this formed a fairly good brake on the fantastic speed we should reach in the following days with the wind behind us.

When dawn came at last, *Haabet* and her crew presented a pretty sorry spectacle. A nutshell completely abandoned to the forces of Nature; rigged with the little storm-sail forward by way of a good joke; the crew, three shadows of themselves. Back we went in a wild chase with wind and sea astern of us, the same way we had covered in four and a half days, toiling to keep ourselves afloat. Gone was all hope of being saved, at any rate in the next day or two. If this weather continued much longer, we could not possibly keep afloat. That was a fact which was more and more strongly emphasized as the hours passed. *Haabet* leaked like a sieve; every hour fresh cracks along the tabernacle were discovered, cracks through which the water spurted in faster than any pump could clear it out again. Rolf caulked desperately. Kaare and I worked shifts at the tiller. As skipper I felt my responsibility more and more strongly; there was no doubt that I alone was responsible for the complete disaster which now seemed inevitable for us all.

For four days and nights the storm continued without interruption; for four days we toiled for our lives, tried to avoid the worst seas, tried to keep the water inboard below the level of the cabin floor. But every time a sea struck us at a wrong angle, the water poured in through the opening in the tarpaulin where the steersman stood, and whoever was at the pump at the moment floundered in sea-water for the next few minutes while working at high pressure. We had now all reached the stage where one begins to get a bit dull-witted, indifferent to what may happen except just at the moment when something unexpected happens and the situation becomes crucial. Everything was soaked—clothes, mattresses, and sleeping-bags; we had not a scrap of dry clothing to change into. We froze day and night till our teeth chattered, but we no longer noticed it. None of us had had a minute's sleep in the last four days; our hands were swollen with sea-water, and toiling with halyards and sheets had removed what little skin we had left. Rolf, who had come straight from a stool in a bank and had not even had the little preliminary training that Kaare and I had had, went about with hands which looked like lumps of raw meat.

On the night of September 22-23 death came knocking at the door in earnest. This was the night none of us would ever forget, even if we never really knew how it was we had remained alive.

It was past midnight; it was pitch dark, and in the course of the last three hours the wind seemed to have increased in strength. Kaare and I were at the tiller, while Rolf lay under the tarpaulin pumping. The water was now over the cabin floor every twenty minutes, and whatever we did in the way of caulking was of little use. It was the steady pressure on the rigging that all the time was pushing down the foot of the mast; soon it would probably go right through the bottom. It was not only the big waves now which broke over the boat at regular intervals; the wind whirled the sea up and from every wave-top, great or small, the water poured in over us as from a waterfall. It lashed our faces; our eyes were full of water all the time as we tried to look astern and steer to avoid the worst seas. What we could see was just nothing. In the last few days we had learned to rely on hearing and nothing else. The rushing noise, louder and louder, from the seas as they gradually approached, rising to a bellowing roar, was the only thing that could give us an idea of where the waves came from. If it was too late to steer out of their way, the result depended on how quickly the steersman was able to judge the direction, so that he could take the sea on board exactly in the direction in which it was moving. This applied also to the following seconds, in which the boat was heaved up with the wave at a fearful pace, completely buried in it. If the boat sheered away, the result was that the water poured in and the boat heeled over on one side. Then the great question was whether the boat would ever come up again. . . .

We hung on to the tiller and made desperate efforts to keep *Haabet* on an even keel. Seas tumbled in over us, each bigger than the last. Rolf had just finished pumping, and I shouted in to him that he was to come out and take Kaare's place. Meanwhile Kaare crept into the cabin to fill three oil bags with oil to throw on to the sea; our last remaining hope was that the advice of our friend the dentist to throw oil on the sea would save the situation. It was all I could do to hear myself give the different orders, all I could do to utter the words.

Rolf and I were now lashed fast to the rail in case we were knocked overboard. The now familiar roaring came from the darkness behind us. We both automatically yelled a warning to the man in the cabin: 'Hold tight! Sea!' Neither Rolf nor I had any idea where the sea was coming from before it tumbled on board. Everything was carried away. The tiller was torn out of my hands, there was a fearful roaring which seemed to deaden all other sounds: water—sea—we're sinking—sinking—sinking! I tried in vain to breathe, only gulped down bitter salt sea-water—everything was black—and so curiously quiet. I felt myself rising slowly, my lungs were near bursting—then I felt the wind tearing at my hair again and gasped for breath. My lifebelt had undoubtedly done its job. At the same time I felt the rope from *Haabet* tight round my waist, and slowly but surely I dragged myself on board. But *Haabet* lay broadside on to the sea, half full of water, and now it was only a question of seconds. Almost at the same time as I climbed on board Rolf came up on the other side. We had been washed overboard when the big sea passed over us. But what had happened to Kaare? I yelled in but got no answer. I yelled to Rolf and asked him to break up the deck planks he was standing on in the steering hole, crawled into the cabin, tumbled over Kaare as he tried to drag himself up on to one of the bunks more or less unconscious, got hold of the bag I was searching for, and paddled out again. There was no time to help Kaare, or find out what had happened; we must just bale—bale—bale!

But where was the tiller? Rolf yelled across to me that it had been carried away by the big sea. In a few seconds two of the deck planks were fastened together round the upper part of the rudder; this would have to hold till we had an opportunity of repairing it properly—if we got another chance. But something else was lacking too. We had completely lost steerage way and speed; we just lay tumbling up and down broadside on to the seas. Then Kaare came scrambling out of the cabin. He managed to say in a feeble voice that he had been flung against the bulkhead and rendered unconscious, and had come to after swallowing a few quarts of sea-water.

'The storm-sail must have gone!' I yelled across to Kaare. Before I could say anything more, Kaare disappeared in the direction of the bows, clinging to the cabin roof. It was madness; if a sea came now Kaare would not have a chance. But there was no time to waste. We went on baling feverishly. Then we noticed that *Haabet* was under sail again; Kaare came crawling back along the deck. 'The foresail wire's gone. I've hoisted the storm-sail on the peak halyard. All under control!' This was just like Kaare. When everything looked blackest the fellow could always produce some little humorous remark.

All under control! But it was not to be for many minutes. Kaare disappeared into the cabin again to try to continue where he had left off. A few seconds after he had vanished, a fresh sea came tumbling on board. This time neither Rolf nor I received full warning. Once more everything seemed to have gone, but we both managed to keep on board by hanging on to what we now called the tiller. But *Haabet* sheered away and heeled over on her side, and when at last we were able to breathe again, we were both hanging half-way over the rail up to our waists in the water. But what was worse was that *Haabet* was lying with her mast in the water and the sea pouring in through the open steering hole. What I yelled to Rolf I do not remember; I only know that next moment both of us were hanging on the weather side as tight as we could, and a moment later Kaare was out beside us. Slowly but sure *Haabet* rose again, this time three-quarters full of water.

Once more we baled, baled as we had never baled before. Kaare tried to use the pump, but this was full of scraps of paper from a stack of *Fritt Folk* which had been lying on a shelf and which had now dissolved in the sea-water. I used the bucket on one side and Rolf his own sou'wester on the other. The situation was hopeless. We had not got the water inboard down even to deck level when the third sea came tumbling over us. All I know is that I gave a yell. I received a blow on the forehead. Everything became curiously still. I held my breath automatically, felt the boat being forced down and myself somehow getting underneath her and sinking even deeper and deeper. My ears filled with a deep rushing noise. Then I was coming up to the surface again.

I can remember that I was clinging to the weather side again with Kaare, that *Haabet* rose again and Rolf was dragged on board, and that we baled. But what happened in detail, and how, I do not know. One thing I remember clearly: I called to Kaare and asked him to say 'Our Father' with me! And at the moment when we went down for the third time I clearly recollect seeing my mother's face before me; she was talking very quietly and calmly, as she always did. And through the deafening roar of the storm and the sea I could hear the words quite distinctly: 'With God's help it'll go all right!' Kaare and I stopped baling; we knelt on the broken deck and prayed, while the seas continued to rush over us.

What happened after that I shall never forget. The third sea was the last which struck us in the wrong position. We seemed all the time to be lying in dead water. Sea after sea rushed past us, now to starboard, now to port. Many smaller seas broke on board *Haabet*, but they were all of a less dangerous kind.

The gale continued for four days longer. Eight days of full gale. Kaare was rather bad for more than a day after the worst night. When *Haabet* heeled over he had struck his head against the bulkhead several times, and in addition to this he had swallowed quarts of salt water as he lay unconscious on the floor of the cabin, three-parts full of water. Rolf had not a scrap of skin left on his hands; they were swollen and full of deep cracks. I was not much better. Kaare remained lying in the cabin for the rest of the night, and slowly but surely he got on his legs again. I was at the helm for thirteen hours on end that night and the following day. Minutes and hours crept away, and time after time I almost collapsed at the bottom of the steering hole. But each time a new sea came along to keep me awake.

When dawn came *Haabet* was a deplorable sight, more so inside than out. The oil which Kaare had tried to pour into the bags had run over and had been flung all over the bulkheads and ceiling along with the water that was on board. Everything was covered with a thin layer of grease, and this undoubtedly contributed further to develop the art of balance in each one of us in the days that followed. But this was not all. The big water container, a glass bottle in a straw basket, which had been quite firmly lashed to one of the bulkheads, had broken loose, probably when the boat was on her beam ends for the second time, and inside the bottle lay the scanty remains of what should have been our iron ration of fresh water. All we now had left was a quart and a half of fresh water in a wooden keg which fortunately had stood the shock. The fifteen bottles of seltzer which Rolf had brought on board at Mandal, and which also were to serve as a stand-by, were smashed.

All the bread we possessed was completely ruined by salt water, and our food supply now consisted of four tins of sardines and a keg containing about two and a quarter pounds of good mountain butter! The situation seemed pretty hopeless.

On the following night, when Kaare was at the helm, there was a sudden shout of 'Light ahead!' For a moment a hope flickered through all our minds, but after we had watched the light for a short time we were none of us in any doubt—the light came from a lighthouse. It flashed steadily—one long and two short! It could only be the Danish coast. Two hours later we saw another light, and while this was visible we had a little discussion in the steering hole aft. Should we continue straight towards the light, and give up now while we had 'safety' in sight? With our storm-sail full it would probably not take us many hours to reach it. But what would happen if we landed in Denmark, occupied by the Germans? Undoubtedly we should all three be captured by the Germans and sent back to Norway for trial. The result of that trial could hardly be in doubt. Was all we had gone through in the last five days, for that matter the last nine and a half days since we had left Norway, to be of no avail? Was the whole of our plan to collapse? On the other hand, how long could we continue this nightmare, without water, food or sleep?

Summing up, we found that the choice lay between two different kinds of death—either being put up against a wall and shot, or finding a common grave in the depths of the North Sea. Further, there was still just a vestige of hope that we might meet a British vessel somewhere out here, especially if we managed to keep a more westerly course.

We discussed the matter, carefully weighing every single point for and against, and came to a unanimous decision: either down to a home in the depths of the North Sea, or England! It was not hard for a 'skipper' to keep his courage up when he had such a crew! Despite toil, thirst, cold and everything else, there was complete agreement. We continued our wild chase before wind and sea.

The wind had now moved more into the north, and it was easier for us to keep a more south-westerly course. We took in the long driving line and at the same time the brake we had hanging out astern. Had it not been for this piece of gear, based on good advice from our friend the dentist, the result would have been quite otherwise.

We could not complain of our speed; the water foamed about us, and at night the phosphorescence stood like a shining curtain over our bows. The sea was not quite so rough now; the big waves gradually became smaller and fewer, but there was still no question of trying to run due west.

On the night of September 24-25 we had another bad fright. Rolf was at the helm while Kaare and I were sitting in the cabin for a moment, trying vainly to find a dry match.

Everything in the way of tobacco was long ago soaked through, and our hope was to be able to dry a little of it on the Primus. Then Rolf shouted *'Mines!'* We dropped what we had in our hands and tumbled out. There! Hardly four yards from us a big horned mine sailed by! Rolf was hanging on to the improvised tiller and had already succeeded in twisting *Haabet* out of the way. But was this the only one?

Low tattered storm-clouds swept by over our heads; now and then, where the layer of clouds was thin, a full moon shone through. It was no doubt the last part of the gale which was passing over. While Kaare took over Rolf's job at the helm, Rolf crawled forward along the deck and remained sitting half-erect in the bows, holding tight to the forestay. Again he shouted: *'Mines!'* Kaare heaved at the tiller and again we just missed a horned mine—number two. It was the fifth mine we had seen in all the voyage, but none of the earlier ones had been so uncomfortably near. In the state we all three were now in, the mental effect of this incident was much greater than it would normally have been. We all three strained our eyes out into the darkness, and everywhere we saw mines. Again and again Rolf yelled out the same word: *'Mines!'* But no more mines were seen. Rolf was on the verge of collapse. 'I see mines everywhere,' he half-sobbed. 'I can't stand this much longer.' It was not surprising that Rolf was the first nearly to go mad. The last time we were flung overboard, Rolf was almost unconscious when we got him on board again. Besides this, he had had a violent blow from something or other on the back of his head. Also, he was the one of the us who had had the least experience of sailing, and in consequence of this he worked a good deal harder.

From now onwards Rolf did nothing but pump. Every twenty minutes in the last three days, and every quarter of an hour on the last day of the voyage, Rolf pumped *Haabet* clear. It was a wearisome task, and I shall never forget how he discharged it. Whenever he had finished a turn, he sank down on the cabin floor between the two bunks, dozed off for twenty minutes, and woke up again when the water stood well above the cabin floor and was washing over his face. By then the water covered the greater part of his body too. Several times we had to shout to him for fear that he would not wake and would drown where he lay. But Rolf pumped.

On September 28, early in the morning, the wind, for the first time in eight days, had dropped to a point at which it was possible to repair the sails on board. While Kaare stood at the helm and we ran due south-west under a forestaysail, I set about sewing together the two parts of the mainsail. It was not so simple, soaking wet as the canvas was, and with hands and fingers swollen and sore. There was another thing that caused us a good deal of worry. The wire we had put in as a foresail halyard before we left Norway had been carried away, and the remains had been torn away out of the block up at the masthead. How should we put in a new foresail halyard?

Once more it was Kaare who saved the situation. A little later in the day he was hoisted up to the masthead with the help of the peak halyard and put in a new foresail halyard. It was a remarkable performance on his part—to be able, in the state he was in, to get to the masthead of a small sailing-boat in the middle of the North Sea, heaved by the swell now to one side, now to the other. But it was done—a last gigantic exertion on Kaare's part. And it cost him all the strength he had left. He lay in the cabin for the rest of the day, hardly able to move. . . .

Haabet was under sail again; westward, always westward. But there was not much left of any of us. This was the last chance we had. If the wind remained where it was, we might perhaps do it. I sat aft in the steering hole, dozed off now and again and was sometimes wakened by the boat having got too far into the wind so that her sails flapped. It was still hard sailing, but nothing compared with what we had known in the previous eight days. We had had nothing to eat of late but butter and sardines; two sardines each at every meal. Our fresh water had come to an end long ago.

The evening of the thirteenth day drew in. Kaare relieved me at the helm. Rolf was pumping. The night was cold, with a bright starry sky; at about one the moon rose. I was sitting out in the steering hole with Kaare. The hours passed without a word. Now and then I dozed off, only to wake each time a bigger sea struck the boat's side to lift us high. Every fourth hour we changed places, and the man who had the tiller tried to concentrate on compass needles and course . . . westward, always westward. . . . Rolf was pumping.

September 29 dawned with sunshine and warmer weather. The wind increased a little as the day advanced and became rather more easterly. We were sailing free again under close-reefed sails. We had butter for lunch; the sardines were finished. Hardly a word was said. We were all thirsty, and the hope that the day would bring a little rain soon disappeared. The sun shone from a cloudless sky. Westward, always westward.

I was sitting at the tiller. Kaare was sitting by me in an attitude of prostration, sleeping; Rolf was lying inside the cabin and the water was already half-way up his pillow. It was 2.35 p.m. I was just going to give Rolf the usual warning shout, 'You must pump!', when something seemed to cut through the air. A queer sound—not from the sea, not from the rigging, nor from Kaare's laboured breathing at my side. It grew louder; I slowly rose, looked up. . . .

'Plane!' I yelled as loud as I could.

In a second we were all three on our legs; steering forgotten, pumping forgotten. The little spot which was approaching from the south-west grew bigger and bigger. Kaare took over the helm while I rigged up a soaking wet Union Jack befouled with oil. The Norwegian flag, which was now ragged and filthy, but which we had hauled down before the worst weather came, went to the masthead. 'He *must* see us—he *must* see us—he *must* see us!' I went round and got everything ready in a desperate hurry, praying aloud as I did so. Kaare just sat and stared at the slowly growing spot high up in the sky. Rolf stood clinging tightly to the mast.

I held our last rocket we had left. The semaphore flags lay beside me on the deck. Kaare sat with pencil and paper in readiness, dry paper from the only container which had kept the water out. A few breathless seconds passed. The two-engined plane grew bigger and bigger. As it drew nearer, I set light to the rocket with a cigarette lighter; it hissed up and burst. The red light sank down slowly and went out. At the same moment the plane swung sharply and came roaring down over *Haabet—it had seen us!* Rolf danced round the mast like a madman. Kaare sat aft holding tight to the tiller, while the tears ran down his face. I myself could hardly see for tears.

An hour later we had three planes round us, flying over *Haabet* mast-high. Three planes! This time there could be no doubt. We received the same instructions as before: 'Will report—follow direction of planes.' And I sent the same reply: 'Have escaped from Norway using call-sign D for David thank you.'

Again and again plane after plane came down over us, flew close by our mast-head and continued for a short time in the same direction. There was no doubt what they meant; we were to sail in that direction. We all seemed to have come to life once more. Rolf pumped and tried to sing a little Sörland song as he did so. Kaare sat at the tiller and just smiled, and I could hardly contain myself.

We suddenly took courage, and in a few minutes *Haabet* was under full sail. It was not the thing for a boat like *Haabet* to sail into port with close-reefed sails! We went so that the foam flew and now, according to the course the planes gave us, ran half before the wind, half with the wind on our quarter. What did a little more water one way or the other matter now when it was all over?

It was past four. Then Rolf, standing on the forecastle, shouted, 'Smoke ahead! Ship!' Kaare and I rose. There! Each time *Haabet* cut over a wave-top we could see the masts of a ship; the masts rose higher and higher and the ship herself appeared; she was coming straight towards us. One of the three planes flew in even curves over towards the ship, and next moment swung round and made straight for us again.

At 4.45 we were about a quarter of a mile from the British destroyer. What a sight! It was almost too good to be really true. I had all the time a feeling that I was dreaming, and

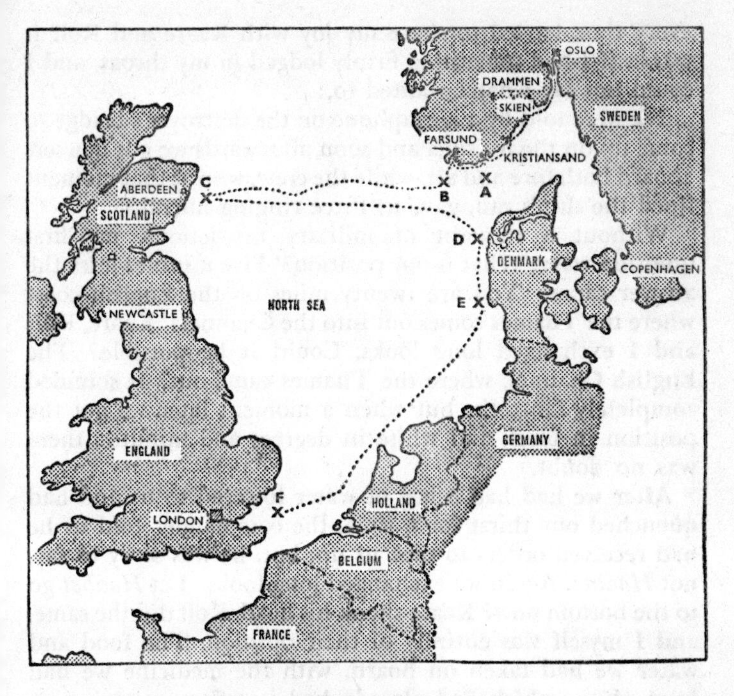

Map of the North Sea Crossing

A. We are caught by a German patrol boat.
B. Two German patrol planes fly over us.
C. Seen by an English plane.
D., *E.* } Lights seen on the Danish coast after six days of storm.
F. We are picked up by H.M.S. *Bedouin* after fourteen and a half days at sea.

every time I tried to share my joy with Kaare and Rolf it was as if I had something firmly lodged in my throat, and I could not say what I wanted to.

We were told by a megaphone on the destroyer's bridge to come up on the lee side, and soon afterwards we got hawsers aboard both fore and aft, while the crew, who at that moment lined the ship's rail, gave us three ringing hurrahs.

Without a thought of military restrictions, my first question was: 'What is our position?' Five minutes later the answer came: 'You are twenty miles off the English coast where the Thames comes out into the Channel!' Kaare, Rolf and I exchanged long looks. Could it be possible? The English Channel, where the Thames came out? It sounded completely fantastic, but when a moment later we got the position in black and white in degrees and minutes, there was no doubt.

After we had had a keg of water lowered to us and had quenched our thirst for a time, the commander told us he had received orders to pick us up, but, he was sorry to say, not *Haabet*. Again we exchanged long looks. Let *Haabet* go to the bottom now? Kaare shook his head, Rolf did the same, and I myself was entirely of their opinion. The food and water we had taken on board, with the medicine we had been given, which had already had its effect, made us all three shake our heads. If *Haabet* had brought us about 1,150 sea miles over the North Sea, first across, then down, and at last across again, surely we could manage the forty miles which remained! We felt big in our shoes, and felt we had good reason to do so. Moreover, *Haabet* was all that we possessed!

The last words we had through the megaphone from the skipper were these:

'I've heard many stories about you crazy Norwegian Vikings, but it seems to me you beat them all! Good luck to you!'

Yes, there was no doubt that we ourselves did not really know what we were doing just then, but our pride in being Norwegians, our pride in having won, was too great.

Two hours later we were hailed by another destroyer with orders to sail up on the lee side. This time there was no question about it: the skipper told us he had received orders from the Admiralty to pick us up, and *Haabet* too. This time we did not have to be asked twice! The food we had taken on board from the first destroyer had made us all sick. Soon after we left the first destroyer the reaction had come, and when we had to begin toiling with sheets and halyards again, with pumping and sea-water, it all seemed twice as hard work as before.

One after another we clambered up the rope ladder and on board H.M.S. *Bedouin*, where officers and crew received us with open arms. What a welcome we had! As we clambered on board, men from the destroyer were down on *Haabet's* deck. First the mast with the Norwegian flag was hoisted on board, after which *Haabet* was slowly but surely heaved up on two strong hawsers. But she was too big to be swung on deck on the davits, as had been intended, so she was made fast, so as to hang outboard on the destroyer's side. Half-asleep I remembered our hiding-place with the map and lists and films—more than a thousand—of German defence works, and with these in my arms I was carried below to the first lieutenant's cabin, which had been placed at my disposal for the occasion. Kaare and Rolf had been treated in the same way and were already in bed, each in a luxurious officer's cabin. With hot-water bottles above and beneath and beside me, and after an injection of something or other by the ship's doctor, I fell asleep. . . . This was England!

I woke eighteen hours later, stiff all over; while I was asleep the doctor had bandaged my swollen hands. After a bath and a prudent lunch I went up on deck, just in time to see *Haabet* torn away from one of the two strong hawsers when a big sea washed over the destroyer's side. No one could do anything about it. The North Sea had won at last and got a prize it had been toiling for for fourteen long days. H.M.S. *Bedouin* was now going at full speed and right against the wind, and when a modern British destroyer goes at full speed, it means about thirty knots. For more than an hour before I came on deck in time to see the end of *Haabet*, the crew had feared that this would happen and had tried to strengthen the moorings. But more than this was needed to oppose the might of the sea! From one steel hawser hung the remains of the propeller and shaft, torn out of the rotten bottom when the sea was knocking *Haabet* to pieces. But *Haabet* had carried out her mission; her crew had been brought through, even if rather wet, weary and swollen. I should like to see the boat which had weathered the seas *Haabet* took.

I learnt from the skipper soon after that they in a 'full-grown' destroyer had had to put into port during the gale and that it was the worst he had experienced in his fifteen years at sea. He had also been told that the destroyer which had been sent out to pick us up after we had been observed by an Avro Anson just off the coast near Aberdeen in Scotland, eleven days before, had been obliged to put back on account of the bad weather. The crew had also heard on the wireless that three fifty-foot fishing smacks from Norway, on their way down the coast of the Shetlands with men who had escaped, had been lost in the gale.

On our way into Hull, where according to plan we were to be landed, the skipper had received counter-orders, and when we came up on deck a little later the same day, we were going at full speed in a north-easterly direction. A British plane, a Bristol Blenheim bomber, had crashed into the sea on a reconnaissance flight over the North Sea on the last day of the gale. The planes which had found us were out searching for possible survivors. And now one of the planes had reported that they had found a rubber dinghy with five men in it a little farther north, and it was towards this that the destroyer steered.

With the skipper we stood watching the perfect co-operation between plane and ship. The planes repeatedly dropped parachute flares to show the direction. When at last we came near enough, we could see a quite small yellow object dancing up and down in the heavy swell. A boat was launched and soon came back with the rubber dinghy in tow. It was a melancholy sight. Of the five men who had been in the rubber dinghy four days earlier only two remained, and only one of these was still alive.

Next day I had a short talk in the sick bay with the sole survivor, a red-haired Irishman. He told me how, on the day on which they had taken off, they had met the remains of the great storm, how they had got into a fog and had been unable to keep in the air in the prevailing conditions. Probably they had got into a violent atmospheric disturbance, and before they knew where they were they were hurled downward and one of the control columns had broken. The next thing he could remember was a crash when they hit the sea. The whole crew had at last managed to get into the rubber dinghy, but one after another they had been flung out by the seas. His friend, who was dead and was lying in the bottom of the dinghy when the destroyer picked them up, had simply been drowned where he lay. For the last twenty-four hours they had both been too exhausted to move. I told him about our eight days of the whole gale, and he just smiled, stretched out his hand and said: 'There must have been someone holding the tiller for you in that gale!'

The destroyer received orders to go north to Edinburgh and we had to go too. I shall never forget the days we spent on board. It was not long before the attention and good food restored us to normal health. We were not allowed so much as to lift a chair; everything was done for us and we were waited on like noblemen. When we landed from the destroyer in Scotland on October 4th, it was with mixed feelings. Such friends as we had made in the short time on board H.M.S. *Bedouin* it would be hard to find. But before us lay England, London and perhaps further training in Canada for the day when we should come back to strike a fresh blow for Norway's freedom.

CHAPTER V

THE SECRET SERVICE CALLS

MORE than two years had passed since our adventurous voyage across the North Sea. And now I had been waiting since the beginning of January 1943 for the decisive word from the British secret service.

The greatest wish so many of us Norwegians had had, ever since the day when we had to pack up and go—to fight directly for those at home and for Norway—had for me been fulfilled. I had been offered the job, and I could do nothing but accept it with open arms. Perhaps I did not think very much about what the task really involved, but that did not matter for the present.

After landing in Scotland in October 1940, I had gone to Canada with my two companions and had been trained as a pilot at 'Little Norway,' near Toronto. In the following summer my friend Kaare Moe had been accidentally killed in an air collision during a training flight. In him I lost a friend, a comrade and a man whose like I had not met before and have not met since. Kaare was buried in the little chapel belonging to the camp and his ashes later removed to Norway, where they now rest in the churchyard at Ullern.

Soon after this I was sent to England with a large Norwegian contingent, and thence to Iceland, where I served for most of 1942 in the 330th (Norwegian) Squadron. Towards the end of the year the squadron had been transferred to Great Britain, but not as we had all dreamed and hoped. The Shetlands were our destination, and we were to get four-engined Short Sunderland flying-boats instead of lighter bombing planes as we had imagined. 'You Norwegians have done remarkably well in your work for Coastal Command and will therefore be the first when it now comes to the question of undertaking such a difficult task as operating a Sunderland squadron out of Shetland!' it was nicely put in a letter from Coastal Command.

We were certainly coming nearer to Norway, but not just in the way we had expected. Again it would be the North Atlantic, fogs and winter storms we had to fight with; not the enemy we all so much wanted to get at with bullets and explosives. Why should all the others get a chance? Why should every nationality fly over Norway and not we, who knew every hollow, every mountain, every fjord in our districts?

My own future task was not yet decided, and in the meantime I did some 'occasional flying' with Bomber Command—'occasions' which I should long remember. But now the secret service had called, and for three and a half months I was to go to school again. Not the kind of school I was accustomed to from earlier days, with ordinary school hours and with stuff one did not take too seriously, but school for eight, ten, twelve hours a day. For many reasons I will not go into details here, but will state the qualifications which were required for the carrying out of the plan: one must be a telegraphist with knowledge of the latest British and American wireless sets which were used in this kind of work; a meteorologist with the ability to send weather reports and make observations as required by aircraft; and have a thorough knowledge of what the Allies knew of the German *Wehrmacht* and its dispositions in Norway.

In connection with wireless and the work as an operator, there were a number of different code systems which one must have at one's finger-ends, and alongside the other main features there were hundreds of further details which had to be mastered.

During this time I made occasional flights, and unfortunately the last ended for me in a fortnight in a Norwegian hospital in London after a parachute jump in which I broke both my legs. Luckily the fracture of my left leg at any rate was comparatively slight, so that in a fortnight's time I was able to continue my work at the school with first both legs and afterwards one leg in plaster. Certainly I had to go to the school each day by car, but time was a decisive factor;

the task I had undertaken could not be started later than the last week in April; after this date an agent could not be dropped over Norway because of the light summer nights. But the great question remained—would a broken ankle and a cracked fibula stand a parachute jump two months later? The Englishmen smiled doubtfully every time this question was raised. Time would have to show. . . .

By April 17 everything was ready. The plan and task were in broad outline as follows. The area Arendal–Grimstad–Lillesand–Kristiansand–Mandal had for a long time been one of those from which the Allied high command had not been able to get information corresponding to its interest and importance. In February 1943 two agents had been dropped up in the Setesdal region to deal with this most important question. But it appeared later that these two fellows had tumbled right into a business of some importance which had blown up in this region and was gradually spreading farther south to Kristiansand, Arendal and Mandal.

Some of Mil. Org.'s arms dumps had been discovered by the Germans, and as a consequence a number of arrests had been made, followed by raids and road controls. More than 150 persons had been arrested in quite a short time, and people on the farms and in the towns all over the district were in a highly nervous state.

It can easily be understood that all this made things pretty hopeless for the newcomers, and the result was that they very soon had to move elsewhere. These two went to Vestlandet, where, instead of their original task, they were to run a wireless station out on an island and report all shipping traffic until conditions in Kristiansand improved. But here too they got into difficulties; the Germans pin-pointed the wireless station and the agents had to move. On their journey to Oslo the train stopped at Drammen as usual; the Gestapo had its agents out on the track of something particular—and one of the men was arrested. He was later sentenced to death three times, but each time something or other caused the carrying out of the sentence to be postponed at the eleventh hour, and the agent was subjected to a fresh bout of torture without any result for the Germans. The liberation of Norway saved his life: his story is one of the many miracles of the war.

A month later a couple of agents were dropped to work in the same region, but this time too the result was much the same, except that these men got to work in another district.

This was the reason why I had chosen to go alone, and also to be dropped at a place which was farther from the district in which I was going to operate. The plan was that I should be dropped without any more equipment than I could cram into a pack—a wireless transmitter and receiver, and the necessary codes, arms, ammunition, a suit of clothes to replace the rough kit I should be dropped in, and a ten days' iron ration of food. Ten days after I myself had been dropped the main equipment, weighing about 1,300 lbs., was to be dropped at a pre-arranged place in Sörland; in the meantime I should have made arrangements with the people from Oslo who were to work at the first wireless station. This was the plan.

I had made twelve parachute jumps, voluntary jumps while training and involuntary included, so that side of the business ought to be all right. The last item in the programme was carried out in the cellar under one of the big buildings in London before I left the city with another Norwegian agent, Evensen, and two representatives of the British secret intelligence service. This was the fitting and measuring of the parachute and harness. The pack too, which now weighed 88 lbs., was fitted into a rubber covering and fastened between the harness and parachute. The whole combination formed the famous 'D-type parachute.'

Late in the afternoon of April 17 we drove into the grounds of an old English country house surrounded by high walls, 'somewhere in England.' Everyone here was sworn to secrecy; every man and woman, from the C.O. down to the washerwoman, was chosen with special care. The same rules applied to all personnel, both ground and flying, at the great airfield half an hour away. From this airfield planes took off every night on special missions, not only to

Norway but to all the European countries. There were planes which dropped agents, planes which dropped equipment for resistance movements and illegal groups, planes which landed unseen on 'secret airfields' in occupied territory and in Germany itself. To locate this airfield had been Germany's greatest wish throughout the war, but it did not seem to have been betrayed so far. From what we saw of the anti-aircraft guns and defences round this airfield, it would be difficult to achieve any great result by attacking it.

The house contained an extremely cosmopolitan collection of persons who were 'guests of honour' in the place; agents from the various European countries. We talked together, ate together, did physical exercises together, but no one knew who any individual was or where he was going. One could only guess from the accent with which he spoke English. No one asked questions; nor did anyone ever talk about himself.

The thing which perhaps we all remember best about the place, apart from our marvellous entertainment by its young ladies, was the so-called 'Operational Egg.' Fresh eggs were at that time largely unobtainable by the English public. Only dried eggs from Canada or America were used. At supper-time it might happen that two fine fresh eggs were carefully laid on a plate before a particular person. The person in question, even if he liked eggs better than anything, seemed suddenly to have lost taste for this previously so tempting delicacy which now actually lay before him. His turn had appeared on the programme for the night's operations; a reminder of this, and a last special piece of hospitality, was the 'Operational Egg.'

That evening I was to sit down in a few seconds and look at two fried eggs on my plate. My appetite was nothing out of the ordinary. There was too much to think about, too many still unanswered questions connected with the coming hours and days.

CHAPTER VI

BACK TO NORWAY

It was a little after eight, and we were sitting together in a little bungalow down at the south-western corner of the airfield, each of us with a small glass of old English rum in his hand. Evensen was in full camouflaged jumping kit, in canvas shoes with big rubber soles over a pair of worn Norwegian ski-ing boots, his parachute harness on, and his rubber helmet and gloves in one hand; the harness was so tight that he could not stand upright. I, similarly equipped, sat in another corner of the little room. Two representatives of the British secret service were there, and the O.C. flying operations from the airfield. There was a feeling of constraint; the other three tried all the time to talk about quite different things from those we were all thinking about; Evensen and I scarcely heard what was said.

The drone of the engines of two Halifaxes was heard from the airfield; the mechanics were warming them up. In the intelligence room the air-crews were receiving their final instructions. The weather report was bad—a strong northwesterly wind over the district where we were to be dropped.

For the third or fourth time I looked into the chamber of my revolver, saw that there was a bullet ready in the barrel, felt to make sure that the commando knife down my right leg was in its place, that the smaller knife in the sleeve of my jumping kit was there, that the parachute harness was on properly and that the electric torch was where it ought to be.

The C.O. rose and lifted his glass: 'To the freedom of Norway and the world—to your success!' A last handshake, and Evensen was driven out to one plane, I to another. We were both to be dropped alone, he in the district round Tinnsjö in Telemark, I in the Eiker forest north of Drammen. But in addition to his 'D-type parachute,' in which the pack is placed in its rubber covering over one's head, he had five containers which were to be dropped. A reception committee was awaiting him on the spot. The aircraft I was going in had containers too, but they were to be dropped to an agent who was operating north of Skien.

One by one the engines were started, were revved up, the magnetos were tested, and the plane began to taxi out towards the runway. Hydraulic brakes whined as we stopped at forty-five degrees to the runway for a final check of engines and mechanism. A green light from the control tower, 'You are O.K. for take-off' over the telephone and then—a combined roar from 6,000 horse-power. Our speed increased—increased—increased—we were airborne!

'From now onwards you are Johansen—Karl Fredrik Johansen, and you were born on April 23, 1917! You are a woodcutter—logger it says on your passport—and you were born on a small farm north of Kongsberg.' . . . 'You are a member of the N.S.*—and are as simple and stupid as the rest of your family. . . .' I sat thinking aloud to kill time.

Only the 'dispatcher' had his place with me in the middle of the plane. He was English like the rest of the crew. He had his job to attend to, and I felt no urge to unnecessary conversation. . . . Without a word he arranged a sleeping-bag on the floor of the plane, just pointed to it and indicated that I could try to get a nap on the way over. But it was no use going to sleep; the parachute harness was not exactly comfortable, and the regulations said that it was best not to try to take it off, as inside an aircraft, because of the darkness, one could not make sure that it was on properly.

From where I sat I could see out through a little square window. The moon had risen now and was sending a river of silver over a rough sea far below. Sitting there, I could not help thinking of that time long, long ago when three of us had floundered about for a fortnight in the North Sea in a too small and too leaky sailing boat, six months after the occupation of Norway, to get across to England. Fourteen and a half days from our leaving Farsund to our being picked up by a destroyer down in the Channel. And to-night we should cruise in over the Norwegian coast less than three and a half hours after leaving that of England.

* *Nasjonal Samling* (the Quisling organization).

After the drop on Svaland Moor (the author and Hjelm Basberg).

The Holmevass cabin in Lommedalen.

Papers from the Ministry of Justice (Jan Tenvig and author).

The time passed slowly but surely. Beneath us now lay a layer of cumulus clouds, grotesque cloud formations, bathed in moonlight. The pilot had had to climb higher to get over a 'front.' I had borrowed a couple of telephones and a microphone mask, and I must say one feels a little better when one is able to follow what is happening from time to time on board.

Suddenly a message came over the intercom: 'Light ahead—Norwegian coast to port!' I could feel my pulse beat more rapidly; a moment later I was sitting on the folding seat beside the captain. There—the faint shape of a broken coastline could just be glimpsed through the darkness, and behind—snow-covered mountains in the moonlight! For a few unforgettable minutes not a word was said. Gradually and surely one mountain top after another appeared through the darkness, and between them the dark wooded valleys appeared dimly. It was like a fairy tale.

We were all suddenly roused by a series of quick flashes down on the ground, followed by bursts ahead of us to starboard, which made the captain turn the plane over in a sharp swing to the left. The anti-aircraft batteries were in full action, but as far as I could see everyone down there must have been kept short of fats in the last few years, and a fairly large percentage was suffering from night-blindness. The puffs of smoke and bursts were a good thousand yards away from our position.

'Do you know where we are?' the captain asked the navigator. 'A mile and a quarter west of Farsund,' was the reply. A brief conversation, and the two agreed to try a little farther east. First a swing southward, and the anti-aircraft fire quickly died away behind us. In towards the coast again, and this time things seemed to be going better. Soon the coast lay far astern; the course was set north-east.

Now and then we passed over inhabited regions. Single scattered lights appeared; the people down there perceived that it was no ordinary patrolling German aircraft that was out at that time of night. . . . Suddenly a string of dots and dashes shone through the darkness from a little mountain farm; a string of V's. Someone had probably been practising this letter for a long time. There was more to come: LONG LIVE ENGL—and then suddenly a stop. What had happened we never found out.

'Another hour to pin-point!' I gave a start; for a good quarter of an hour I had totally forgotten what was going to happen. It was a message from the navigator. 'Pilot to "Norway"—pilot to "Norway"!' It was for me this time. I answered, and was told I had half an hour in which to eat a bit of food and drink a drop of coffee before it was time to get ready. Hungry? No, I could not strictly say I was, but perhaps it would be sensible to have something inside me—it might be some time before the next meal. The dispatcher and I sat and ate. He was trying to tell me something about his last operations over France, but it came to a stop, on account partly of the noise of the engines, partly of an inattentive listener.

The pilot called up again over the intercom; the navigator this time. There seemed to be one question which bothered them both—wind force. Every time the navigator took the drift of the aircraft in relation to the ground, the result gave a force of between thirty and thirty-five miles per hour. It was certainly possible that the wind force was rather less lower down, but in all probability it was twice the maximum allowed for parachute jumps. To me, that side of the operation was a thing for the captain to worry about.

'We've just time for a last cigarette!' It was the dispatcher who offered it, and he did not need to offer twice. We sat in silence.

Then: 'Twenty minutes to target!' . . . 'Pilot to "Norway"' . . . 'O.K., Captain, go ahead.' I hardly knew my own voice. 'Get ready—and good luck!' Again I replied automatically: 'Thanks for the trip: we'll meet again in a year or so—I hope!' I broke off the connection, put on my rubber helmet, fastened it securely, found my gloves and put them on.

I got up, stepped over a lot of parcels containing leaflets, which were to be dropped on the return journey to conceal the plane's real mission, and sat down on the forward edge of two large doors in the floor. The dispatcher was busy checking over the parachute harness and hooking it on to the large rubber-covered pack which now hung in a slip arrangement right over the doors.

What was to happen now, in theory, was this. I was to jump out first. When the straps, thirteen feet long, from the harness to the pack were drawn tight, the pack would break loose and fall more or less straight out of the hole. On the top of the pack the parachute itself lay packed: in this case a parachute thirty-two feet in diameter. The top of the parachute was in turn fastened to a steel wire sixteen feet long by a kind of string which would bear a weight of 225 lbs., and the steel wire was fastened to the plane. When the jumper had gone thirteen feet out into the air, the pack would fall when the straps from the harness were drawn tight. Pack and man would then fall the length of the steel wire, and the wire would begin to draw out the parachute, which was about thirty feet long. In other words, when the whole thing had fallen thirteen feet (straps) plus three feet (pack) plus sixteen feet (steel wire) plus thirty feet (length of parachute before opening), i.e. about sixty feet, the string which fastened the parachute to the steel wire would be broken by the weight and—the parachute would open!

'Ten minutes to target!' The dispatcher leant over from where he stood on the after-edge of the doors and passed on the captain's message to me. My brain had quite ceased to function normally; there was just one sentence which repeated itself automatically: 'You're going out through that hole!'

Then the dispatcher opened the doors. An icy blast blew up through the hole—and ran still colder down my back. There, far below, lay Old Mother Norway—mountain on mountain, valley on valley—jagged, repellent and cold. Seconds became hours as I sat with my legs half-way over the hole, ready to jump.

The pilot had gone down to a lower level. The Halifax heaved itself violently over the mountain tops. I tried to find a clue in the terrain, some place I had seen before, but it was too dark. Only the contours of water, mountains and valleys could be distinguished against the deep blackness.

I looked back to the dispatcher's face, from which the signal would come together with green and red lights from two small lamps in the roof. He was standing with the microphone mask over his face, and from his movements I could see that he was talking to the captain. The plane was swinging steadily—rising a little, but sinking again: something was not as it should be—something was wrong.

It was the wind force. In the last minutes over the hole I had just sat and wondered how in the world the thing was to come off: the plane was being heaved up and down so that it was hard to keep in the right place. The dispatcher found the headphones I had been using earlier on the trip, and made signs to me to take off my rubber helmet. 'O.K., Skip, go ahead!' But there was a thirty-five-mile wind force, and the captain told me rather curtly that he refused to let me go.

So it was all to be for nothing—all the seconds and minutes to me had been like hours. Cursing fate, I wrenched off the parachute harness, crept into the sleeping-bag and did not wake till we had landed on the airfield in England five hours later.

We were to try again the next night: again I should have to undergo much the same sensations; again I must accept the refusal and cancelling of the jump for the same reason as before; this time the wind force was nearer forty miles.

It was the night of April 19–20, 1943; the time was 1.45. For the third time I was sitting at the edge of the hole in the after-part of the Halifax. This was the last night of the full moon, the last night before the summer months, in which agents could not be dropped into Norway. It was the last chance I really had of carrying out the task I had undertaken.

The aircraft had a Polish crew. I sat staring hard at the dispatcher, trying to guess his thoughts from the movements of his features. Again we circled round, again the plane was flung from side to side by a too strong wind; again I sat for seconds and minutes on the edge of the open hole, undergoing the worst mental torture. The plane began to climb again!

There must be some limits to what a man can endure. This time it was not at a dispatcher's request that I took off my rubber helmet for a talk with the captain on the intercom. He gave three reasons for not letting me jump: (1) there was a good thirty-mile wind force, i.e. fifteen miles too much, (2) he could not find any stretch of open moss which should be there according to the map, only mountains and forests everywhere, (3) he dared not go too low because of the violent gusts of wind, and he could not reduce speed to less than 160 miles, against the normal 115–120 miles, because if he did he would lose steering way in the violent air currents.

I will not report the discussion that went on for a quarter of an hour, but will only state that in the hearing of witnesses —the rest of the crew by intercom—I took the whole responsibility on myself.

I was sitting on the edge of the hole again; the time was 2.7 a.m. This time the dispatcher had inherited my nervousness, and for me there was only one thing to do: to take the chance of things going right, and jump. The Halifax went lower—the contours of water, mountain and forest grew sharper—there was a terrible lot of snow—the plane swung—went straight for a few seconds—swung again—speed was reduced slightly, and the propellers set at high pitch—we went steadily lower—I was heaved to and fro—I stared at the dispatcher—green light, and 'action station' from the dispatcher, who had now raised his arm—I flung both my legs into the hole—fractions of seconds—red light . . . 'Go!' I started and—was out. . . .

The wind howled in my face. I was slung round—struck my head against something, the rear wheel of the Halifax—I saw stars—many stars—a terrific jerk—more stars—a sharp pain in my back, my head—everywhere—the night was dark—I became unconscious.

The next thing I knew was that I was being jerked and flung about pretty violently; it was a little while before I really paid any attention to what was happening—and there—a few yards away, against the fearful wind, I saw the rear turret of the Halifax and the rest of the plane silhouetted against the sky. I was hanging from the plane!

If it was fear or pain which made me faint again, I cannot say, most probably both. I recovered consciousness, feeling that I was still hanging, that I was being flung up and down, to and fro at a furious pace—and I fainted again.

Before I finally recovered consciousness, a miracle must have happened: I was on my way to the ground far below. I looked up instinctively: yes, the parachute was open, but only partly. It looked to me as if some of the many silk cords which went up to the parachute had got entangled in the material and divided the whole 'umbrella' into several sections.

I looked down—far below in the darkness lay water, mountain tops and forest. I could only feel that I was falling a good deal faster than I had ever done before. But there was nothing I could do about it one way or the other. Yet there was something seriously wrong with my right foot or leg. It was hanging all wrong in relation to the left, almost at a right angle. I tried to lift my leg as I hung—but the only reaction was a stab of pain.

It was blowing hard: I was approaching a ridge just below me—dense wood—no, I was caught again by a violent gust, passed the top of the ridge and went at full speed down into the valley on the other side. I held my breath—now for it! A bunch of big fir-tops came rushing at me—the noise of branches breaking—something like a big besom hit me in the face—everything became still and strange—I had fainted again.

How long I was unconscious I do not know, but gradually and surely I came to myself again. A strange noise in my ears, a strange silence, and for a few seconds, minutes perhaps, I felt that I was dreaming—felt that I had come into quite a new world. At first I dared not move, but at last I tried. A burning pain in my back brought me back to reality, and I looked up, sideways and down.

I had landed in the top of a tree: I was hanging with my back against the trunk, and above me, a dark mass against the lighter sky, hung my pack. The fir-top itself was broken off and lay across a tree next to it and beyond, while the remains of the parachute were entangled in another. What a fantastic piece of luck! So fantastic that it could hardly be true.

It did not take me long to get hold of my commando knife

and cut away the parachute straps: at the same time I twisted myself round to face the trunk, and slid down through the fir-boughs as carefully as possible. I now understood what was the matter with my right leg; the knee had been dislocated and the whole lower part of my leg, with the foot, had been twisted ninety degrees out to one side. I could only hope that nothing was broken; but that a knee out of joint could be so horribly painful I should never have believed.

I just collapsed at the foot of the fir-tree like a pile of wet rags and lay there with closed eyes. I stretched out my hand, caught hold of a piece of reindeer moss, and inhaled its scent. Never, never, would anyone make me do another parachute jump; indeed, I never wanted to see a plane again!

This was Norway: Norwegian fir and pine. Norwegian bilberry and reindeer moss. Despite the burning pain in my back and knee I could not help enjoying their familiar scent, taking long draughts of the night air. Everything was so strangely quiet; only the noise of the wind in the fir- and pine-tops came down to where I lay. The long hours in the Halifax and the mad descent through the air afterwards now seemed like a bad dream. But every time I tried to move in order, if possible, to be rather more comfortable, the burning pain emphasized the merciless reality of the situation.

How long I had lain I do not know, but it was beginning to get cold. Thoughts raced feverishly through my brain. Was this to be the end? Was the task I had so lightly undertaken to end in failure before it had even begun? Would the Polish captain of the Halifax be proved right in having held that it was madness to jump in the prevailing conditions? I willingly admit that I have seldom felt so utterly miserable and helpless as on that April night, when I lay with my knee out of joint in the midst of the Eiker forest, in a temperature of fifteen degrees Fahrenheit and as much as a foot and a half of crusted snow.

I must have slept a little after all. I woke shivering, and every quiver sent a knife-thrust through my knee. My foot had become completely numbed as it lay, apparently with a separate sprain of its own. The knee was a good deal swollen. I suddenly noticed that it was beginning to grow light.

Again I tried to think with some degree of clarity. Something *must* be done now, and that *something* must be done quickly. 'The first thing you do, on landing in an area occupied by the enemy, is to remove every visible trace.' That is the first commandment for an agent who is dropped into territory held by the enemy.

I lay for some time looking up into the fir-top where I had landed, and thence on into the next tree, where the greater part of the parachute lay caught up in the branches. If the aircraft had been observed *en route* for the dropping-place and the Germans sent a Storch over, it would not be difficult to find the place. The parachute was indeed camouflaged, but it would be easily seen against the white snow underneath. And then? I should hardly be able, with my bad legs, to crawl many yards before the Germans were on the spot, and after that all they had to do was to follow the tracks.

If I could only slip my knee in again, there was at least a chance. But could I do it without help? Close to the stem of the tree I had landed in stood a fairly thick birch sapling. Between them they formed a sharp fork. I lay looking at this fork for some time. Was this a possibility?

How long I tried and how many times I fainted, I will not say. I have broken a few bones in my time, but I had never till then experienced anything so infernally painful as putting a knee into joint oneself, getting a purchase the while with a broken-off stick. If any one had told me it was possible, I should have refused point-blank to believe it; so, perhaps, will many who read this book. But he who has experienced anything like it, and been in a situation in which his life has been at stake, will understand that a man will do what in everyday life would be unbelievable.

I lay looking at the parachute in one tree and the pack in the other. Now at least I could move my leg, although it was swollen higher up. One thing was certain: I must climb up and get hold of the pack which hung up in the tree-top. Its contents formed the whole basis on which my work was to start, and without it I might just as well stay where I was. The parachute must be got down too.

How long it took and how I did it I will not attempt to

explain here. But when the sun rose over the ridge to eastward, I was quite ready to start. I had repacked the pack and, on account of its weight, thrown out a number of small things which I could do without at a pinch. Among the things I had kept were a wireless transmitter and receiver combined, a battery vibrator, a set of code-books, two revolvers with ammunition, a suit of 'town clothes' and provisions for two days. These 'provisions' were packed in a watertight half-pound tin, and consisted of pressed concentrates. Tins like this were used as iron rations in all R.A.F. planes in case of a forced landing.

When I left England my pack weighed 89 lbs. The weight I had kept I guessed to be about 80 lbs., and as the reader will certainly understand, extremely heavy for a walker with a bad leg. The great question was: where was I and in what direction should I go to reach Darbu railway station? How far had the plane dragged me from the place where I had first jumped out, and what course had it kept? I lay down and studied the piece cut out of a map which was supposed to cover the area round 'pin-point.' It was difficult to see anything, and I soon found that it was little use to try to guess any position. I must begin by going north-north-east towards the top of the ridge on which I had landed, and if I could only get a bit of a view over the country round about it ought to be possible to fix the position fairly accurately.

It took me a good hour to reach the top. An hour of alternate crawling and staggering, an hour to cover about 500 yards. The whole thing seemed completely hopeless. The view from the top raised my spirits somewhat. To judge from the map the position was about thirty miles north-west of where I ought really to have landed, and so a good deal nearer Darbu railway station. But, on the other hand, I should have to cover much more difficult ground to reach that place.

I had in my pack a little pocket flask of the strongest kind of English rum, and after a good draught I set off again, half walking, half crawling. In the hours that followed, I tried to keep away from all northerly slopes to escape the snow, which was there about three feet deep.

The hours passed, and I do not know how many times I lay down and just thought that it was all over with me. But every time I lay down for a little while, it grew so damned cold. The right knee was now double the thickness of the left, and after each rest it felt as if someone had stuck a knife through my leg when I tried to use it again. Several times I thought of making a fire, but rejected the idea on account of the smoke. If the drop had been detected, this would be just inviting a speedy end to the game.

The whole day passed, and night approached again. I was soaked from the waist downwards from crawling over the ground where there was snow, while the upper part of my body was wet with perspiration. As long as the sun was up it was not so very bad, but later in the evening it grew clear and cold—the same weather as the night before, with a strong wind. There was no question of doing a mile an hour; I ought to be satisfied if I could manage a few hundred yards. What became steadily worse was that I began to doubt if I was taking the right direction. It seemed impossible to make the ground agree with the map. Where according to my calculations there should be a biggish lake, I came, as likely as not, on a river of such dimensions that I had to make a long detour to get forward at all. Where I had expected a valley and a small stream, a good-sized lake barred the way.

It was a little past ten on that first night when I lay down to sleep under a fir. One thing was clear, that if I was not to freeze to death and lie there for good and all I must have warmth, without regard to the light and the smoke a fire would create.

This made things better, and for a good hour I lay there and dried my stockings and boots, had a change of underclothing and ate a slab of chocolate and a few raisins. And on top of this a good draught of English rum. I have never been addicted to strong drink, either before or since, but I maintain that the pocket flask of English rum played a decisive part on that walk. Hard by the fir stood an old rotten pine stump, and after a lot of trouble I managed to break off some pieces for fuel. I put the whole lot on the fire, wrapped myself up in my raincoat and went to sleep.

What was that? The snap of a twig. I started and, only half-conscious, caught hold of the revolver which lay in the side-pocket of my pack. I was so cold that my teeth chattered, and it seemed to me that an echo came from the wood around me. Were there people about? The moon was up and it was fairly light. I strained my eyes in the direction from which the sound came. Another crack! I huddled myself together and lay as flat as I possibly could. Something was moving behind a clump of dwarf birch. I loosed the safety-catch of my revolver, raised my arm cautiously and aimed as well as I could. I lay quivering in this attitude for a few seconds. There! I was on the point of firing, when out of the swamp came an elk, quite calmly and placidly; he snuffed a little, then went on rooting in the snow for something to eat. The wind was blowing straight towards me from the animal, and the elk was obviously quite unconscious of any danger.

I collapsed. 'You damned fool!' I called myself. 'You prize specimen of a damned fool! Yes, you're the right man to send on a secret mission to occupied Norway, when you're almost scared to death by a wretched elk! . . . Clear off, you brute!' I yelled, and the king of the forests swung round and vanished, leaving a cloud of snow behind him, while I quaked at the sound of my own voice. There was no absolute necessity to shout at the top of my voice in my predicament.

It was half-past two. The fire had gone out a long time before, and it was miserably cold. A slab of chocolate went down like lightning; just a sip at the flask, and on I went, my knee protesting loudly. North-north-east, yard by yard, hour after hour. I moved in my sleep and recollect few separate details; I only remember that time and again I wanted to lie down for ever—but I grew cold, so on I went.

It was a little after nine when I rolled down a short slope and lay cursing to myself with both legs completely hidden in a bog-hole. But—I gave a start—did I not smell smoke? Yes, certainly—up on a hillock on the other side of the swamp lay a little wooden hut, and smoke rose from the chimney. People! I drew my legs in and almost yelled from the pain it caused me, crawled behind some bushes and lay watching the hut. Fancy being able to get into a nice warm hut, perhaps have a bit of food, and, moreover, find out where I really was! Not a sound was to be heard; only the smoke told its plain story.

I lay still for twenty minutes. I had slipped off my pack, put the revolver in my shoulder-holster and now lay counting on my buttons whether I should take the chance or not. . . . Yes, things must take their course. With the help of sticks, and making a violent effort, I limped the fifty yards up to the hut door and knocked. A chair scraped, and to judge from what I could hear, someone suddenly became busy inside and went to and fro across the floor several times. All was quiet for a few seconds; then the person moved towards the door, a bolt was drawn inside, and the door slowly opened a few inches.

I gave a start at the sight of the person who appeared in the doorway: an elderly man in full *hird* uniform! 'Good——' I checked myself and very nearly forgot the rehearsal I had gone through to myself before I knocked. I don't know which of us two made the queerest figure as we stood staring at one another. 'Good morning,' was my cautious opening. 'Good day,' the answer came slowly. 'I suppose I couldn't sit down for a little while,' I continued. 'I had a nasty fall into a hole up on the ridge and twisted my knee, and then got soaking wet!"

The man in *hird* uniform opened the door an inch or two wider and looked me up and down from head to foot. 'Where have you come from then?' 'If I can only sit down for a little while, I'll tell you how it all happened!' I replied. Then, reluctantly: 'You may come in then.'

It did not take me long to comply with the request. The man was obviously alone, at all events for the moment, and I was too weary to think what would happen if there were several of the same kidney in the neighbourhood. I sank into one of the two armchairs in the hut, taking a rapid look round as I did so.

One rucksack—one hat—one empty coffee cup on the table. No, there was certainly nothing to be afraid of at the moment. A fowling-piece indeed hung on the wall, but otherwise the man did not look particularly dangerous.

'Well now, tell me where you've come from!' The man obviously meant to hold his ground, and it was just this question I was perhaps best prepared to answer. 'Well, I was on my way over from Sandsvaer to Darbu, and I fell into a hole up on the ridge and twisted my knee a bit!' And to spare him further questions in the same key, I continued at once: 'I'm a forestry pupil, you see, and am going over to mark some timber for Mastebogen.' 'Yes, but surely Mastebogen doesn't own any timber near Darbu?' 'No, that's quite true, but I've got to go to Darbu station to fetch some maps, and at the same time I'm going to meet an inspector from Oslo who's coming up to look at some timber that belongs to Mastebogen. We're going down to Hakavik together and shall go in from there.' It was a good thing I was grounded in the details of local affairs, and this last statement seemed to convince the man that I, so to speak, belonged to the district.

It was now my turn to ask questions. 'So you're one of the sensible fellows who belong to the party?' I began, opening my wind-jacket and showing a National Socialist party badge which adorned my own lapel. The man jumped up, beaming all over his face, and held out his right hand. 'Yes, I thought as much—you're very welcome! *Heil og sael!*'

I almost laughed, but confined myself to a 'friendly' smile. The man suddenly set about dishing up all the good things the hut afforded. The coffee pot was filled and put on to boil; home-baked bread, good butter, bacon, bannocks, jam —I cannot remember all the good fare the man proudly set before me. Real good coffee! Three cups one after the other performed miracles in a worn-out body. And while I sat there and ate and drank, the fellow's tongue worked like greased lightning. I found out where I was, which was the best way to Darbu, that he had had a festival all on his own the day before on the occasion of Hitler's birthday, that most of the people thereabouts belonged to the cursed '*jössing* class.'* and so on in the same key.

I had produced my pipe, but naturally had no tobacco. Then I had only to help myself! German tobacco! It made

* A term applied to Norwegian patriots by the Quisling party.

my throat sore, but I put the best face on it. Naturally the tobacco was first-class. I was just dropping off to sleep where I sat when I was startled by a sudden question: 'Did you hear the plane that was over here the night before last?' No, unfortunately I had not; I had heard people down in Sandsvaer say there had been a British plane over in the night, but I had slept so soundly that I didn't hear anything! Had he heard it? 'Yes, indeed I did——' And then I heard a story which emphasized the suspicion I had already that the man was not quite sane. It was a British plane that had tried to bomb his hut, he declared, so vehemently that the tobacco juice from the quid ran out of the corners of his mouth. 'The plane wasn't more than thirty feet over the roof. It came twice, and I had a shot at it with my gun. I'm quite sure I hit it, for it didn't come again!'

For a good two hours I sat listening, half-asleep, to the various stories the fellow dished up. Just now and then, when he got on to the N.S. and the development of the Great German Reich in Norway, I put in some more or less intelligent remark. He had explained to me that he preferred to live alone in the forest, so there was no danger of our being disturbed by possible visitors. From the name he gave the hut and its surroundings it was clear that I was a good deal too far west of the route I had laid down. If I continued along the ridges right up to Darbu, as I had begun, I should never be able to get there. If, on the other hand, I could get down to the road which ran from Hakavik up to Darbu, there was at any rate a chance of a lift from some peasant or perhaps a wood-carter.

It was nearly twelve o'clock when I took my leave. But when I tried to take the first steps across the floor, my leg simply would not bear me, and I fell to the floor. The man burst into lamentations: 'No, oh no, you can't get to the village in your state! You must lie down here in the hut, and I'll go down and fetch two or three *hird* lads, and then we'll carry you to the village!' I did not know whether to laugh or cry: but the situation was rather tragi-comic. It might sound tempting, but there must be some limits. Two or three others of the same type might, at any rate in combination, be able to think rather more clearly than this arch-idiot!

I went out and down the field, while the man stood on the hut steps protesting. Across the swamp, past the spot where the pack lay hidden, and on and up through a little gully. There was no need for the fellow to see what kind of a burden I had. It was not till a good five minutes later that the hut door shut again, and I was able to proceed. The hours passed and the day passed. I did not do many yards an hour, but I did them in the right direction.

It was about eleven that night when I reached the northern end of a long lake. According to my reading of the map, it should be Store Oeksne, but the contours could not be made to agree with the map. The shape of the lake was wrong, and the ridges round it did not tally with those marked on the map. I wish I had known then that the map of the district had not been revised in the last twenty years, and that the original Store Oeksne had been dammed up since the time when the map was made. Where the map showed a serviceable cart track from the end of the lake down to the village, I did not find so much as a trace of a road. But I assumed that I could not find the right spot in the dark, and began to look round for a place where I could spend the night. Half an hour later I was well buried in shavings in the loft of a comparatively new hut. For once it looked as if my fortunes had taken a better turn. . . .

At five next morning I went on. My knee, which I had bound up with an elastic ankle bandage, was now quite stiff and more than twice as thick as the other. I don't know if it was the exercise that did it, or simply that my senses had become dulled, but the fact was that it seemed a good deal better. And now I was really on my way down towards the village.

There was the Eiker, and there was the scattered village. I lay out on a mountain ridge and enjoyed the sight. It was nearly light, and the sun was just creeping up over the crest of the ridge on the other side. It was almost unbelievable. But what next? At a distance all looked so smiling and gentle, but what kind of people lived in the farms down there? Were there Germans in the neighbourhood? What had really happened in this time, almost three years, that I had been away, cut off from day-to-day developments here at home?

At eleven o'clock I reached the first fence and lay for half an hour up in a patch of wood, whence there was a good view over the farm below. It was not a big farm; well-kept, red-painted outhouses and a white main building. A man was chopping wood over by the shed; shortly afterwards an old woman came out on to the steps and called out something or another. Two boys were doing a bit of carpentering behind the barn. But what sort of people were these? Should I bank on their being so-called *'jössinger'* and go down and ask for something to eat?

The man had a bit of a shock when he saw me come limping down across his field. He stood axe in hand and stared. When I greeted him, and not till then, he seemed to recover, and after a few words about the weather, he also asked where I came from. I told the same story, and he too at first seemed rather doubtful. But it was not long before his tongue got working and he asked for news from Sandsvaer. It gradually became clear from the conversation that the man's patriotism could not be doubted. When I asked if he had heard aircraft over those parts a night or two before, he gave me a long look and only nodded. It looked as if he had his suspicions, but he seemed to be satisfied with the story I had dished up. I will not deny that I embroidered the story about the plane—now more than two days old—a good deal, as is usual in the countryside. But I myself had neither seen nor heard the plane, so nothing else was to be expected.

The question of food arose of itself when the man asked me to come in, and it appeared in a short time that the family was going to have dinner. A lorry was then carrying wood down to Vestfossen, the farmer told me, and if it came back for a new load later in the day, I could have a seat on it as far as the crossroads, and then I should have to walk from there to Darbu. But it was never certain how many journeys these wood-cutters would make.

At two that afternoon no lorry had yet come, and after a cordial leave-taking from the kind farmer's family, I limped on. Five miles along a high road—I shuddered at the thought! People I met on the road seemed a little taken aback at the rather queer apparition. Peasants in those parts were evidently accustomed to know the people they met on the road. Certainly I was dressed like a genuine wood-cutter, and the treatment my clothes had received during the last few days would at any rate not weaken this impression. But it was not hard to see that the rucksack I was carrying was too heavy, and furthermore I was limping rather badly.

But people must stare and think what they liked. Only three times along the whole length of the road did I take cover at the sound of an approaching car. I must admit that the sight of the second car gave me a bit of a shock. It was German and open, with eight men on the deck behind. They all wore helmets and carried rifles. It was the first time for nearly three years that I had seen them at close quarters: it did not look as if they had changed much.

I shall never forget that high road along the Eiker to Darbu. It was no use to crawl there; I must just limp as far at a time as was possible. And when people passed, either in one direction or the other, I had to pull myself together violently in order not to show how bad I really felt. With the last ounce of strength I possessed I dragged myself up the slopes to the main road that ran down to Darbu station. Only a few hundred yards more. The train, from what I had learnt at the farm where I had been, went about six, and just as I reached the main road it entered the station. There was no question of catching it. I just collapsed into the ditch. This put the lid on it. What should I do now?

The nearest house was all that interested me—no matter what sort of people lived there, or what happened. I shambled into the yard, slipped off the rucksack on the steps and knocked. An elderly woman opened the door. Could I sleep over in the barn, as I had just missed the train and was going into Drammen? I supposed there was no hotel in the place.

Yes, I could come into the kitchen and sit down for a little while, and she would talk to her husband. I sank down on to a chair, and the woman disappeared into the next room. What sort of people were these? . . . I had not completed the thought when the strains of 'God Bless our Good King,' jerky and uncertain, issued from the room whose door stood ajar. To judge from the sound someone was playing on a child's xylophone. At the same moment the woman returned. She also immediately heard the notes that issued from the other room. Without saying anything she crossed the floor quickly and shut the door, giving me at the same time a long searching look. 'That's my little boy who's ill!' The words came from her cautiously. I only smiled a little: 'Nice to hear the tune he played.' The woman gave me another searching look. 'You can sleep in the barn to-night—but you must talk to my husband when he comes in.' Unasked by me, she put a jug of milk and a glass on the table and began to butter bread.

The husband was, if possible, a little more cautious even than the woman. He asked few questions, only listened closely to the story I had to tell. This was the same as before, except that I was now going on to Drammen from Darbu. But I added that even if there was a place at Darbu which received guests generally speaking, I had some interest in avoiding too many people. We then moved into the living-room, and here the farmer had a photograph of the royal family hanging on the wall, with the Norwegian flag draped round it. I offered him English tobacco, and asked if he had heard the plane which was over a day or two before. He just nodded, and we did not touch on that subject again.

It was not the barn that night, but a delicious warm bed. Through conversation with the farmer I had learnt of some of the changes which had taken place in those three years, and I can only say that I felt completely out of touch. There was another thing which I noticed repeatedly and with alarm: in conversation I continually used English words and phrases, a thing which might be very troublesome in certain situations. But it was not so easy to avoid this after I had been to English schools for three years and been with Englishmen every day. To put off one's own personality at a few days' notice and change completely into a new skin is not as simple as one would think, and this I found more than once in the months that followed.

I was too tired to think out any further plans that evening and fell asleep at once. I had covered about twenty miles in three days!

The housewife woke me at about seven next morning with breakfast in bed. Bless her! She did not say much, and so far comment was superfluous. The booking office at the station opened at nine, and as I wanted to be there early so as not to meet too many people when taking my ticket in case there were any difficulties, I was the first man at the window when it was opened. There was no one else in the waiting-room.

'Where to?' the booking clerk asked.

'Drammen,' I replied.

'Have you a travel permit?'

Travel permit? That was something I had not reckoned with. Nor any of the others over in England. It was something new. In the meantime I had caught sight of a number of posters which adorned the walls of the waiting-room. 'Norwegian youth for Norway with Quisling!' . . . 'Join up as front-line fighter.' 'With N.S. for Norway'. . . .

I boiled inwardly. They had not got as far as this when I left home. Without thinking of what I was saying, I asked the man: 'Surely I don't need a travel permit to come back to Norway!'

The man was silent for a moment. Then: 'What did you say?'

I gave a start and corrected myself: 'Surely I don't need a travel permit to go back to Drammen; I came from there five days ago and then at any rate no one asked me for a travel permit!'

'No, that may be so, but if you'd read the papers in the last month you'd have known that the new travel regulations came into force on the twentieth, and according to them one must have a travel permit if one wants to travel for a distance of over twenty miles from home!'

'Regulations or no regulations—I want to go to Drammen very badly!'

'Have you a passport?' the fellow asked.

'Of course I've a passport,' I replied and produced my legitimation papers.

'Oh, I don't want to see it,' the man continued, 'I only wanted to know if you had a passport.'

This is a remarkably inquisitive fellow, I thought, and the man seemed to understand that he had made me furious. With a smile he stamped first one ticket and then another, handed them both to me and explained: 'One's from Darbu to Vestfossen and the other from Vestfossen to Drammen. Regulations are there to be got round, you know!'

This man was the telegraphist at Darbu, and there was certainly no doubt where he stood. Nor was this the last time I was to make use of him.

But the train would not go for almost another three-quarters of an hour, and to avoid people I took my rucksack, sauntered down to the main road, and sat down by the wayside. There was little traffic that morning; only a German vehicle passed now and then. Most of them were ordinary lorries; a small Opel saloon car passed and also a convoy of five cars together. They were all going towards Kongsberg.

Then a green open car came down the road at a comparatively slow speed. I must admit that I was so 'green' at that moment that I did not notice that it was a police car. In the back of it sat six Germans in full equipment with a tarpaulin over their legs. The car stopped where I sat. Involuntarily my pulse quickened.

'Got any matches?' The soldier in front leaned out and asked in a mixture of German and Norwegian. Matches, I thought—only those which are made over in England, exactly on the Norwegian pattern, but the best were good enough, no doubt. I handed him the matches without a word.

Then I had a sudden inspiration. The car was sure to be going to Drammen. Yes, quite, right, the car was going to Drammen. Could I have a lift? The commander, an *Untersturmführer*—it was he who had used the English matches with good results—demurred a little at first, but finally nodded consent. I could get in with the others on the deck behind. It was not impossible that there might be trouble on the train because I was travelling with two different tickets, so this arrangement seemed an excellent one.

I man-handled my rucksack up first and climbed in myself behind it.

That was a drive I shall never forget. Beside me sat a little elderly soldier in a green uniform, who talked quite good Norwegian. What was I doing, where had I come from, what was my name, how old was I, where was I going, what were my political views, and did I know of any places where he could get some eggs in exchange for tobacco? He talked all the time with a good-natured smirk on his lips. Having satisfied his curiosity, he began to hold forth, and it was then that I first realized what kind of travelling companions I had got. For a good two days his party, along with two lorry parties from Kongsberg, had been combing the woods west of Darbu for parachutes reported to have been dropped from an English plane on the night of the 19th–20th.

I grew rigid with fear where I sat, and still more rigid when he went on to praise the style of our Norwegian rucksacks. It was the pocket in particular that was so conveniently shaped—and he demonstrated his opinion by turning and twisting the rucksack this way and that. I puffed feverishly at my pipe and tried to appear as calm as possible. (The fact was that never in my life had I been in such mortal fear as just in those minutes!) Then the conversation turned to the war, and we discussed whether the invasion of England would take place this spring or if they would wait till late in the autumn.

When we reached Mjöndal station I was not slow to take my leave and thank them for the lift. Quite remarkable how much better my knee felt during the first fifty yards away from that car! But I still believe that none of these eight police soldiers had the slightest suspicion. They had been toiling around in the woods for three days, searching in vain for what they had in their midst; they were utterly sick of the whole business and did no more than what they had been ordered to do. But if the same situation had arisen after a month of illegal activity in Norway, I would not have been the man to ask for a lift! There was certainly no doubt in this case that my good luck was better than my intelligence.

My train journey on to Drammen went excellently. There

were many people travelling, and a good many Germans. But no one seemed to take much interest either in me or my rucksack. Drammen railway station had the reputation of being rather an unhealthy spot, and I did not waste time unnecessarily in putting my rucksack into the cloak-room. According to the time-table there was nothing to prevent my going straight on to Oslo, but the fact was that I did not want to go into places where I was known in daylight. I had, moreover, thought of taking the train on to Sandvika, and the 'local' from there into Bestum. That meant a long wait at Drammen, and this I spent in Drammen church, well hidden away in a corner.

The train went on towards town a little before six, and an hour later we were at Sandvika. It was still too light to continue my journey, so I had again to wait for an hour or two. My first idea had been to send the rucksack on from there as luggage, but on applying at the ticket office I was told that luggage was not sent by the local train. I had, therefore, to put the sack into the cloak-room, as I had a good deal of business at Sandvika and would take a later train in. I hoisted the sack up into the window, and the man behind the desk took it over.

'Beastly heavy, this thing of yours.'

I held my breath at the thought of the wireless set, seeing him on the point of dropping the whole outfit on the floor on the other side.

'Been collecting iron?'

'Well, what do you collect when you stay a fortnight with a grandfather who's got a country farm?'

He did not reply, and wrote out the cloak-room ticket . . . 80 lbs.!

At Bestum station I gave the sack into the charge of the stationmaster personally. I knew of old that the man here was a first-rate fellow, and I had had confirmation of this in England. There had evidently been no changes, as the same woman who had been there for years opened the door. I am sure she did not recognize me, and doubtless did not regard one sack more or less as a matter of great importance.

It was with a queer feeling that I walked along the old

familiar roads towards Smestad. Three years is a long time, and then, when one comes back at last to the part of the world for which one has been desperately homesick, one is a sort of hunted unwelcome animal which has to lie hidden and sneak along under cover of darkness. Whenever I met people, I got busy wiping my nose or doing up a shoelace; if a car came along, I turned and went the same way as the car was going . . . Ullern station, Bekkefaret, Ullernchaussee, to the Montebello road. I stood down at the crossroads and looked up towards the white house at the top of the hill, my own home. Did my family still live up there? Should I walk past the door? Of course it was dead against all security regulations, but all the same——.

A minute later I stood outside the door, leaning against one of the posts. It was past ten, and all was quiet. If only I could just drop in for a minute, greet my mother, who no doubt, that evening as on every other, was sitting inside wondering what was happening to her son abroad—greet the rest of the family. Fancy being able to creep into the good old bed up in my room, dark now behind a lowered blind. Faint streaks of light issued from the cracks round the black-out curtains in the two rooms; the dining-room window stood open.

Then the dining-room door opened, and in the light that came from the sitting-room inside I could plainly see my mother's figure. The telephone in the house was ringing; she hastily shut the window, and the sliding door of the sitting-room was closed again. I felt faint as I stood there; nearly called out, nearly ran in through the open door.

I had meant to spend the night with a clergyman's family in Smestad. They were a first-class family, and I had thought of using the son in the 'office' of the Oslo section. But there was no one at home at the clergyman's, and after a short rest under some currant bushes in the garden, I went on to Ris, where my first contact lived. My plan had actually been to inquire into the circumstances of my contact at Ris before directly approaching him, as the family was most probably up to the neck in illegal work already. But again I had to bank on things being all right.

I saw a German sentry in the green police uniform in front of the drive up to a house opposite where my contact lived. For this reason I went on and round by Ris school to use the garden entrance from the lower road. There was a German sentry also in front of the school, which was next to my contact's house on the other side, but he was obviously an ordinary soldier.

I went up through the garden slowly and cautiously. A faint light glimmered through the black-out curtains on the first floor and from a window on the second, so there were people there anyway. But what kind of people? I did not ring for a little while. The damned German sentry stood there in an easy attitude on the other side of the road. If only he could make a little round, everything would be much easier. But there he stood—and of course the bell was in the front of the house, and the main door too. The kitchen door was a little better concealed; but there was naturally no bell. My solution, therefore, was to ring twice at the front door and then move cautiously over to the kitchen door—and hope that the right kind of person would come out. If a German opened the door at half-past eleven at night to a person who first rang the front door bell and then asked for a conversation via the kitchen door, he would undoubtedly be suspicious. But it had to be. I was worn out and hungry and already utterly sick of playing hide and seek, so I must risk it.

Someone came and opened the front door first. Curiously enough the door was shut again at once, and the same person came through the kitchen to the kitchen door. Those short light steps could be those of no German: it was Wencke, the daughter of the house. Before she recognized me, I had slipped inside the door and shut it again, took off my hat and spectacles, and not till then did she open her mouth. 'You're crazy!' she said.

It was a joy to meet them again—both the daughter of the house and the shipbroker Tenvig himself. We sat up far into the small hours, with food and drink and endless talk! I had a Goulard water compress put on my knee and finally went to bed in the son's room, as he was engaged on so-called 'volunteer work' arranged on his own account.

A week after the day on which I was dropped I was to be present with the 'reception committee' at a fixed spot down in Sörland to receive a parachute drop with all the equipment for the summer's work. May 2 was absolutely the last possible day for the drop, because of the light nights and the danger of being seen by unauthorized persons. There was no question of my doing this in the state I was in at the moment. Four days had gone already, and instead of starting right away and organizing the whole thing, I had to reconcile myself to sitting at Ris for a week with my leg on a chair and my knee in a compress. A doctor ordered me to hospital for a month to have the fluid drained off; the hospital, which I visited on two occasions, maintained that I should have a stiff leg for the rest of my life if I did not do this—but time was running short, and this too had to be risked. The nurse and the Red Cross doctor were splendid. 'And what name shall we put on this gentleman's prescription and card?' That was all they asked. They both guessed the cause of the trouble, in spite of the elaborate story which had been dished up, and I was obviously neither the first nor the last patient of the 'incognito' class they had had.

The name of a shopkeeper in Oslo had been given me in London as my first contact. Through him I should make the necessary further connections. The password, however, proved to be very dubious, and I shall not forget our first meeting. It was a good week after I reached Oslo, and till then I had been confined to the early hours of the night for the little movement I could attempt. Conditions in Oslo were at that time relatively quiet, and there was little danger of bumping into anything unexpected. There were masses of Germans everywhere; but there were also plenty of civilized people to mix with. But after all, Oslo was my own home town, and ordinarily, in peace-time, one can hardly go for a walk in the town without meeting some acquaintance. The time of day was usually the decisive factor in this respect, and I got into the way of cycling into town about nine o'clock, when most of the 'unpleasant' type would be well tucked away in some office or place of business.

I went up to the shop by a roundabout route. I had never

met the proprietor and naturally did not know what he looked like. When I went in two Germans and one Norwegian were standing by the counter looking through some books. I did not feel inclined to ask for the proprietor while they were there, so I followed their example. A woman behind the counter asked if I was looking for anything in particular, and I replied 'French books.' Now I had found out in advance that there was a shortage of French school-books, so that it might take a little time to find what the shop contained in that line.

The Germans did not appear to find anything particularly interesting, and left in a few minutes. 'The proprietor promised to try to get hold of some French school-books for me,' I now explained to the woman behind the counter. 'Is he in?' No, unfortunately, he was not, and was not likely to be back till about eleven. Very well, I should have to come again.

At a quarter to twelve I opened the door of the shop again and went in. I did not even have a chance of talking to the saleswoman, for I noticed a man standing with his back to me looking at some books—my old friend and form-master from the middle school at Ullern. I could not well go out by the same way as I had come in; it would obviously arouse the suspicions of the woman behind the counter, who had already seen me, so the next five minutes were devoted to an intensive study of picture postcards in the farthest corner of the shop.

My form-master at last finished his business and left the shop. Yes, the proprietor had come in now; would I wait a minute, as he was on the telephone. . . . Quite incredible how many things turn up to hinder one just when time is short. . . . People came in and people went out—and again I was to have occasion to study the collection of picture postcards over in the corner. This time it was the mother of one of my most intimate friends, who knew both me and my family quite well. . . . Then a man in the forties appeared in the doorway from the inner part of the shop. The saleswoman went up to him, said something and nodded in my direction.

'Yes,' I said, 'it was about those French books which I came in and asked about some time ago, and which you promised to try to get for me.'

The bookseller gave me a long look. 'What French books?' he asked. But there were two other customers standing beside me at the counter, and I felt no urge to ask for a private conversation so long as they were there.

'Are you sure it was to me that you spoke about these French books? I'm sorry, but I can't recall your face—nor having promised to get any French books.'

Yes, there was no doubt that it was he who had promised me to get the books, but it was so long ago that he might be excused for having forgotten it. The bookseller, still deep in thought, went over to a shelf and produced the little collection of French books which the shop possessed at that moment. I had been shown the same collection twice before. Then at last I had a chance of asking him for a private conversation.

'Won't it do if we stay here?' the bookseller asked, and now his face had assumed a rather harder expression.

'No,' I answered briefly, 'haven't you an office?'

We just stood there in the office looking each other searchingly in the face. I took the liberty of shutting the door which led out into the shop. 'I've a message for you,' I began. 'Andreson, the plumber, asked me to look in and remember him to you!'

The bookseller's face did not change in the least.

'I'm sorry, but I don't know a plumber called Andresen, and, to be quite frank, I must ask for an explanation of your rather intrusive behaviour.'

I began to feel rather uneasy. 'Oh, that's curious—you are the proprietor of this business, aren't you?' Yes, he was. 'Well then, you must know Andresen the plumber,' I went on.

But no, there was no change in the bookseller's stony face. I began to hesitate. There was only one thing to be done—to use the right name of the person in England who had given me that address. But no, not a sign of comprehension; only, if possible, a rather more hostile expression on the bookseller's face; a storm seemed to be gathering. The game had gone far enough.

'Well, there must be some misunderstanding, and I will just ask you to forget the whole episode. Before I go I should like to ask you if you know a man called Preben who Andresen the plumber says used to come in here a good deal; but we might leave that till another time.'

The last sentence was decisive. The bookseller pulled me back hastily into the office, and this time he asked me to sit down. Then he said, still without a movement of his features: 'After that I think I am justified in asking for a further explanation of all this mystification. Who are you, where do you come from—and what do you want with me?'

It was my turn now to be a little suspicious, but I came to the conclusion that there could be no misunderstanding. The bookseller was only being cautious, as indeed he had every reason to be; and so I laid all my cards on the table. Not till next day, when the bookseller had questioned England as to my identity, did I receive the handshake I had awaited from the moment I entered the shop.

The bookseller became our chief contact in Oslo in 1943, and the work he did was first-class. A whole lot of identity cards and ration cards had to be obtained. Certainly I had a false identity card which I had brought from England, which was good enough for the time being; but the necessity of having a number of different names and professions, behind which one could take cover on different occasions, was quite clearly shown during the work of the summer and autumn.

In addition to identity cards valid for Oslo and all the inland districts except the frontier zones, frontier dwellers' cards for the various frontier zones had to be obtained. For this purpose the bookseller had a contact with a quite young lady employed in the police passport office, who did this job admirably.

To build up an organization from the beginning in conditions of which I had only partial knowledge was not as easy as I had thought. Most of the people who at that time were capable of doing a job efficiently were already up to their necks in illegal activity elsewhere. Of necessity, absolutely reliable men were wanted in the key positions, and the only possibility of getting these was to turn to people I had known myself in earlier days and whom I could guarantee. But it was important that as few as possible should know the other workers, and that was not so simple where former friends were concerned.

A few chosen persons were now approached through the daughter of the house up at Ris. Like herself, most of them had long been occupied with other illegal work, but the question now was 'either—or,' without any names being mentioned.

There was one principle which I regarded as of decisive importance from the very beginning: I would not let any man work for me and in other organizations at the same time. This was a mistake to which far too many fell victims all through the war. People were caught who possessed information far exceeding all reasonable requirements, with the inevitable result that hundreds were kept in prison for a great part of the five years of war.

I myself was to have an assistant in running the wireless station. It was at first not easy to find this man. I had made an arrangement with one of my best friends before I left England; but on arriving in Oslo I found that he had made a short stay at Bredtveit and later had nearly been arrested again. The result was that he, like so many others, had had to go to Sweden a week before I came. This was a nasty setback to my plans, for it was not easy to find a man who I knew would stand up to the conditions in which we should have to live out in the woods. He must be a man on whom, above all, I could rely absolutely in these difficult circumstances, a man accustomed to the woods and able to make himself comfortable in primitive conditions; a man with plenty of common sense and strong nerves, who could handle firearms if necessary, and, most important of all, who could receive and execute an order. Further, he should be able to slip quietly away from his daily work without attracting attention.

Rolf Millang, a former member of the Scout troop I had

had before the war, proved to be more than willing, and as nearly as possible satisfied my requirements. He was felling timber at the time up in Nordmarka, as he was to take a degree in forestry and wanted practical experience; he was working for a very considerate chief, who did not ask any unnecessary questions on his leaving.

The conditions at the shipbroker's house at Ris were most peculiar. The German police had requisitioned the house opposite; another neighbour was a Nazi, and the school just below was packed with Germans. Nevertheless, every other evening during the time I used the house as a retreat, a number of persons came at different times. These formed the editorial staff of one of the most widely circulated illegal newspapers in Oslo. The daughter of the house was on the staff, also two of my best friends, the Elligers twins, from Nils Juelsgate in Oslo, and one or two others whom I did not know. At 6.30 p.m. the wireless was brought out of a secret room, and the printing press was working down in the cellar all the evening. No one but the daughter of the house knew that I was staying there, and it was not intended, for the time being, that anyone else should find out. I had counted on using these twins, but not as long as they had to work on the paper.

One evening—the day before I was to leave—the shipbroker and I were sitting out in the kitchen having a snack. The editorial staff had strict orders not to go anywhere in the house but into the cellar, where the printing-press stood, and the room up on the second floor where the wireless was usually kept. This was because the family was expecting a visitor from the country. The 'old man' and I were sitting and chatting, quite quietly so that no one should hear anything. Suddenly the door was thrown open, and there stood one of the twins, Ottomar. Seldom have I seen a question-mark in human shape as I did then! In the days before that famous sailing trip to England in 1940 we had talked, more in fun than anything else, of my perhaps coming back and our carrying on war on our own account. Well, now that one twin had found out, of course Carl Sigurd must too.

It was something of an experience to me to come into the midst of this hive of activity. For three years I had longed to get home to my own people, and often regretted that I had ever left the country. I seemed to have got so far away from where anything was really happening; at any rate many of us had that feeling. Even if in many ways we were more in the war, when up in the air and out on the sea, than most of the people at home, it was in quite a different way. Then, the result of what one did was not so visible to the individual; one flew for six, perhaps sixteen hours hunting for submarines or over a convoy far away up in the Arctic or out on the Atlantic, and often things nearly went wrong. But when one came back from an operation, the war was over for that day, so to speak, and one felt that one was outside the whole thing, could not see any result of what one had been doing. That was just why I often longed to get back to my own country, where the conditions were such that one was right in the middle of events every day, perhaps indeed every hour of the day.

There was one severe setback to our plans which we should have difficulty in making good: the parachute drop of all the equipment for the summer's work, which we had not been able to receive before the time had run out. Now our first chance of getting it would be in August, and the great question was what we should do in the meantime to get hold of material, clothes and food so as to be able to work on a fairly large scale. Ration cards were all right, but, as everyone knows, there was not too much to be got on them in those days. It was no doubt possible to get into contact with other local organizations and obtain help from them, but for the time being we must refrain from this, for I was unwilling to involve in our work others who had enough to think about already and also were in much greater danger.

CHAPTER VII

TO SÖRLAND

AFTER a fortnight in Oslo all our provisional arrangements had been made. We could not do much towards the setting up of an office there; but the twins, with the shipbroker and his daughter, and later his son on his return to Oslo, were to look after this side of the business when we were able to give the O.K. from Kristiansand.

Our contact on the railway had been given to us from London. It was he who was now to get us travel permits, and it was therefore necessary to stop at Drammen; our contact was head clerk at the station and brother to a Norwegian captain in London. There was no doubt about the password this time; but we were obliged to spend that night in the porters' room at Drammen station. The travel permit had to be obtained through an official in the central police station in Oslo.

The whole thing went astonishingly well, and at 12.10 next day we left Drammen by the ordinary Sörland train. We had sent our sacks as luggage for safety's sake, in case of an examination on the train. Kristiansand S. was the address, plus two different names and street addresses, chosen more or less at random. The train was filled to overflowing, and we had to find ourselves places out in the corridor. Rolf sat on a box and I on a good-natured fellow-passenger's trunk.

On our arrival at Nelaug station we were to have rather a fright. In the refreshment room, where we obtained two bottles of inferior mineral water, I noticed a man who seemed to be taking a marked interest in us. When I went out of the refreshment room to look round the station, he followed me. With anxious misgivings I steered for the station lavatory. The man followed me, looked round to see if there were other people about, came up to me and said: 'Regards from Drammen and I was to give you this.' He pushed a scrap of paper into my pocket and went out.

'Don't go to Kristiansand; there is a check on all travellers into the town.'

That was all, but more than enough as far as we were concerned. Three minutes to do it in—take out our sacks which were on the train as luggage, ditto our bicycles, the whole amid vehement protests from a porter, who could not understand why we did not know where we were going.

But what were we to do now? Our travel permit was to Kristiansand. I will not say that the station-master believed the story we dished up as a reason for the change in our travel plans; but 'an aunt dying at Arendal' was a thing that might happen to anyone! But according to the 'law' at any rate we should have no occasion to go to Arendal. How the man who had brought us the message could have known that it was we who ought not to come up against a control, have known our exact description, and have received the message from Drammen in so short a time, remained a mystery.

From Arendal we went on by bicycle via Grimstad and Lillesand. It was tiresome that no tourist or summer traffic had begun, and two men of the 'dangerous' age on bicycles with heavy packages seemed to kindle a novel and suspicious interest among the country people. This we noticed clearly at every place we entered in search of food. The same thing happened when we knocked at the door of a little farm a mile or two on the near side of Lillesand, soaking wet after bicycling for several hours in pouring rain. We asked if we could sleep in the barn or in the shed, and there was a low-toned conversation between us and the farmer's wife with the door opened to a width of four inches. When we had explained that we were wood-cutters on our way to Setesdal to get work there, the door was slammed and we thought for a moment that we had met with a blank refusal.

Then we heard something moving slowly across the floor inside, and this time the man of the house came out. The whole story was repeated; there was a few minutes' discussion, while the man had time to look rather more closely at the two travellers, and then at last we were given shelter. But not in the barn or in the shed, but in a small hut which lay a little farther from the house itself. Intentionally? Yes, from the man's suspicious, wrinkled forehead there could be no doubt of that.

We were pretty comfortable in that tiny hut; from the posters on the walls and the general style of the place there was no doubt that the family was O.K. Evidently the son of the house was running his little secret patrol; the Scout movement, of course, had long been prohibited by the Germans. . . . So we slept pretty well that night, with no idea that our nearest neighbour was one of the strong Nazis of the place.

CHAPTER VIII

UNDER A FIR TREE ON RÖYNAAS MOOR

THE goal of our journey began to draw near. Through Lillesand and Birkenes, down through Tveit, Kjevik, Aalefjaer, Eidet and—Kristiansand. We had been three days coming from Arendal, taken it easily and had an opportunity of studying the ground in the country round our future field of operations pretty thoroughly. No control, no one who showed a sign of wanting to stop us. As we went on there were a fair number of Germans to be seen along the road, but they all seemed to be busy with their own affairs. At last we were close to Oddernes church and quite near the clergyman, our first contact.

But things did not go just as we had intended. Conditions were far from quiet, and we were most strongly advised to work at a safer distance from the town. People were evidently nervous after what had happened before; our contact himself still had his youngest son 'inside.' That we had met no control on the road into the town was regarded as a piece of good luck.

So we had to cycle back over the same road to find a place where we could set up the wireless station and organize communication with the town by messenger. But it was not easy to find a suitable place along the high road, or better, a short way into the woods, where we could steal current from an electric cable to run our wireless sets, and where at the same time we could count on being able to work undisturbed. Further, we ought to be somewhere where people could not come upon us unexpectedly, somewhere where we could have a fairly permanent camp.

Many alternatives were suggested and rejected, and during this work we naturally bumped into a road control which looked like ending badly for me. So, after learning that the Tveit district and the southern part of Birkenes were free from Nazis, we moved farther northward.

Röynaas moor, seventeen miles from Kristiansand, was the place from which the whole business was to be organized in its first stage. Our quarters were under a big fir some way into the woods; we had no tent at this time, on account of the great weight of all the other equipment we had to carry with us from Oslo. There were now three different contacts in the town itself with whom we were to co-operate, three contacts who were all to operate independently and at all costs not to know about one another.

These three main contacts were to have direct communication with the station: a clerk in Oesterveien whom for the sake of simplicity we will call Arne, an official of the Kristiansand customs house called Johan, and a business man who had a job at the lumber factory out at Bellevue. Through these men an efficient intelligence network was to be organized; each man had his special field of work.

On May 15, early in the morning, Rolf and I walked down towards Kjevik airfield. We had been combing the ground along the east side of the valley to find a suitable place for the station. We had to have a wire with an alternating current of 220 volts, of the type which normally runs between posts along most main roads in inhabited districts. To anyone considering this question quite superficially it will perhaps appear fairly simple. But most of the wires on main roads are telephone wires; there are also several other types of wire—high-tension wires, and wires with direct current from local electricity installations, and a faulty coupling here can easily mean that the whole of your wireless is fused without any sound at all being heard.

But try and tap a wire running along within sight of the main road! I think myself that an attempt would have had unfortunate results. The Germans were as a rule very observant as regards electric wires along the main road. . . . At last we had found a suitable place. It was a mile and a quarter from Kjevik airfield. The wire ran to a school from a transformer a little farther along the road. The school lay at a short distance from the main road, and to take the shortest route the posts passed through a patch of woodland for a distance of three hundred yards. It was a fir wood with thick deciduous foliage below; it was rough going with large heaps of stones in the background, so that the possibility of people coming just through this little patch of wood was small. Behind rose a high steep ridge with a fairly straight rock face turned towards the south-west. This last feature played a very important part as regards the strength of the wireless signals which were to be sent and received, since the rock face served as a reflector and increased the strength of the signals.

What we did not know at this time, however, was that the wires continued farther south and supplied a number of German huts with current. The huts had at any rate long-wave receivers, and they probably had short-wave sets, too, which under normal conditions would pick up the tapping from our station not more than three-quarters of a mile away.

I rode with the wireless sets in my bicycle bag ten minutes ahead of Rolf, who followed with the code-books and other necessary material. There was nothing to gain from local people seeing us too much together. We had learned that rumours were already in circulation about the two strange men who had been seen with large parcels a day or two before, and who were later seen every day cycling to and from Kristiansand.

It took a little while to fix up the station; this was indeed the first time in real operations that we should try to make contact with England—the first time we were to set about

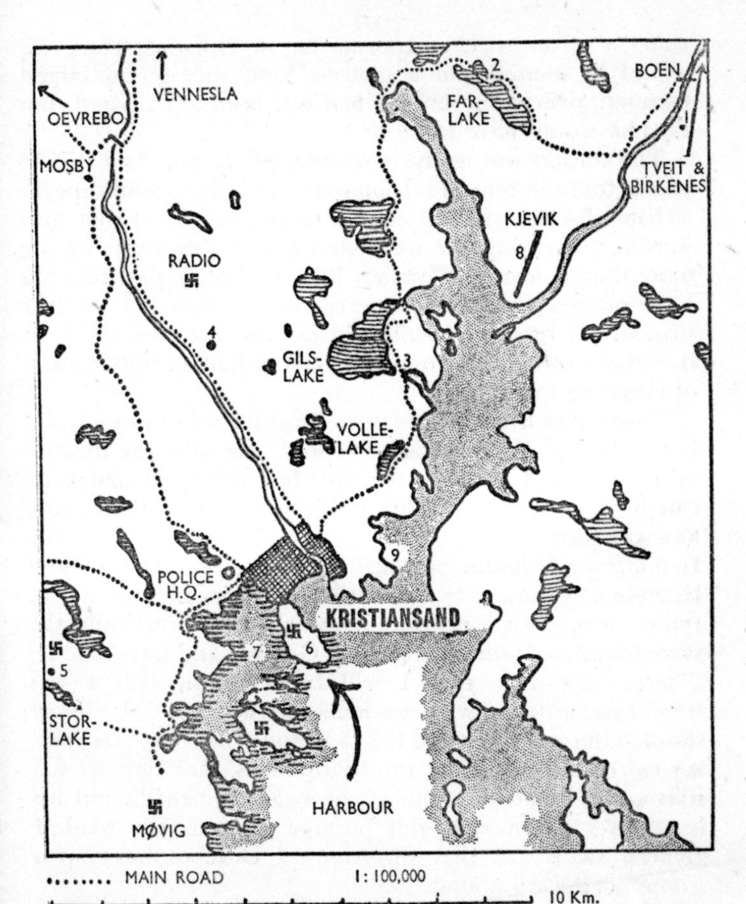

1. One of the first stations we established south of Boen bridge overlooking Kjevik Airfield (Chapter VIII).
2. The bridge over the Farvann where under-water swimming was useful (Chapter XVI).
3. Eidet Café. 4. The "Upturned Boat" (Chapters XI and XII).
5. The location of the radio station north of Stor Lake where the German lookout-station was just some 200 yards away
6. Odderøya, the peninsula where the German H.Q. was situated and from where all traffic into and out of the harbour was controlled.
7. The harbour guarded by the anti-submarine nets where all convoys were formed.
8. Kjevik Airport. 9. Marvigen—the German submarine base.

using a secret wireless transmitter in Norway. That this would be a mile and a quarter from the second largest German airfield in Sörland had not been anticipated, but the risk would have to be taken.

The station was ready. A quarter of an hour had still to pass before the central station over in England would begin to listen for our signals—that is to say, we hoped that they were still listening, for we should have given a sign of life more than a fortnight earlier. Rolf sat keeping guard on a little mound about fifteen yards away, with his revolver loaded and ready for action, in case we had visitors. I sat listening to the news from London and had an opportunity of checking the time.

There were five minutes to go. In three minutes we could begin. Would it be all right? Would they hear the signals? Were they still listening, or did they think we had been caught long ago? One minute—thirty seconds—there: AKY AKY AKY AKY: — —.— —.—— ...—...—...— AKY In a minute I should call, turn the switch to reception and listen on the frequency on which Central in England would reply: PBO. Two other stations worked on practically the same frequency—one of them was German and quite strong. There!—no—yes: PBO. I will freely admit that I was trembling a little with excitement. 'Contact!' I simply shouted the word across to Rolf and could not hear how loud my voice was because of the headphones. Rolf just gave a start and a broad grin, but at the same moment he put his hand over his mouth and pointed towards the road. I glanced swiftly in that direction—a German lorry with troops northward bound.

Two telegrams were sent, one received. The whole thing was over in less than half an hour. Dots and dashes came clear and distinct through the headphones; nor did it seem that Central had any great difficulty in understanding me.

The difference it made to our spirits—after our weeks of toil and increasing setbacks, cannot be described. It was like a breeze of encouragement blowing through all the blackness of things at home in those days.

We were to keep this scene of contact more or less to ourselves for about two months. It may perhaps be asked how a secret wireless station could be run a mile and a quarter from Kjevik airfield without being located by D/F and captured. We asked ourselves the same question when we opened the station. Later information explained it completely; it was just a matter of calculation. The Germans had three D/F stations in the neighbourhood of Kjevik; the three formed a rough triangle. Our position was almost exactly in the middle of the triangle, and when these three stations tried to locate us by D/F, they more or less located each other and confused the result in the highest degree.

One day, after contact, when I was in a country shop west of the river, a short way below Boen bridge, I got talking with a German who proved to be an operator at one of these three D/F stations. Our conversation began by my asking him if he could sell me a little tobacco. I could have tobacco, but I must get him some eggs in return. We sat on a wooden bench outside the shop and talked about quite everyday matters. I told him I was a wood-cutter; he told me he had been a farmer, and was now an operator at one of the wireless stations at Kjevik. Of course I was much interested in the last-named branch. The man, who was well over forty, was very talkative and told me a good deal more than he should have. Among other things, he asked twice if I had seen any suspicious men while at work in the woods. I had, of course, but not just round Kjevik. On the other hand, I had reported to the police three fellows whom I had met in the woods on the way over to Vennesla; these had no doubt been dealing in illegal newspapers.

Well, the thing was that at the wireless station where he was working they had picked up signals from an illegal station which, according to him, must be quite close by. His chief maintained that it must be quite a long way off and that it was transmitting with very strong signals. Every night for more than a week an extra man had been on duty listening all the time on the frequency on which the signals had been first heard. They had heard the station twice since, but it had not been possible to D/F it on account of disturbances.

Herr Schultze—that was the operator's name—got his three

eggs a day or two after this first conversation, and I got a packet of cigarettes. After that the barter transaction was repeated several times. Each time he asked me the same question, and each time, when in the course of our conversation we got on to 'this damned Norwegian wireless station,' he informed me of the same negative result. We continued to change our frequency at irregular intervals, and altered our times and call signs.

For a good month we had run the station practically every day from the same place. We had only two visitors. One was a boy who had a call of nature, jumped off his bicycle as he came along the road, and squatted about ten yards away from us. Apart from an unlucky westerly wind no harm was done, and we continued to transmit after a delay of ten minutes. The other was a woman looking for a strayed sheep. She, too, was seen before she could reach the station.

There was another great advantage about the position of this station; we could keep a very close check on the planes which took off from and landed on the airfield. The Germans had evidently sworn to catch the illegal wireless station. They began direction-finding with 'Fiesler Storch' and D/F cars. As a rule I got a good way through the first telegram, and occasionally had started the second, before anything happened.

'Storch taking off!' Rolf came in cautiously from the look-out post. It was a Sunday afternoon, with a light breeze and fine weather I sent 'wait ten minutes,' and we hastily withdrew under the foliage with the wireless well covered by a jacket. There it came—sixty to ninety feet above the fir-tops—circled and swung, went on right over the spot where we lay quite still—up the valley—circled round farms and woodlands—came back again—over—and in to land.

It had not touched ground before we were at work again on the 'ticker.' The Storch started afresh and again I sent 'wait,' after having reduced the strength of the signals. Again it landed with obviously bad results—and I went on sending. Playing hide-and-seek like this was really quite entertaining and at times quite humorous. But it was quite obvious that one day we should most likely come off worst. My friend Herr Schultze, too, was able to tell me every day that now it would not be long before they had it. Poor fellow, that station had become a positive obsession with him—and the bad results secured by his own branch really distressed him. I offered sympathy and eggs, and got information and cigarettes in return.

People began to be seen in the woods; not ordinary people, but 'photographers' and 'zoologists' wearing German Air Force uniforms. And not only in the woods, but also along the high-road into Kristiansand and up through the valley. In other words, something was being done by a lot of snoopers, whose intentions were unmistakable. One man in particular we both had the pleasure of seeing time and again—a rather short, thickset fellow with stripes corresponding to those of a Norwegian sergeant.

This fellow had a certain propensity to hide in the ditch along the road, and every time we caught sight of him he was lying taking photographs of some flower or stone. Now and then he had fixed up a regular stand with two cameras.

During contact one morning Rolf and I had a narrow shave of becoming patients for heart treatment at a more or less celebrated 'sanatorium' in Kristiansand. I had sent two telegrams and was just beginning a third. As usual, I looked up and across to where Rolf sat to make sure that things were all right. One look was enough: Rolf had huddled himself up and lay with his revolver ready—aimed at something or other. I just followed the direction of his gaze and—sank down into the little hole dug among the boulders—took off the earphones slowly and noiselessly—slipped out my revolver—pulled a leafy branch over myself and aimed.

The 'photographer-zoologist' from the Air Force, Kjevik! . . . The minutes which followed were those which last for hours. He went slowly up the slope—between Rolf and the place where I lay—under the aerial which hung about ten feet up! And, upon my soul, he had not done yet: where it began to grow steep he turned and came down again. But no, there was a limit to everything—he made another turn of ninety degrees and disappeared along the side of the ridge. He was looking for flowers, or perhaps it was stones; I do not know for certain, but I still think he was after something else. But the main thing was that he had walked with his eyes fixed on the ground and therefore had not seen the aerial when he went right under it.

There was no more sending or receiving till late that evening, and then from quite another place. We waited for ten minutes, and then Rolf took a little walk round about. All was quiet again, and the station was dismantled in record time.

But there was to be no end to the fun that day. The adventure with the 'zoologist,' together with news of visits to houses in the districts farther south on the previous day, caused us to hide the wireless in a place prepared in advance. With it we hid everything connected with illegal activity. Rolf went on northwards along the road towards the camp; I went the other way to see if I could get a few more cigarettes.

Just below the shop a shock awaited me; a black German police car came by at a good pace and stopped abruptly. Two men jumped out, pressed a tommy-gun against my stomach and rather roughly demanded to see my identity card—to be more precise, my frontier dweller's card made out in the name of Karl Fredrik Johansen. Where did I live? How old was I? When was I born? Where did I work? For whom? My telephone number? (unfortunately I had none, nor had my employer), etc.

Could I give any other proof that what I said was true? I thought of the only resource—the shopkeeper who had previously declared that he knew me and my family and who also ostensibly came from Kongsberg. I went ahead on my bicycle, the police car behind me, and I had all the time a strong feeling that one of them had me well covered.

I started when I perceived Herr Schultze sitting on a bench by the roadside just in front of the shop. With that prize idiot about there was not much hope. Then I had a little idea—it might work! 'Walter!' I cried. He rose at once, did not notice that the car behind was interested in me, just came up to me as I stopped and shook hands with me. Before

I could say much one of the policemen was on the spot, and Herr Schultze, somewhat taken aback, was asked if he knew me. Oh yes! He spread himself about where I lived and what my name was, and declared that he had known me a long time! The police car went on northwards—unfortunately there were no cigarettes that time—and no eggs!

That was the last time we had contact from the place a mile and a quarter from Kjevik. Later that evening we went down and fetched the wireless equipment and the rest of the material. Next day, at two in the afternoon, a German party about 200 strong went all over the ground, and according to rumour they found various things. But we missed nothing. . . .

CHAPTER IX

THE HUT AT GULLRINGSTJERN

Our first camp under the fir up on Röynaas moor we had had to abandon long before. It had poured with rain for several days on end, and there was not much pleasure in lying out of doors with what few clothes we had wet through. A barn with no door where cows were accustomed to seek shelter was our next habitation, until we were visited one day by two boys and a girl who looked after the herd. As was to be expected, the whole neighbourhood knew next day that we were living in the place, and when, one stormy night a week or so after we had packed up our things and moved, the barn was struck by lightning and set on fire, we were naturally the first to be accused.

The food question was still about the same. To begin with it was, generally speaking, hopeless to try to get anything, and in our attempts to get a little extra from the farms round about we came into contact with a rather singular family at one of these. One of the nearest, we were told, belonged to a man who 'anyway was not a Nazi.' With him lived his brother, who had formerly been chairman of the council up in Birkenes and had evidently been turned out of his post when the Nazis took over. Which was in itself a recommendation.

'Could we buy a little milk?' Yes, after some negotiation we got a glass each. A few days later we went up to the farm again. First milk, and then came the question of our chances of buying a little cream. The farmer considered this long and well, trying by every means to 'place' the two unexpected visitors. He would not show his colours, and we were gradually compelled to disclose our general political sympathies. When I think now of all the questions the farmer asked and all the stories we told him, I can only smile. In our hearts we had condemned this family as some of the biggest rogues we had had to deal with so far, and at the same time as stupid fools who had not the smallest understanding of current affairs.

We were students who had gone off on a long summer excursion for fear of forced labour, and this attitude seemed to be accepted by most people, including the family at the farm in question. We got milk, we got cream, and after long and crucial negotiations we got a more or less regular weekly supply of butter. This continued for a time, till we moved to other regions, where the fetching of the valuable product became too laborious and we simply had not time for it.

We little knew then that the two brothers up at Röynaas had done a very good job after the wave of arrests in February. A doctor at Drangsholdt had been one of the local leaders. He escaped at the last moment with some of his fellow-workers, and these were all hidden for over a month by the brothers.

The peasant family which was to play the most important part in our lives throughout the operations of the summer and autumn lived on a farm in Söndre Birkenes. They also kept the local shop, and their name was Aabel. Our acquaintance began with two bottles of mineral water and a very sceptical attitude. Not one question, either at the beginning or later, only an obvious reserve. For us the upshot of this connection at that time was almost a life and death matter. Here again it was we who had to show our colours to some extent by 'loose talk.' But days and weeks were to pass before we were in any degree accepted. As what? Rolf as a law student and I as a medical student. Whether the family believed this story I will not say; we never got a reply.

But the result became increasingly visible: we got food, always more and more of what usually passed under the counter. And as time passed we gradually got more than food!

It was no simple matter to get co-operation from the peasants round about. There was no one who knew us as individuals; no one who could give us a recommendation or 'certificate of patriotism.' This was our greatest difficulty throughout the summer. It was clear that if we were to work in peace and decent conditions, we must get hold of a hut some way from an inhabited area, but this in itself proved to be a matter of great difficulty. The peasants whom we approached had no guarantee whatever as to what kind of people we were, without regard to the stories which were dished up. Rumours were afloat in the neighbourhood; some thought we were police spies, others that we were control agents, and others again considered that we were 'dangerous' and were carrying on illegal work.

Nor had we ourselves any security whatever for the peasants we talked to. Certainly it was said that there were no Nazis in Söndre Berkenes, but we had no guarantee. Nazis were one thing—another and much more dangerous type were the people who agreed with both sides and could in no circumstances hold their tongues about what they saw and heard from one day to another. This last type was perhaps in the majority; I do not mean exclusively in Birkenes, but in most parts of Norway.

Besides the Aabel family, the Birkenes, Daland, Hauge and Rogsland families were to give us the support we so sorely needed throughout the summer's work. We became acquainted with these one after another through negotiations about renting huts and requests to be allowed to buy country produce. Every time we wanted to have contact with England at night we applied to Hauge to let us sleep in the barn. The reasons were usually different.

When the farm people had gone to bed and all else was still, we usually got busy setting up the wireless station in the barn. Electric current was only to be had by a 'stolen connection' after the bulb of the light circuit had been taken out. The aerial was stretched across the floor, the length and direction of which suited it extraordinarily well. And while the people slept, we had our little 'chat' with the other side. At this farm, too, we had cautiously admitted that we were 'students'—a comparatively harmless category, which could be helped without any great risk.

Both the farms on the other side of the river had huts inside the wood. At first neither of these had any great desire to let the huts, and thought of a number of things which prevented them from doing so just then. And certainly they had every reason for reluctance. But when Jörgen Birkenes heard that we were students in hiding, he returned to the question, and everything was arranged in a short time. We were not to rent the hut—that is to say, we were not to pay him anything, but to borrow the hut for as long as we wanted it. And the hut at Gullringstjern was constantly used in the weeks and months that followed.

The equipment which should have been dropped by parachute a week after myself, and on which we depended to some degree for an extension of our activities, we tried to get over by the most varied methods. But the British absolutely refused to fly; not so much because of the danger to themselves as for fear that a reception committee for the things was fairly sure to be captured and the drop itself observed. Not even our proposal that they should send a Mosquito with only one parcel, consisting of the most important material, was accepted.

The only solution then was to get the most important things sent by ordinary plane to Sweden and on from Sweden by messenger. These were in the first place a vibrator, so that we could use the wireless set on six-volt batteries and not be dependent on wires. Next meteorological equipment for the weather forecast station—and tobacco. Every day, after our meal, whether it was three boiled potatoes three times a day, with a little bread and butter, or a mackerel or herring, we had sunk down apathetically on the one 'bed' in the hut, muttering, 'If only one had a pipe!'

Collaboration with our contact in the town went quite well, even if the result at this time was not all that could be desired. The trouble was that we were too far outside the town itself, and the whole business was too laborious. We had indeed arranged a so-called 'potato code' which we used over the telephone: situation reports on movements in the harbour from one day to another. But even these were not what they could have been, and a customs official who ordered potatoes, parsnips, turnips and swedes, or inquired for eggs, could not always get the exact information over to us. And almost every day there had been rotten potatoes in the previous day's consignment, which meant that one of us must go into the town. That meant thirty-five miles on a bicycle and a seven miles' walk every day; on bad food, that became rather too exhausting in the long run.

But there were also the guard's son Arne and his friend Thorstein, who now and again cycled over from Kristiansand with important news and with such food as they could get from the town. These two covered a different field from that of our contact with the 'potato code.'

CHAPTER X

'YOU NEVER CAN TELL'

WE WERE notified by wireless that the things which had been specially ordered had been sent off from Sweden. I now had to go to Oslo myself in connection with the unfortunate end of our place of contact a mile and a quarter north of Kjevik, the forwarding of goods by messenger from Sweden, and the organization of a head office in Oslo.

I took the day train to Oslo, provided with an ordinary travel permit which Arne had got through one of his connections.

As usual on a train journey with a regular travel permit

and as an ordinary passenger, I chose one of the middle compartments of the carriage. In the event of a control, I should at any rate be aware of it in good time.

At Lunner station I had a strong feeling that something was happening on the platform. There were an unusual number of Germans and also a great many Norwegian State police officials who seemed to be fairly busy. I rose, with uneasy anticipations, from my seat by the window, made my way past the three ladies and two men who were sitting in the same compartment, and went out into the corridor.

Nothing unusual was to be seen. The train started again. Then, almost at the same time, the doors at both ends of the carriage were opened, and in rushed a party of the minions of the law, with tommy-guns and all their professional outfit. Almost at the same moment I went back into the compartment, and shut the door as quietly and calmly as possible so as not to arouse unnecessary suspicion among my fellow-passengers.

I was in a tight corner. I had on me not only a revolver, but also three different passports, not to mention two envelopes containing altogether 3,000 Norwegian crowns to be distributed in Oslo.

I wish I could describe the expressions on the faces of the other people in the compartment when I stepped across, pulled down the window and—as the train was crossing Lunner bridge—got rid of these rather troublesome pieces of evidence. But the best part of it all was what happened when I was about to pull the window up again. A man sitting next to the door had not said a word throughout the journey, and we all regarded him with great suspicion. Evidently he too had seen what was happening out in the corridor; he watched what I was doing for a moment, and then rose quickly, took a small attaché case which was lying on the rack, stepped across and, with a 'one moment' to me, flung it out of the window!

The ladies, who throughout the journey had shown themselves clearly to be the most thorough-going *jössinger,* sat paralysed with fear, too paralysed to say anything at all. The other man went on reading his newspaper—reading it upside down from sheer fright. We were not a minute too soon; the door opened, and in came two of the State police. Ladies could sit down—men must stand with their hands up—personal search and check of each person's frontier dweller's or identity card. Examination of each man's luggage. 'All right!' And they went on to the next compartment.

When we reached Drammen one of the men seemed suddenly to get bothered; he remained sitting for a little while after the train had stopped, but then abruptly got out. The man in the corner followed immediately after. He leant over towards me with the words 'Thanks for your company and a pleasant journey.' Whether these two men were together, or whether the second had been alarmed by the sudden hurry of the first, I cannot say. In any case, I did not feel over-comfortable and had little desire to see Oslo West station that evening. Contrary to my original plan I got out at Sandvika.

I had to wait for some days in Oslo because the despatch of goods from Sweden had been delayed. German raids were going on in the district along the frontier, and the messenger's package had remained at one of the 'post offices.' These days I spent up at Röa with my friend the bookseller and had the opportunity, with the twins and the shipbroker's son Jan, to organize the Oslo section and also the messenger and postal communication between Oslo and Kristiansand.

One afternoon I went up to Lake Bogstad for a bathe with the bookseller's sons. A number of logs were floating on the water in a boom, and we amused ourselves by running about on these. Unluckily I got some splinters into my right foot, which was to cause some trouble later. They caused blood poisoning, and I left Oslo three days later with a temperature of 101.4 degrees, after arranging for the dispatch of some of the stuff from Sweden, as well as two six-volt accumulators.

I left by boat this time—to be exact, in the *Kristiansand* on July 13. The reason for my not going by train was that the boat was still free: in other words, no travel permit was needed so long as one had a frontier dweller's card or other pass for the western zone. Moreover, I did not want to run into anything like what had happened on the journey up;

it would be very difficult to get two suitcases full of wireless parts, weapons and other equipment out of a train window.

The doctor up at Röa had given me a bottle of pills which he said would keep the poisoning in check. This was all plain sailing, but directly I came on board I hung over the rail and parted with the little I had eaten that day. 'Poor man,' I heard an old lady beside me remark, 'he's sick before the boat's left the quay. It must be awful to be like that!'

Yes, it really was awful—and I was not worth many rows of beans when the police came on board and demanded frontier dwellers' cards. This was very curious; people said it was the first time this had happened on board the *Kristiansand*. I cannot say that I felt very happy as I sat on my two suitcases and went through the various points on my frontier dweller's card with an idiot of a policeman. But I was really too ill and weak to pay very much attention to what was happening.

But as soon as the police had finished something happened which woke me up. I caught sight of three young fellows just crossing the gangway and showing their papers—three former Scouts from Ullern, lads of eighteen or nineteen—the father of one of them, I had heard, was a strong Nazi. What views the other two had I had no idea, but this was the worst of all unlucky meetings.

A game of hide-and-seek all over the *Kristiansand* began. I am afraid I lost it. First one of them noticed my face as I sat on a hatch on deck with my head in my hands, on the point of vomiting. Of course the fool called the other two at once, and they stood together whispering. Evidently none of them was sure; but the one who had first noticed me was determined to have his opinion confirmed, for he walked slowly towards me. I contorted my face, pulled down the corners of my mouth as if I had St. Vitus's dance and in general behaved like an idiot.

The boy changed his mind, blushed and went back to the others. An eager whispering continued. Sick and tired of the whole thing, I went below and sat down at a table in the alleyway, again with my head in my hands, to try and get a little sleep. The boys did not give up. One by one they passed the place where I was sitting, stopped a little farther on and tried to get a glimpse of my face. At last I grew furious and suddenly got up, when the one who had started this game was standing three yards away from me and staring.

'I've had enough of this,' I hissed in the best Bergen dialect I could muster, 'I'm sick of being stared at like a circus animal! Clear off, before you and the other two go overboard!'

He looked quite astonished; the St. Vitus's dance and the Bergen dialect had evidently made an impression.

'I—I'm—only looking for the lavatory!'

'You've been past the door six times at least, so go to——!'

Kristiansand! It was a relief to be there, although the doctor at Lund assured me that I should die in my bed within two days, perhaps sooner, if I did not go into a hospital where they could open up my foot. The red streak up my leg had long ago reached the groin; the gland was like a nice little tennis ball, and the whole thing looked very bad. But—I had things with me that ought to go over the wireless the same evening, and so I had the usual seventeen miles' bicycle ride that afternoon. And, very curiously, the blood poisoning eased, and four days later the whole trouble was more or less cured.

CHAPTER XI

THE 'UPTURNED BOAT'

UP IN Tveit and Birkenes all was quiet. Rolf, besides a good deal of other preparatory work, had taken a job as farm boy with the Aabels and thereby strengthened our position as 'students' quite considerably. Now it was full steam ahead again; the station was to be moved, and we could begin to work on a broader basis.

The country round Kristiansand had long ago been combed in every direction to find the best position for a station. It ought to be in a place from which there was an unimpeded view of the whole port of Kristiansand, so that we could send, besides situation reports, the exact time of ships' arrival and sailing. But at the same time it ought to be somewhere where there was less chance of its being quickly discovered: that is to say, somewhere off the beaten track. There was a further very important factor to be considered: it must not be too far away. Each battery or accumulator, full, weighed nearly 60 lbs. These would have to be carried up to the station from wherever we could get them charged. Along the high road this could be done on a bicycle, but through the woods the means of transport would be on a man's back.

And naturally, this time we were not so keen to place the station right under the noses of the Germans. A look at the map of Kristiansand and surrounding district will make the reader understand why we chose the 'Upturned Boat.' It was the highest point in the neighbourhood of Kristiansand, only about three miles outside the town along the road over the side of Södalen. Certainly it was a summit about 750 feet high, rising straight from the road, and it was a hard job to get up it, but the various 'shady sides' of the 'Upturned Boat' far outweighed its disadvantages.

We spent several days on end up at the 'Upturned Boat' and in the country round about. There was not much sense in moving the whole apparatus up to this new place, if we were to be compelled to move again a few days later. We found the place for the camp above a little moss, thickly covered with birch trees, on the farther side of the actual top. A path ran across the moss and continued down the precipitous side of the ridge to the road in the valley. But the path was obviously little used and originally trodden out many years before.

On the edge of the moss stood the remains of an old shanty and beside it the foundations of another house. The shanty had collapsed, but a large part of the roofing was still whole. Before any of the technical equipment for the station was moved up, we built a little shelter for the wireless station up on the rocky slope, on a ledge above the moss. The place was fairly inaccessible and well covered on all sides by leafy trees. We ourselves lay in a tent a little farther along the same ledge.

There were, however two things about the position of the station which we did not care for. About a hundred yards below the top of the 'Upturned Boat' and south of it began the German area which had formerly belonged to the shooting range. About a mile and a quarter north of our own wireless station, up on Skraastadvarden, the Germans were installing a new main wireless station for Kristiansand. In other words, we had to use the utmost care for twenty-four hours in every day so as not to be detected by Germans from these two places, picking berries, going for evening walks or on other errands.

The only possibility of getting the accumulators charged proved to be, after many vain efforts elsewhere, to have them done at the house of our contact Arne. Among the things sent from Sweden were a charging transformer and an oxygen meter, so this side of the business was in order. But to have a six-volt accumulator standing buzzing down in the cellar under the prevailing conditions in Kristiansand was no joke; the whole family in Oesterveien behaved splendidly and were to continue to do so through much unpleasantness later in the summer of 1943.

Telegrams began to stream out from the wireless station up at the 'Upturned Boat.' We kept watch at our look-out post every morning from before light till about eleven a.m. In the afternoon we were on watch from five o'clock until dark.

In this way we could observe all shipping that used Kristiansand, and the Allied Supreme Command usually knew the most important details about one hour later. Kristiansand was of such great interest because, as the Germans' chief naval base and port in Sörland, all the convoys which were to go south, west and north along the coast of Norway with supplies for the various towns in Vestlandet and Nordland were formed there. In the harbour, too, all the convoys for the voyage to Denmark were given escorts. Convoys coming from the west also usually came into Kristiansand.

Simultaneously with reports from our direct observation, details concerning the same ships, sent up from our contacts in the town, were sometimes telegraphed. As soon as the British were informed of the number of ships, their size and escort, what time they had weighed anchor, and their speed and course, they could decide whether it was worth while to make an attack, or whether they should wait till they had got the whole convoy farther along the coast of Vestlandet. From the reports which were sent out they could easily calculate where the convoy would be at any time, and deliver attacks, which often had astonishingly good results.

From the 'Upturned Boat' we had a view in fine weather, practically speaking, right over to Mandal in the west and past Lillesand to Grimstad and Arendal in the east. With such a view the position reports on convoys were sent up to one hour after they had sailed.

But the 'Upturned Boat' was unfortunately something of a paradise for people who were fond of woodland and open country. We thus had a good many visitors, and on a Sunday there could be as many as fifteen or twenty people at our look-out. At these times we had to 'go for a walk' too, take a little rucksack with some food in it and sit down up on the top. That we disappeared from the place several times in the course of the day and came back again a little later did not seem very unnatural. As long as they were Norwegians we did not take these visitors very seriously, but it happened quite often that there were Germans in uniform or in civilian clothes, and the last category in particular we did not much care for.

We gradually built up a very nice little station. We fetched 'building materials' every Sunday from the German wireless station on Skraastadvarden. As a rule there was no one there on a Sunday, except a sentry who was obviously asleep.

One thing was quite clear—two men could not carry on this work alone and at the same time run it at all securely. Now and again we might, for a few days at a time, get a little help from one of our contacts in the town, but that was not nearly enough.

When one of us was in the town fetching reports, food or something else, and the man who had stayed behind had to leave the station for the look-out post, we had no guarantee that some unauthorized person would not in the meantime inadvertently hit upon the station itself and the camp. The person in question, if he was one of the wrong sort, might go quietly to the nearest farm and ring up, while we on our return would unconsciously walk into the enemy's arms.

I telegraphed to England. The man with whom I had planned to co-operate before I first left England must now, I said, be sitting in Sweden, most horribly bored. Why not send him back? The plan and the wish expressed by us were approved, and we were told that we might expect Hjelm Basberg in a month's time; further information would be sent to us.

We, therefore, had only to try to keep the station fully active until then. This was easier said than done. The Germans knew perfectly well that there must be a secret wireless station in the immediate neighbourhood of Kristiansand. Time after time convoys left the port; time after time they were attacked in practically the same place, off Jaeren, where there was neither harbour nor shelter for a ship that became a casualty. Ship after ship was sunk; cargo after cargo failed to arrive at its destination.

Their efforts to find the sinner were perceptible to us from time to time. Direction-finding planes were now very freely used; another had been transferred to Kjevik from Sola to take part in these efforts. There were days during our contact when we had to lie flat in the heather up on the 'Boat'; there were times when we were quite convinced that a plane had found the station. It would circle around the top four times, flying low; from where we lay behind a bush we could see quite plainly two men on board searching every square yard with glasses.

Once when it seemed that the Fiesler Storch had received our signals on its apparatus before it started, while still standing on the airfield, and had probably made a provisional D/F, we had the chance of trying a new system. The word 'Plane!' from Rolf, who was keeping watch above the station itself, followed by 'Making straight for us!' made me jump. I did not send 'wait' this time, but continued my signals, though suddenly reduced in strength. The result was visible immediately; the Storch turned abruptly, flew several times round the place where the signals had suddenly become weaker, and then returned on an exactly opposite course. I raised the signals quite slowly to maximum strength; the plane turned about again and started afresh. Then I did send 'wait,' and after that I had to give up a later period of contact as the Storch would not abandon the search.

But it was not only planes that interfered with our activities. There was a control on all roads into the town, and sometimes actually a control on Lund bridge. These controls were tiresome, especially when one had an accumulator on one's luggage carrier. That things often went all right was hardly due to any cleverness on our side, but to incredible stupidity on that of the Germans. It became necessary, therefore, sometimes to send people ahead when something 'dangerous' was to be transported. We had thus at all events a chance of finding out what lay ahead of us and could act accordingly. But when a motor-car patrol came along, or some other mobile form of control, there was nothing we could do before we were 'right up against it.'

The farmer at whose house we kept our bicycles while running the station at the 'Upturned Boat' was *said* to be a good fellow, but we were never able to make quite sure of this. We were out on the moor picking berries, we said, but anyone must have been able to see, for example, that the biscuit tins we used for carrying accumulators were heavier, or at least just as heavy, when we went up on to the moor after a visit to the town. That twelve or fifteen Germans were busy every day carrying loads to their wireless station, a few hundred yards farther up along the road, was not to make conditions any better.

CHAPTER XII

THE 'POACHER'

FOUR good-sized ships in westbound convoys had been sunk in the course of a week. Things began to grow lively in the country round the 'Upturned Boat.' As far as we could gather, the Germans were now sending a number of patrols, mountain troops, out into the area every time a convoy of any size was to leave Kristiansand. It began to be pretty hopeless to try to run the station so long as we were only two. We were up to twenty hours a day on our legs, for to sleep while it was light could easily have disastrous consequences.

But fortunately the end of July was approaching, and if we could hold out for the rest of that month, conditions would certainly improve.

We had twice been forced to close the station completely for several days at a time; a company of mountain troops had held manœuvres in the area east of the 'Upturned Boat'—the area in which the Storch had evidently established that the station lay. And the end was to come one day.

It was a Friday morning, the time was about 4.30, and we were both on the look-out on the top of the 'Upturned Boat.' We counted the ships with the aid of our glasses: eight cargo boats over and nine under 4,000 tons. In other words, it was pretty certain that a large convoy was to sail westward. We had already, at one a.m., sent an advance report based on the observations we had made the evening before.

And there they went out slowly, one by one, between Odder island and the anti-submarine defence outside. The escort was coming from Marvika in the Toppdalsfjord. Rolf sat and wrote while I sat with the glasses and dictated each ship's size and appearance. In our eagerness we did not notice that we were not quite alone. It was not till the last ship had left the harbour and we had half an hour before the next contact time, that I rose rather abruptly to run up to the camp and get the telegram coded and sent. Then I noticed something moving behind some trees on a hillock about 350 yards away. As I rose, something white disappeared behind a thick fir-tree; I went on as if I had not noticed anything at all, just whispering to Rolf, 'There are people about—just go on as if nothing had happened!'

I sauntered very slowly in a more or less opposite direction to the place where the white object had moved, entered the wood, and then—ran up at full speed.

I looked about very carefully—not a trace, not a sign of

life. For a good half-hour I sat quite still above the place, but still there was not a sound to be heard, except the usual concert of birds hailing the sunrise.

This was rather curious. Had I been as badly mistaken as all that? Was I sleepy to that degree, or were my nerves really beginning to give way? It could hardly have been an animal, or perhaps—no, I had seen a face quite plainly through the fir branches.

We should have to miss a contact and send the most important news two hours later. But to be on the safe side I took a long walk in the country round about before we made our way to the station. The whole day passed without our hearing or seeing a soul. The traffic down the road, 750 feet below the look-out post, was going along as usual—perhaps a little busier than was usual. We did not feel comfortable; we felt that someone was watching all our movements as soon as we were outside the camp.

It was about two o'clock when a twig snapped a short way below the moss. We had just eaten a slice of bread each, and were going to try to get some sleep in turn. We both started up—someone was coming up the path!

In a twinkling I had the sack containing the 'holy of holies' fastened on my back—all the code-books, the crystal set we were using and the plan for the running of the station generally. And there we lay, each on one side of the way up to the little shelf with a good view down on to the moss, ready for what might come. If there were many of them, we had not a chance. . . .

A man was breaking through the undergrowth on the lower side of the moss—a man in civilian clothes—yes, he was 'only' a Norwegian and to judge from his clothes one of the local peasants. He went on slowly up the narrow gully towards the 'Boat' and passed the top ten yards from where we lay. I think we both had the same thought: how lucky that during the time in which we had lived on the ledge above the moss we had been so careful not to make any tracks in the grass, which a snooper could have followed to our retreat. We had jumped from stone to stone behind thick wild raspberry bushes close to the rock wall; even down at the beck we had always taken water at different places.

Again we kept watch at the look-out post in the evening; again a number of ships of different sizes assembled in the harbour, probably to sail the next morning; and again an advance report of the number of ships went by wireless to the Allied Supreme Command.

At a quarter past three next morning we were both again at the look-out post. It was still dark; there was just a suggestion of daylight over the mountain tops to the north-east. It was cold. Over on the moss east of the summit a belated blackcock was calling. It was quite clear, and the sky still strewn with stars.

The blackcock's calling ceased quite suddenly; there was a snapping of dry twigs as it rose and flew off northward. We had both noticed this, but had not very much time for further reflection. We heard anchor chains rattling and steam winches working; for some reason the ships down in the harbour were off early that day.

I sat straining my eyes through the glasses; it was almost hopeless to try to distinguish details—I could only just make out the number as they passed out. Rolf made notes and endeavoured with the naked eye to find out which ships they were, corresponding to the notes we had made the evening before.

Then we both started—a twig snapped somewhere down in the direction of the German area. I lowered my glasses quite slowly. 'Don't show you've noticed anything!' I whispered. Rolf just nodded in reply. Then I said, aloud to Rolf: 'It's beginning to get light—we'll soon have to see about picking some berries!'

Humming the Horst Wessel song, with my hands in my pockets, I sauntered down towards the place from which I thought the sound had come. But there was nothing to be seen, everything was quite quiet—oppressively so. Back over the fence which marked off the German area and up to the top. Rolf was sitting with his back against a stone humming to himself. 'Not a thing!' I whispered.

Again we thought that we had deceived ourselves, but to be on the safe side we remained lying where we were, glancing now and again towards the harbour, where the details were becoming clearer. The convoy of twenty-two ships was proceeding westward—if only we could get our report off!

We remained lying where we were and looking cautiously down towards the German area. I was whistling aloud when Rolf's leg moved slowly towards mine and I received a quite gentle kick. 'There! look there! towards the big fir by the stone down there a little way inside the fence!' Rolf whispered; he found it hard to control his voice.

'I'll go down and have a talk with him,' I whispered back; 'perhaps he's only a Norwegian. If there's trouble try to get round behind the man—if there are many of them, go cautiously up to the station—take the "holy of holies," warn the boys and clear off to Oslo—get news over to England!'

I loafed across into the German area with my hands in my pockets. The white of the man's face was visible through one or two bushes; he was standing quite still. 'Is there any reason for playing hide-and-seek so early in the morning? Is your watch right?'

There was no need to shout; the man was standing hardly ten yards away. No reply: I went on a few steps, and suddenly went hot when I thought that I had neither passport nor revolver on me—only a stout birch stick.

Then at last the man sprang out. 'Halt!'—I trembled. So after all it was a 'green.' 'Hands up!' He did not say the words, but hissed them. I still stood with my hands in my pockets. 'Hands up!' he yelled, with his rifle pointed forward.

I racked my brains; it was a *very* unpleasant situation. Was he alone, or was he yelling so loud to attract the attention of others who were close by? He yelled for the third time, and this time I thought the rifle would go off. Only a gigantic bluff could save the situation now. I continued to stand still with my hands in my pockets, and just stared the man in the face. At last I answered in German as calmly as I could:

'But, sir, this is a queer way to greet a friend so early in the morning—a very unpleasant way! I ask you politely what the time is—and get a rifle pointed at me by way of reply!'

He replied, if possible still more furious: 'Your passport!'

'What right have you to ask for anything of the kind? I'd like to see your papers first! I don't walk about in the woods at this time of day with a timber cargo in my pockets. If you want to see papers, you must come with me down to the farm where we're staying now.'

The man went on, scarlet with anger: 'Three mornings running I've stood and watched you up on the top; you've spied on the harbour with glasses, noted the ships leaving and disappeared as soon as they've all gone! Give me an explanation—why are you up here so early every morning?'

I tried to smile as I replied: 'In the first place we've *not* been spying, even if your idea is quite a good one. Glasses are necessary to see that poachers like you don't shoot game. And as to taking notes, may I tell you that my friend writes poetry?—by the way, sir, would you mind not talking so loud—I'm not deaf!'

The conversation was carried on on my side in very bad German, but there was no doubt that the man understood what I said. 'Hands up!' he yelled again, 'and come down to the guard-room with me, and we'll soon settle that part of the business!' His words were emphasized by a movement of his rifle.

The only chance was a bluff. I glanced over my shoulder at the man who stood there fuming with rage, stood for a moment looking across towards some trees in the background, smiled quite noticeably, nodded several times, and turned to the German again:

'I don't think so—it would most certainly be very unhealthy—perhaps for me—perhaps for you!'

The man, who was about forty and thickset but small, fell straight into the trap. 'Where's the man who's with you?'

'Men, you mean,' I replied. 'There are six of us keeping watch up here now—and three of them are in the wood behind you at this moment!'

The German was in great doubt. This was the only chance for me now. I nodded towards the bushes in the background again. The man's voice had suddenly begun to quaver; he grunted something incomprehensible, and did not dare turn right round. With my hands still in my pockets I turned my back on him, quite slowly. 'Good morning!' I said, and went as calmly as I could up towards the top of the 'Boat.' I expected the shot every moment, and I will willingly admit that I was trembling with nervousness. Not a sound—not a shot—not a word.

Over the top and down on the other side. At the same moment Rolf came crawling out from behind a rock. At the critical moment he had flung a stone into the bushes behind the spot where we had stood, and the noise of it had given me the idea—although for a moment I thought there were more Germans on the way up. Now the only thing was to put the best face on a bad business; we walked openly as if nothing had happened, and sat down for a few minutes on a large rock. For safety's sake I shouted the names of one or two fictitious people, received no reply, and remarked in a loud voice that the others had probably gone for a bit of a walk round.

The German had followed us and was sitting on a rock a little lower down; he also, in all probability, wanted to show that he was not afraid. 'Let's go down to the village and get some milk!' Rolf proposed, so loud that the German could not help hearing it. 'Good,' I replied, and we started down together—the German some distance behind.

'The devil!' Of course we could 'fix' him, but on the other hand what would the result be? Shooting which undoubtedly would be heard; the German would be missed when the guard paraded at eight o'clock; the countryside would be gone through with a fine comb; extra controls would be put on all roads. No, this was a case in which one's personal desires must be kept in check and reason allowed to prevail.

On the edge of the steep drop down to the valley the German gave up. We had passed the ledge with the wireless station at a distance of a few feet; all was peaceful there. Half-way down the hillside we stopped and listened; all was quiet. At the farm we took our bicycles and went up the valley. Behind the first bend and well covered by the woods, we left the road again, hid our bicycles and proceeded up the slope towards Skraastadvarden.

Not till three hours later, having combed the country between the German wireless station and our own to be sure that our retreat was clear, we cautiously and quietly slipped down the rock wall to our camp. The report on the convoy which had sailed that morning went in record time, together with a message that we were closing the station for a few days—on account of 'disturbances.'

With the whole of our equipment, except the accumulator, we went back the same way, and then on our bicycles, with all the stuff behind us, into the town. As a measure of precaution we started with a quarter of an hour between us in case of control. We met again farther on, nearer the town. We then continued towards the town with Rolf fifty yards behind, out of consideration for the 'holy of holies' which was hanging upon his chest. If I were stopped, he at all events would have some small chance. But all went well—we went through back streets of Lund over to the Sörland road, deposited our sacks in Oddernes churchyard, and for safety's sake cycled up Kongsgaard Allé to Volle Lake to have a look at the general situation.

CHAPTER XIII

'COMING TO-NIGHT'

It was eight that evening when, worn and tired, we came into the Aabels' farmyard. Yes, there was room in the loft, and we had just to creep in. If we had come with fifty men, I think the answer would still have been the same. We were able to eat a decent meal for the first time in two months. That evening the two men of the family were to some extent enlightened—that is to say, we told them straight out that we were not really 'students' and were not hanging about the roads for our common amusement. I do not think this was any news to the two men; they had long before put two and two together and got a result of pretty near four. But great was their astonishment when from the bicycle bag, which they themselves had handled on several occasions, we produced the wireless. In a few minutes news came from London.

'Four German cargo boats out of a convoy of twenty-two were sunk this morning by British torpedo aircraft off the south-western coast of Norway. The aggregate tonnage of the vessels was about 20,000. One aircraft did not return.'

I just held out my hand to Rolf and smiled. 'We'll get there some day!' Counting the four last, there were fourteen notches in the birch stick now.

The time for the parachute drop with the supplies we had been dreaming of all the summer began to draw near. By reason of its many advantages a moss in the Svaland moor was chosen, a place about three miles west of the Sörland road at Aabel. We knew the ground thoroughly from the time we had stayed up by Gullringstjern in the hut in Birkenes. We still wanted to be able to avail ourselves of this hut, and Jörgen had as usual no objection to this.

But there was another hut which was now more important to us while we were waiting for the drop: Rogsland's hut, which lay on the edge of the moss where we meant to receive the drop. There were no difficulties about this either, and next day the necessary equipment was moved up.

On August 12 Hjelm Basberg arrived. He had been delayed somewhat on the journey from Sweden on account of the steadily increasing difficulties on the frontier and in Oslo, but all had gone well. It was three years since I had seen him, but he was not much changed. A fellow who knew what he was about, a woodsman who knew the conditions better, perhaps, than most others and who, above all, had his nerves in good order and was sure-handed if it came to shooting.

The day after Basberg's arrival we received this telegram: 'Coming to-night. Keep watch at time agreed. Seven parachutes and one separate parcel.'

There was feverish activity that evening. We had planned every detail in advance; a cave half-way down a rock wall

Packing container parachutes (Carl Sigurd Elligers and Lars Larsen).

Examining weapons after drop: May 7, 1944 (Lars Larsen and author).

The main station in Oevrebö: Jan Tenvig coding telegrams.

Jan Tenvig on guard.

nearly a hundred feet high, nearly three-quarters of a mile below 'pin-point,' had been chosen as a dump for the most important things dropped. Everything, too, which had any connection with wireless activity was hidden on the ledge there of an evening. The place was very inaccessible, and anyone who did not know it well would have to use a rope to come down. It was impossible to see the ledge and cave from above; nor could they be seen from other directions. A carefully thought out plan of retreat was made in case anything unexpected should happen.

We had made an agreement with Daland, the schoolmaster, who lived in Birkenes and who had gradually been 'put in the picture,' that he should give us a hand with the actual drop. Thus there were four of us sitting waiting at twelve o'clock. It was a clear starry night without a cloud in the sky; there would be a full moon in two days. The wind was blowing from the north, between ten and fifteen miles an hour; it was cold. Out on the moss were pegs with white labels, marking the places where the different men were to stand, each holding his light, so as to form a triangle for the pilot. In addition to the torches which were to be held by each individual, we had fixed up two tins containing shavings soaked in paraffin.

The minutes passed. Now and again I took a short walk up on to a hillock above the moss, partly to check the direction of the wind, partly to listen. But all was quiet. Twice I thought I heard the sound of aircraft farther south, but I must have imagined it.

One o'clock came. Still all quiet. Half-past one: not a sound. The wind had increased in strength and shifted a little to the north-west, so that we had to change the direction of the triangle a few degrees. I cannot say I much liked this turn of events; in the first place it would be more difficult for the pilot to estimate the wind and therewith the actual drop; also, the direction of the wind was now such that the plane would fly low over the only farm in the district. This was rather tiresome for the special reason that Nazis lived at that farm. But that risk must be taken, now or never!

It was nine minutes to two. I sat up on the little hillock

and listened, dozing off once for a bit. Then—I gave a start—the sound of a plane! Yes, there was no doubt this time—but was it the plane that was coming to us?

Yes! I bounded down to the moss, where the lads had heard the noise already. All stood ready, torch in hand; there it came, a four-engined Halifax! What a sight—like a black ghostly bird against the paler starry sky.

A loud whisper from me, '*Light!*'—and three beams from well-shaded lights were flung up towards the plane. One circle—run in—there! One parachute after another, like pearls on a string—one, two, three, four, five, six—and seven! But what about the parcel? The plane swung round and came back, but turned away sharply in the middle of its run in. What had happened? Why didn't the fellow clear off as fast as he could? There he was coming in again—but again he turned away. 'All lights out!' I shouted furiously. That chap up there was bound to wake at any rate half the neighbourhood before he went off!

At last he himself had evidently made the same discovery. The plane vanished to the north-west like a black shadow.

Unfortunately the wind had caught the parachutes and carried them southward at high speed. They were found about two hundred yards from the triangle. It was dark inside the wood, but the parachutes, all of which without exception had become entangled in boughs of good-sized trees, stood out as dark silhouettes against the sky. Every man worked in silence; this was a business that must be done quickly. In the event of the parachute drop having been observed, it was hard to say at what time a visit might be expected. Nor could 1,000 lbs. and more be unpacked in a short time.

Not till four a.m. had all the hardest work been done. Till then all around had been quiet. Each container had in it three tin boxes, in which the gear was packed; the most important, which held new sets of code-books, wireless equipment and new crystals, was marked with a large white X, and these things were the first to be placed in the cave. As a safety measure the schoolmaster Daland was now sent home. In the event of a 'visit' it was arranged that he should if possible send a message to us by his son.

At eight a.m. all the most important items had been distributed; everything of technical importance had been stowed in the cave, while all food, clothing and other things of a personal nature were distributed among a number of different hiding-places well covered by fir branches.

Among the things dropped were 270 lbs. of chocolate, 5,000 cigarettes, tobacco, tinned meat, dried plums, apricots and apples, and many other things we had only been dreaming of for months past. Although we were all dead-tired, we were in the highest spirits. How much chocolate each of us ate in the course of those hours, and how many cigarettes we smoked, I cannot say, but it was a wonder none of us were sick. For safety's sake we took a bundle containing chocolate and some cigarettes, and laid it on the ledge along with the most important things. After this we all took sleeping-bags and lay down in the heather on the top of the cliff. All the automatic weapons and ammunition which had been dropped were also stored on the ledge. In the event of there being 'trouble' there would hardly be 'positional warfare'; it would be a question of who was quickest on his feet.

CHAPTER XIV

A LIFE AND DEATH CHASE ON SVALAND MOOR

Rolf and I were going to try to get a little sleep, with Basberg on guard. We lay in our sleeping-bags fully dressed; we had taken off only our boots.

It was 9.30, and we had been asleep for half an hour. I had really been only half asleep, and the moment Hjelm touched my shoulder I was wide awake. Hjelm did not say a word, only handed me the glasses and pointed; he was lying doubled up and hardly moved. I lay where I was in the same position, took the glasses, and—there, straight across the valley on the other side of the beck and at about the same height as ourselves, about two hundred yards away, stood a German, gazing across at the top where we lay. Mountain troops!

He probably saw us at about the same moment as I saw him. A few seconds, and a bullet came smack against the rock wall between Hjelm and myself—a miss by inches only. Another—and another! We lay flat for a moment, while the bullets pattered against the rock above us. Rolf was sleeping as soundly as ever; I wriggled up to him and shook him till he woke, forced his head down when he tried to raise himself, and in a few valuable seconds made him realize the situation.

'Put your boots on quick—we're spotted!' I have seldom met anyone who can really sleep as well as Rolf at any time, even if the moment is most critical and his own life hangs by a thread. 'When I count three we go, and you follow about five yards behind!' The same orders were given to both men.

'Three!' As we got on to our feet we saw behind us, a little higher up and about twenty yards away, a whole party of these green-clad devils! When they first saw us, it seemed that for one valuable moment they did not believe their own eyes: in any case there was perfect quiet for a few seconds. Then came a hail of fire from tommy-guns and rifles; we hardly noticed the bullets which sang round our ears; one thought only possessed us: 'Keep ahead! Run for your life!'

Off along the route we had planned in advance in case anything should go wrong: down a steep mountain cleft to the sheer drop—a jump into the top of a fir which had grown up close the wall—full speed one after another through the fir branches to the bottom of the valley.

There we gave them the slip for the first time; the Germans evidently dared not jump, but had to go round. But the German who had first detected us had made for the same valley bottom and probably followed the direction of the firing. He came crashing down through the undergrowth twenty or thirty yards above the tree just as we reached the ground.

The hunt which now went on for hours in every direction across the moors will never be forgotten by the three who ran for their lives. Down cliffs and up slopes, over pools and becks, now lying doggo on our stomachs, now in a wild chase under a rain of lead. It soon became clear that we had to deal not with a few small patrols, but with several hundred men posted according to a freshly drawn up plan over the whole district between Toppdal and Torridal, the two main valleys to west and east, and between Ogge Lake and Aalefjaer to north and south. Now we first realized why we had been allowed to remain in peace so long after the actual drop.

We had been running for a good three hours, and still had some of our pursuers close behind us. We tried by every means to shake them off, but without result. That we were already pretty well exhausted need not be said. We were crossing for the second time the same great moss south-west of Gullringstjern; we had gained on our pursuers over the last ridge and down the cliff. We were following the same track across the moss which we had made the first time and which the Germans had now turned into a broad street. But—instead of continuing up the valley on the other side, as we had done the first time, we turned back at a sharp angle along the edge, walking on stones all the time so as not to make tracks. Until we could hear the leading pursuer grinding up the slope to the moss, we followed the edge, then turned off sharp into a narrow little cleft and flung ourselves down behind a large rock.

We fought for breath and lay still: we dared not even hope for any outcome. There came the first man; he stopped for a moment, visibly tired, and then made off across the moss along the same track which we had followed. It worked—he disappeared at a dangerous speed up the valley on the other side. For a moment we thought of firing, but realized at once that it would be madness. There they came, more of them—they also followed the track and disappeared up the valley.

Four men so far—obviously four men in incredibly good condition and well accustomed to Norwegian forest country. Had we eluded them? For the time being at any rate. We lay still for some minutes; we hardly dared move. If we could only get over to Trolldalen or Refsdalen, as the local people call it, we should be a long way on our journey. It was not far in distance, but how many posts and patrols had the Germans between us and that valley?

Revolvers in our hands we crawled up the mountain cleft. The same rule still held good, and we had just repeated it anew to one another: if one of us was wounded, it was the duty of the others to finish him off. Not only were our own lives at stake, but each one of us was responsible for many families and individuals, apart from the many secrets of the work. If one of us was captured, no one could know what would happen to all these; perhaps a lot of people down in our district had been arrested already.

Up we went yard by yard—on our stomachs through low scrub and bushes, over the ridge itself in light, open wood and down again in the same way. One more valley and one more ridge before we were on the side of Trolldalen.

There! We jumped up again: a machine-gun post—a hail of bullets—and there was another wild chase down hill with new, well-rested pursuers hot on our heels. There was firing also from a summit a little farther off; where it came from none of us knew. Another hour passed—two hours—three hours; again we left our pursuers behind.

Along the east side of Trolldalen, a little north of Steane, the mountainside falls almost sheer from a height of some three hundred feet; we should get another chance there. We were already well ahead and had reached a narrow cleft which we knew from previous experience to lead down into the valley, but which, seen from above, seemed to end abruptly in a sheer drop. We slid down, round a corner, and got on to a ledge screened by low trees. Here we remained lying without moving a limb, afraid to breathe. A number of our pursuers remained on the edge of the cliff, furiously discussing where we had gone; at last they agreed to separate, some going north, others south, and a few remaining where they were. Fifty yards away!

We were in a hole: how long should we wait before the dogs, which we had several times heard baying on our track, came up and showed which way we had gone? How long would those fellows stay up there? If only some wind would come and make a little noise in the trees, so that every tiny sound was not heard!

We lay as still as mice, listening. Shots were continually being fired, now near, now farther off. But they were mostly scattered shots, probably meant to frighten us; only now and again came a burst from a tommy-gun whose owner thought he had seen something.

Someone was moving again up above us, was beginning to run southward; evidently they had received a signal, or had suddenly thought they heard something. We waited a few seconds—a few minutes—and continued downwards, crawling one after another to the next ledge, where we lay down again for a spell. All three of us were pretty well done; our nervous systems were on the verge of breakdown; and, clean against all common sense, a lighted cigarette went round to each of us in turn and we simply swallowed the smoke.

While we lay on this ledge rain began to fall; at first only single drops, increasing to a steady downpour. This was our salvation—for the time being! The trees began to drip, and the stillness of death, which previously had made the whole affair so completely hopeless, was replaced by the pattering of raindrops on leaves. At the same time there came a faint breeze which increased the noise.

We went on down towards the bottom of the valley. It was steep and rough and consisted of loose stones. It was a quarter past five; the hunt had lasted for seven hours and continued almost without a break. We were all three soaking wet, first with perspiration and later from the rain. It was beginning to get cold: the jerseys we had on when this game began had long been thrown away and we were only in our shirts, which were now torn to rags.

Which of us set the stone rolling I do not know, but one stone took others with it and caused a miniature landslide. In our ears it was a fearful noise, and we lay breathless without moving a finger. . . . A shot—two—three. We still lay where we were, till we could hear one, or perhaps two men, coming up from the bottom of the valley. Again we rushed downhill—along Trolldalen northward, with one or more pursuers after us. This time they did not seem to be men in good training; at any rate we managed to keep our distance. Down to the very bottom of the valley; up the river in its actual bed, sometimes in the water and sometimes on the stones. If dogs were used, we should have a chance.

All three of us were now as good as done for; our legs would not carry us any longer—they grew heavier and heavier each minute. We had stabbing pains in our chests, and I for my part felt that my heart was going to burst.

A gigantic rock on each side of the river closed the valley; at this point the path was made three feet wide to enable people to get through at all. On each side of the gigantic rocks were sheer walls. This must be our last chance. Hjelm and Rolf went on a little farther and took cover, whilst I remained lying behind one of the huge rocks.

The man came along; it looked as if he too had difficulty in running; now and then he almost came to a stop. A hundred yards—fifty—I fired three shots in quick succession. The German flung himself on the ground, and next moment, as though shot from a cannon, ran up the side of the valley among some big rocks. Three shots were fired back—he had only a rifle, no automatic weapons. The shots went far up into the hillside, on the opposite side to where I lay. The man was not aiming at all; he must have been in considerable fear for his life, or he overestimated us.

Under cover of the great rock I ran on farther and joined Hjelm and Rolf, who had found the place we knew from earlier times: a narrow cleft in the hillside, invisible from the path up through Trolldalen, running south-west at a sharp angle towards the top of the next ridge. With an effort we reached a point about a hundred feet up and lay there behind some bushes, from which the path was in sight. We had lain there for five minutes when the same German who had been first up through the valley, and at whom I had fired, stole past! He was an oldish fellow and hardly a 'woodsman,' nor one of the best turned-out of the mountain troops. We lay there for another quarter of an hour without stirring. All was quiet again, except for scattered shots farther east. Then came another series of shots from a machine-gun, but this time farther north in Trolldalen.

What happened up on the moor after that I recollect only in broad outline. We reached the top of that ridge, got past a machine-gun post without being detected, down on the other side, and lay under some bushes till it was nearly dark, while the rain poured down without a break.

During this time we had a chance to work out some kind of a plan based on a variety of alternatives. While Hjelm and Rolf lay where they were, I made a little reconnaissance down to Bjor Lake, a little farther south. Here all was quiet, and it did not look as if the Germans had had any idea that we should get so far west by that time.

I tried my luck at an out-of-the-way farm, but found only an old woman of eighty or more. As she was almost stone deaf, and I did not want to ask my questions about local conditions at the top of my voice, the result was poor. But I was given a mug of milk, which did wonders.

When I regained the spot where the others lay hidden, all was still comparatively quiet. Only the occasional firing from farther east continued with varying strength.

We made our way cautiously to the farm where I had been. And now we decided to take a last chance. With about 500 yards between each man, we walked down the open road past Bjor Lake and Steane down to our own neighbourhood, Raen and Aabel village shop. It had stopped raining, and there was no doubt that the machine-gun posts on Bjorvass moor and the other high ground in those parts heard people going along the road. A few shots were fired, and the bullets struck the water fifty yards below the road. But we went on walking, openly, without checking our steps for a moment, as if we ourselves were Germans or people with perfectly clear consciences from the farms round Bjor Lake.

Impudence pays! The Germans found no reaction to the shots fired to scare us, and stopped after a few attempts. That we walked with our hearts in our mouths every second I will not deny.

Now the great question was: the suspension bridge over the river—was it guarded? If it was, we could all swim, and this would be the only possibility. We came to Raen, the group of farms which lay close to where the suspension bridge crossed to Aabel. There was light behind the curtains, and as we passed, someone peeped out curiously and drew his or her head back again at once. The bridge; not a soul to be seen. Yard by yard I went over to the other side, while Hjelm and Rolf stood waiting for a minute. If no shot came, the road was clear, and they could continue up to Aabel.

Our plan, based entirely on impudence, had succeeded. Just as we had all reached the farmyard the first car passed —a German car—the police patrol on the Sörland road.

It was nearly twelve, and the people at Aabel had gone to bed long before. But it was not long before we sat with Anders and Sören round a well-provided table down in the cellar, while the two women of the family did all they could to stuff us with food. While we sat there eating, we told them what had happened. Cars were continually passing the window; the Sörland road ran close by. Police cars had been about all day, the family told us; twelve persons had been arrested, including members of the Birkenes, Rogsland and Hauge families. What had happened to the schoolmaster Daland no one knew for certain at that time; but it was rumoured that he had been in bed when the Germans came (for the best of reasons, it must be said!) and his wife had told the Germans that he was very ill and had been in bed for the last few days, and so they had left him alone. (This rumour proved later to be correct.)

In short, it was now only a question of time as to when the Aabel family would be visited; we three, therefore, by way of precaution, agreed to Anders' proposal that we should go for a little walk up on to the moor towards Röynaas, i.e. on the opposite side of the valley, where the great hunt was still going on.

For two days we lay buried in the hay up in the outside loft of the Aabel farm; Anders kept us informed of the latest developments in the neighbourhood and supplied with food. Our clothes were in a very sorry state after the chase, so when we decided to make a trip into town we had to borrow clothes from Anders.

But how should we get to the town, with the road patrolled and all the guards and the rest of the police who were concerned in the affair driving up and down at all hours of the day?

Spaced at half-hour intervals we sauntered down the road from Aabel to Drangsholdt, about twenty minutes' walk. Rolf started earliest that morning, for it was intended that he should take another bus down at Boen, which went into town by a different route.

Hjelm was to go last, as he was to take the same bus as myself, but from a stopping-place farther down. There certainly was a good deal of police-car traffic on the roads as we went each to his own place in the early morning hours. But who could suppose that the persons for whom hundreds had now been searching for three days and nights would be following the same road which the police used most—especially when the last track led northwards through Trolldalen and the men had probably tried to get to the Sörland train somewhere in the neighbourhood of Oggevann? It was there that the patrols were concentrated in greatest strength.

While I sat on the steps of the shop down at Drangsholdt waiting for the bus, and one police car after another passed, a solitary workman came down the road. It was Hjelm. An uninitiated person could not have seen that he was in any way different from all the other workmen who had to go out at that time in the morning. Hjelm passed the place where I sat without moving a muscle, and went down to the next bus stop.

It was almost comical when we were sitting in the same bus—Hjelm and two senior German officers, who had got in at Boen, and another workman, identical with Rolf. Something unforeseen had occurred, but what it was that had prevented him from taking the other bus we did not find out till later.

Rolf got off at Justnes, seven miles outside Kristiansand; Hjelm got off at Eidet, four and a half miles outside, and I went right on in. At the beginning of Kongsgaard Allé, just before the entrance to the town, there was a control, but it was fairly superficial. Everything went astonishingly well, and we all met the same evening at our contact's house in Oesterveien.

The great question now was, how to get away from Kristiansand. Would the railway be watched? Would the Kristiansand–Oslo boat be watched? Most probably all communications from Kristiansand would be controlled for the time being; but the question was to what extent. Telephone communication between Arendal, Grimstad, Lillesand, Kristiansand and Mandal was stopped.

It was decided that evening to send Rolf east by train to Oslo next morning, as he was very well known to people in the countryside and to those who had already been arrested. Despite the risk of a police visit to the house at any hour of the twenty-four, the family offered to keep us for the night.

Arne's father, a guard on the line from Kristiansand to Oslo, was now, as usual, willing to take Rolf with him on the train in his 'special way.' He was one of the many people in the service of the Norwegian State Railways who did indescribably brilliant work in the war. He was over sixty-five, but as vigorous as a young man and always willing to take over a share of the duties which during those years were specially imposed on the youth of Norway. As usual Rolf's journey went well, despite snoopers and police at a number of stations.

During the week we started contact from Oevrebö, and communicated the unfortunate result of the parachute drop. At the same time we sent off important reports and information in reply to a series of questions we had received from London immediately before the drop. These questions related to the net defences of the port of Kristiansand:

Were the nets anti-torpedo, anti-submarine, or anti-surface vessel?

What sort of buoys were used to keep the net up?

What was the distance between the buoys?

Length of net in the different sections and position of moorings?

How were the nets moored and what kind of yielding system was used?

What influence had ice or other objects had on the net?

How thick was the wire between the buoys, and how many strands were used?

Depth of the net? Size of meshes? Thickness and number of strands in the mesh wire? Anchored to the bottom and if so by what means?

Was the net connected with acoustic or magnetic mines outside it?

The reader will most certainly understand why the station staff scratched their heads reflectively on receiving this string of questions. At first the whole thing seemed hopeless, but in a little while a number of lucky circumstances made it possible to answer them all. By using the three main contacts, who in turn used every source they had, we got the answers one after another.

The amusing part of the whole business was the way in which it became possible to obtain the answers. A Swedish ship which was to enter Kristiansand for examination 'unluckily missed the opening in the net when entering after dark.' At a good pace she went straight into the net and took a whole section of it with her in to the quayside. It had to be sent to the naval yard at Marvika for repairs—and at Marvika there were two men, one of whom was a contact of Arne and the other of Johan, the customs official. The last-named in particular did an excellent job, as he himself was working on the repairs. Our contacts in combination did all the work, and we had only to put together the results.

Months later I found out what lay behind the questions. The *Tirpitz* was the objective. Certainly this ship had at that time no connection with the port of Kristiansand; but information collected from various sources indicated that nets of the kind used at Kristiansand and Stavanger were also in use at Altafjord to protect the *Tirpitz*. The difference here was only that the nets were double and in places were connected with mines. In the Altafjord it was practically impossible to get any detailed information about the nets, and the only chance was to get this from Kristiansand and Stavanger.

CHAPTER XV

WE MOVE THE 'SHOP'

THE situation in Kristiansand was quite untenable. People were for the most part very nervous, and rumours flew round as never before. One day I was sitting in a barber's chair in Dronningensgate getting my hair cut, as a slight alteration in hair-style seemed necessary. Two Norwegian civilians and three Germans sat waiting for their turn.

'That was a hell of a business up in Tveit!' I led off in a low voice to the barber. I was interested to hear the general opinion of what had happened, and that one generally hears very well in a barber's chair. Without apparently giving the Germans a thought, the barber continued:

'Birkenes, you mean, don't you? Yes, that was a hell of a business—eleven parachutists were dropped—there was a big fight—a lot of Germans were killed—and according to what I heard, only one of the parachutists. The others got away—to somewhere in the north—in any case they were reported to have been seen by Ogge Lake. A double guard has been posted at Fiskaa factory—the Germans are afraid of an attempt on it.'

And he went on: 'There were three students all the summer up in the country where the parachutists were dropped, and it was they who organized the action by the home forces. At least two of them were shot, too, in the fighting up there.'

There was no need for me to ask questions; it ran out as from an open tap. The barber's hand shook just a little when I exclaimed angrily: 'The whole lot ought to have been hanged!' The barber evidently thought I meant the three 'students' and the eleven parachutists.

We felt it was hopeless, in the prevailing conditions, to try to go on running a station at Kristiansand or in its neighbourhood. We had indeed our contact in the police, who passed on daily all reports connected with the search.

But even if 'three suspicious persons' had been observed in the street at Grimstad at a quarter past two one morning, and the same at Arendal, which had caused the Germans to close those towns and comb them as well as they could, we had no guarantee that they were not hunting the same persons in Kristiansand. The last report we got ran: 'A man about six feet tall, in a light coat, with fair hair, believed to be identical with Karl Johansen, alias Oeyvind Fredriksen, for whom search is being made, seen on the boat to Bergen. Bergen warned and inquiries set on foot.'

One thing had to be done before we both left Kristiansand for the time being. All the stuff which lay hidden on the ledge up on Svaland moor (the most important part of the consignment), was necessary if we were to continue working in Oslo. It *must* be fetched. Of course there was a very good chance that the Germans had found it all; but there was also a chance that the spot had been too well hidden and that, after finding all the food, tobacco and clothes, they had taken this for the full cargo.

But this part of the work I insisted on doing alone. As 'chief' I could not help blaming myself for the result of the parachute drop and for the twelve people from the district having been arrested. There was no doubt that the actual drop could have been better prepared, that 'pin-point' was too near a farm where Nazis lived. Of course I could hardly have known that the 'chairman,' or whatever he was up in his district, was going to a party just that night and would come home to his farm just as the plane came sweeping in over the tree-tops and the parachutes fell in a shower, clearly silhouetted against the sky. Nor that the 'parcel' of 135 lbs. of white flour, which was to be dropped immediately after the containers, had stuck in the hole and the pilot had made several attempts to get rid of it before he disappeared after making an unnecessary amount of noise. But, in spite of the coincidence of many unfortunate circumstances, I was undoubtedly in part to blame.

Hjelm had to go to Oslo, and this time we had to risk the journey by boat, as the situation on the railway had become considerably worse. Hjelm went on August 25 and had one or two scares *en route*. Tired and worn after the last weeks, he lay down to sleep in his cabin, only to be woken a few hours later, when the boat called at Grimstad, by a rude German with an electric torch in his hand. 'Papers, please!' —it was the first time this had been done on board the coasting steamer at Grimstad, and the reason could hardly be disputed. Hjelm pulled out his frontier-dweller's pass: 'Harald Jorgensen, born April 26, 1917, at Oslo, resident temporarily at 7 Odinsgate, Kristiansand: profession, seaman.' Where was he going? Hjelm produced a letter dated a week before from the Oslo labour exchange telling him of a job on a German steamer which was to sail from Oslo in a few days or so. Hjelm was allowed to pass—calm, as he always was, and with his papers in order—and the German police proceeded to the next man. In Oslo there was a drastic control by the Norwegian State police, but as Hjelm had only a small suitcase and a rucksack containing nothing dangerous, this also went well; the police did indeed try to ring up the labour exchange for confirmation, but got no answer. Several other people, however, were to have the pleasure of going up to 19 Möllergate for a 'more detailed interview.'

Next day a fearfully tousled fellow was cycling northward along the Sörland road towards Birkenes. Clad like a beggar, bearded, crooked-backed and bow-legged like an old man of the woods, I was off to pick cranberries on Svaland moor.

There was still a fairly dense traffic of men in uniform along the road, and it was not pleasant having to pass these cars, especially at the beginning when it was still light. But it grew dark before I reached the worst stretch—through Tveit and up to the Aabel shop. Of course, as usually happens on such big occasions, I met people who had formerly had contact with the 'students.' But it is remarkable what a little disguise can do. They were interested now too, as they always were when a stranger travelled through the district, but all went well.

The Aabel family were a bit scared, but the door stood open as it was wont to do. Certainly there had been exciting times up there since we last met. And I was now able to get more details of what had happened. Among other things, Anders and Sören had walked up to Birkenes once or twice and talked to Nils Daland, the schoolmaster, who had now evidently recovered from his most serious illness.

From what I was told it appeared that the Germans had begun to surround the farms about the same time that they took us 'in our beds.' Daland had tried to keep his promise to send up a warning to us by his son. Aamund had set off along the moor as fast as he could; but close to the moss where the drop had taken place the Germans had begun to fire at random, and it was all he could do to save his own skin. He assumed that we were already caught and had a narrow escape from being arrested himself on his return to the farm.

Of the twelve who were arrested only two really knew anything, Jörgen Birkenes and Sigurd Rogsland. And even what they knew of the kind of work we were really carrying on could hardly make the situation much worse. But—as we were to find out later—these men, and most of the others who were interrogated, had played their parts excellently.

A thing it was unpleasant to learn just then was that the Germans were still patrolling the Svaland moor district at regular intervals. How it would be possible to reach the ledge, where it might be hoped that the stuff still lay, the next day would show.

Before it grew light again I was on my way up to Steane by Bjor Lake, along the same road we had come down on that unforgettable night. It was half-past three. I did not see a soul till, at about half-past five, I reached the farm where the path to Trolldalen branched off. The people at Steane were up, and two faces, like living marks of interrogation, appeared against the window; the woman of the house came out on the steps, followed by a child.

It is thought bad form to go past a house without having a chat at many places out in the country, and especially at a remote farm like this—and at half-past five in the morning. 'Are there many berries up in these parts?' It was undoubtedly a rather silly question, and it must have sounded even worse when put in a bad mixture of east and south Norwegian! But I had to think of something. The woman's reply was in keeping, and I found that there was little sense in continuing the conversation.

It was with a queer feeling that I went on up the valley, and passed the spot where the last German had been in contact with us, before starting to climb to the top of the ridge in the direction of Gullringstjern. There really were a lot of berries, and they tasted very good so early in the morning. But if I met a patrol now—would it not be rather unusual to be picking berries at six in the morning?

As a measure of precaution I lay for an hour and a half on a small ledge in the rock wall, dozed a little and took things easily. Not a sound. At eight o'clock I began to pick hard, and it was not just for amusement. I needed berries in my pail to cover later on what I might be bringing down with me again. I picked and picked, moving steadily northward, slowly but surely, with eyes and ears every moment directed elsewhere than just on the ground.

Yes, there had certainly been people about! Along every sunken track over mosses and fells there were marks which suggested the autumn migration of a great herd of reindeer. When I had reached the moss west of Gullringstjern the sound of voices made me start. I cannot say I felt inclined to wait, but I moved behind some big rocks and remained sitting there for a few minutes. I still heard the voices, but they did not come closer. Were there still Germans, then, down by the hut? Was a patrol in occupation of our old retreat?

I went on picking cautiously in a curve northward, over one or two low ridges and on towards the valley on the same side where the first German had stood and fired at us.

Yard by yard I went on: as many leaves and scraps of rubbish as berries went into my pail—this was the crucial moment. Were one or more of the green-clad soldiers sitting on guard round about? I had a nasty feeling that one or more rifle barrels were following me; I had had the same feeling ever since I came up from Trolldalen. But of course it might be imagination—most probably, perhaps, it was: my nerves were not quite in order that morning, up in the same country where we three had run for our lives hour after hour only a week before.

Half an hour passed. Still there was not a sound. Three-quarters of an hour—there—someone was coming up the valley. I pulled myself together and took out my revolver. There were several of them. Quite right—a patrol in the mountain troops' uniform—seven men came up the valley and passed the spot where I lay about thirty yards away.

To judge from the sounds they went on up the valley; it was quiet again. The great question now was: were they following a regular route at regular times, or was the whole thing a matter of chance? Another half-hour passed—three-quarters—a whole hour. Then came voices, and the noise of several men walking. This time they came from above. The same patrol, at the same pace.

The same interval passed. I had now been sitting, at times lying, in the heather behind a large fir for nearly three hours when the patrol came up the valley. This time there were only six men. They passed, and to judge from the sound of their voices they were discussing something. They certainly were not taking their task very seriously; most probably they had been at it for the whole week and were tired of searching for the birds which had flown.

As soon as the voices had died away for the third time, I went on picking berries. Down into the valley, where now a regular 'road' ran, to the other side, up a little gully, past the hill behind the ledge and on towards the moss itself.

I did not go quickly. There were many berries—and still more leaves. I did not get right to the moss; I was only interested in knowing what the chances were of anyone taking me in the rear while I was engaged on my job. Right over by Rogsland's hut there were obviously people—Germans. But someone there was sitting and playing on a mouth-organ, so I was warned in time.

Back to the rock wall and cautiously down to the spot where we had been surprised. I almost laughed aloud: there, in the same place and in exactly the same position in which we had abandoned them, lay the sleeping-bags! I carefully pushed my hand into my own and drew out the slab of chocolate I remembered having hidden there at the moment of discovery. A trifle gnawed by mice, but otherwise good.

But this was curious: either our first pursuers had not troubled to search where we had been lying, or they had simply not found the exact place, or they had weak heads and did not dare look far enough over the edge. For one moment I had the nasty feeling that at that moment ten or twenty men might be sitting amusing themselves over my triumph, taken a little too much for granted!

But there was not a sound to be heard. I shinned down carefully. There were two tins which had been inside the containers, three soaking wet camouflaged parachutes, and the cave with the things in just as we had left them last time. It was almost too fantastic to be true. For a week the Germans had been searching, had combed the ground right from the moss and had made roads down in the valley where they had passed, while here, in the midst of several hundred men, all this splendid stuff lay undisturbed. One slab of chocolate went straight down; another disappeared into my trousers pocket. Suddenly I thought of the time; ten minutes more, and the patrol would come down again. To be on the safe side I lay quite still. Ten minutes passed—twenty. Not a sound. What should I do?

They came down a quarter of an hour later than I had calculated. But of course the devils must set my nerves more on edge than they were already; they stopped almost below the ledge; one man drank from the beck, while the others sat down on the rocks and had a smoke. Twenty yards away —I was afraid they would hear my heart thumping against my ribs. Were they simply play-acting? Was I in a trap? Did the men sitting down there know quite well that they had the fish in the net—and were just waiting for a few more to haul it safely in?

Then one of them got up, and the others followed immediately. They went on down the valley. I did not waste any time. Code-books and crystals, a wireless set and a vibrator, as well as the twelve slabs of chocolate and a few boxes of cigarettes we had stowed away for safety's sake, were stuffed into a rucksack, and some down into the pail, after the berries had been emptied out. A piece of paper on them, and the berries on top again. Down into the valley again and up on the other side. Again I made off southwards, this time rather faster than earlier in the day. Everything was quiet again, and not a human being was to be seen on the way to the steep drop into Trolldalen. Here I lay down; the last part of the way back could not be covered before dark.

CHAPTER XVI

A MISCALCULATION

As usual I did not get away from Aabel till I had had a meal. Again they ignored the strong possibility of their being shot if I were found on the farm. It was nearly two in the morning when I reached the hut up in Oevrebö with my valuable load. All went well.

I was to make two more journeys up to Svaland moor without any disturbance worth speaking of. Three journeys in all with loads of nearly 80 lbs. to take back to Oevrebö. Up one evening, on to the moor next morning by different routes, and back the same evening and night. The only difference from the first journey was that I did not look in at Steane or engage in any unnecessary talk, and that the last time I did not see a sign of a patrol, although I waited for three hours on the edge of the valley.

It was the fourth and last time which nearly finished me. It was about three in the morning; I had found that, time being short, I could just as well cycle from Oevrebö about eleven at night, so that I need not put up at Aabel, but could go right in early in the morning. This proved to be a bad miscalculation on my part.

Past Aalefjaer and on up to Far Lake it was pitch dark. A car came at a good speed up the same road as myself, slowed down a little, passed and went on. I had nothing on my back, only a little food in a haversack. I glanced automatically at the number-plate as the car passed; but owing to mud and a bad light it was impossible to see the 'nationality.' I went on cycling, and took no particular notice of the car. About five minutes later a car came down the road. It was curiously like the first—and the number-plate?—POL 159!

My brain worked at high pressure for a moment; the heavenly peace of night-time in the valley had disappeared at one blow. Get off the road at once? No, there would hardly be much sense in that if the car should come for a further look at the man who was out cycling at a quarter past three in the morning. If I had got off the road in the meantime, the police car would have given the alarm, and under no circumstances should I have been able to take that road back to the town after having been up on Svaland moor for the last load. If, on the other hand, the car passed again without doing anything, it would at any rate look as if I had the best conscience in the world. So—I must take the risk of continuing and just hope that the car would not come back at all.

Seven or eight minutes had gone. I still maintained my speed, had perhaps increased it slightly after reaching Far Lake from Aalefjaer and thus getting free of the steady uphill grind for a little while. My heart inevitably began to beat a little faster when the beam of a headlamp shone through the night from a car going in the same direction as myself. Was it the same—the police car?

For a few minutes I thought it was another car and breathed a little more freely. I had just reached the place where a small creek of Far Lake shoots out to the northward and the road goes over a bridge; it was another hundred yards or so to the bridge itself.

The car came close up and slowed down: I swung over to the side of the road to let it pass, but it would not pass—only followed me at my own speed about ten yards behind. What was I to do? For the moment my only thought was that I formed an excellent target and that an attempt to resist would hardly turn out well! The only thing I saw ahead was the bridge—still about twenty yards ahead. Then the car accelerated, dashed past, and swung round on the farther side of the bridge at the moment I reached it.

I cannot say exactly what happened, nor which of us shot first. I only know that I jumped off my bicycle, snatched my revolver from my shoulder-holster and let fly at the first man to get out of the car. A man in Norwegian State police uniform fell flat, pressing his hand to his right side as he did so. Another man, I think in German uniform, was close on the heels of the first, while a third was setting up a searchlight on the roof of the car. The second man stumbled over the bicycle and fell, his revolver nearly hitting me in the face. I fired two more shots before jumping over the railings into the water under the bridge; it was quite shallow water and I floundered for a few seconds before it was deep enough to get under; everything was pitch black; someone was firing a tommy-gun; under water it was gloriously quiet and refreshing.

My lungs were almost bursting when I cautiously raised my head above water to inhale and at the same time get a glimpse of the searchlight on the car, which was sweeping round in the immediate neighbourhood of the bridge. Then I swam under water away from the light, this time with rather slower strokes so as not to be completely exhausted. Up again, and this time it seemed that the greatest danger was past. A few minutes later I came to land in the little creek and lay panting at the water's edge for a few seconds. There were two possibilities: I could try to make my way northward through the woods to Boen, cross the bridge there and go south towards Kristiansand on the other side. Otherwise, I could try to reach Vennesla and thence go on up to Oevrebö. The latter alternative was undoubtedly the best, though it was pitch dark and it was hard to make one's way through the woods.

I was not, however, to do either. Someone had thrown away a milk-pail or paraffin can, and in the dark I did not see it. With a crash I tumbled on my head, while the milk-pail or whatever it was rolled down the slope and fell into the water with a splash. And I was supposed to be walking quietly—damned fool that I was!

Over by the car two men were still searching in the beam of the searchlight, evidently thinking I had been hit and drowned. They could not help hearing the rattling of the can. With torches on they rushed along the path beside the little creek. I heaved myself round and rushed up through the wood; I could not see a yard in front of me and at last went head over heels over a big stone. I swore and came near shouting aloud, for I had twisted my foot. I lay where I was behind the stone: things must take their course. I grabbed feverishly for more ammunition and stuffed the magazine full.

There they came, no longer running, but walking fast. Now and again they ran for a few yards and then slackened speed again, turning their lights round about and down towards the water. They passed a few yards from me and went on up the path. I was in a hole. I had only one chance; it was indeed a very good idea, if I could only put into effect the inspiration I had had in the passing of a few seconds.

I stole cautiously back along the path. I no longer felt the foot which I had twisted. On to the road—up on to the bridge—over the man who lay there moaning, probably almost unconscious. Then, up with the bonnet of the car and out with the distributor-head. No more motoring in the next few hours! And then—my bicycle was all right—off at full speed down the same road we had come up by, along the road across the moor to Vennesla, down to Mosby and up the steep ascent to Oevrebö.

The fellow who crawled into bed a few hours later up in the hut in Oevrebö was not worth many rows of beans. There must be an end to these risks. This was in any case the last occasion for a long time that I should enter that district, whether the work in hand was important or unimportant.

But we still had a load of stuff which must be brought down, among other things two Sten guns for which we had good use now that we meant to continue our work in Oslo. The whole thing was arranged in a most ingenious manner by Arne and some of his friends.

Berry-picking trips were very common in those days, and when a Christian youth association went out with baskets and pails nobody could suspect that it had any connection with 'illegal work,' even if the district chosen was called Svaland moor!

All the equipment was packed now; some was left in charge of Gunnar, one of the men who owned the hut and who had also already done a great deal for us. Gunnar also undertook to send off everything which was to go on to Oslo and which was necessary for the running of the wireless station there.

Once more our friend the guard was to have an extra passenger to Oslo from Kristiansand, after everything had been arranged. This journey too went pretty smoothly. Before I left Kristiansand I received the last report from the 'Archives,' where the Norwegian lackeys of the Gestapo, Pedersen and Vehus, presided at the interrogations. The inquiry had taken a very favourable turn, thanks to the splendid behaviour of those who really knew the details of our work. Seven of the persons arrested were liberated after a time, as the Gestapo had no case against them. The other five, without there being incriminating proof against them, and more as a reprisal than anything, were sent first to Grini and then to Germany.

But it was quite clear that Rolf, Hjelm and I had these five to thank that things had gone as they had, and that it was possible for us to continue our work. Well done, Jörgen Birkenes, Erling Hauge and Sigurd Rogsland, Bernhard and Einar, and thanks on behalf of the cause for which we all had to make sacrifices.

CHAPTER XVII

WE START A STATION AT OSLO

In Oslo all the organizing work had been completed. The twins Carl Sigurd and Ottomar had been working all the time with Jan and Wencke and several others. On regular days in the week, the 'post' had gone from Oslo in the most varied ways to the three main contacts in Kristiansand, to be forwarded to the station. I say 'post' because most of the code messages were really sent in an 'almost' ordinary way as open post, so open that it was not even amusing! But not one of the many hundreds of messages was lost on the way; not one was sent to the wrong address.

Contact from Oslo was opened from a villa up at Röa, to be more precise the boys' room at 'Uncle Hans'' house, with the gutter as aerial. This was excellent for occasional use, but the house unfortunately had a number of major or minor Nazis as neighbours, and as it might be assumed that these had been allowed to keep their short-wave wireless sets, it was scarcely a tenable position. The tapping from the transmitter would undoubtedly interfere with the Nazis' sets.

We had to make a further search for a suitable headquarters somewhere outside Oslo, far enough out for us to be able to count on running the station more or less undisturbed through the coming months. We first had a try above the big German camp at Woxen; but unfortunately we discovered that we had tapped one of the main lines which supplied the camp with current, with the result that this, experimentally, was cut off in the middle of our contact, turned on again and again cut off. The tapping had evidently again been heard, despite double filtration between the key and the apparatus. For reasons I need not explain, we packed our things and vanished at top speed.

A hut up in Lommedalen finally satisfied our requirements as a 'stationary station.' The hut was lent us by a landowner named Lövenskiold, of Vekkerö, with whom we had been in contact earlier. The 'Holmevass cabin' was a place with every possible advantage and, at any rate to begin with, very few disadvantages.

We obtained the necessary co-operation through the forest official whose district it was and some of his staff. To protect the landowner and his servants, this time a number of formal letters and documents were drawn up. There was a letter from the Land and Forestry Department to the landowner with an 'order' to get two 'forestry pupils' somewhere to live in the district north of Guriby saw-mills. The intention was that the two forestry pupils 'should study tree diseases and take samples of earth for analysis from different places in the neighbourhood.' Of course the forestry students were members of the National Union (*Nasjonal Samling*).

In case anything should happen the papers were deposited ready for use, provided with all the necessary stamps and in the formal language of the Department.

Three-quarters of a mile from the Holmevass cabin lay Lövenskiold's private electricity works, which supplied parts of Lommedalen with power, an alternating current of 220 volts. In a line with the electricity works lay a little hut which was generally used by the watchman; but as he now lived in Lommedalen and preferred to come up by motor-cycle every day for the necessary inspection, the key of the hut was handed over to us. Electric light having been put in, this was the place which was used for regular contact in the first week.

But one day during our contact we were to have a visitor—an ordinary Sunday tripper out walking, who was interested in electro-technical matters. Luckily he was observed in time, and he, thinking we were the watchmen at the works, embarked on a very advanced electro-technical discussion. Whether he was much edified by our more or less intelligent remarks about the functioning of the works, I cannot say; but at any rate it was clear that a repetition of the experience might have unfortunate results.

Above the Holmevass cabin, on the other side of a small valley, lay a fairly high ridge with a pretty steep drop down to the valley in a south-westerly direction. Into this hill-side ran a gully which in the course of time had become filled up with rubble. This was the place, and in a week an 'underground' station had been excavated. The roof of the station ran level with the ledge in the face of the rock, and was covered with exactly the same kinds of moss and heather. A few small firs were planted on top of it all.

While this work was being done contact was maintained direct from the Holmevass cabin. But here too we were to have visitors repeatedly. The road up from Guriby to the summer farm on Mosberg moss and to Mattisplassen up in Krok Wood went right past, and there were people everywhere on a Sunday. We were now working solely on batteries, and these were charged down in the hut. They could stand there buzzing only at night, and early in the morning, or late at night, they were carried up and down by bicycle to and from the station.

Regular messenger communication with Oslo was maintained by Jan and the twins, and the bookseller's shop served as a central office, with a number of 'post boxes' in different places.

It was not very long before we got into difficulties. Conditions in Oslo began to be more 'disturbed' than usual; German traffic increased on the roads leading up from the town, and there were more controls; it was different, too, from down in Sörland, where one could more or less tell in advance where the controls would be. Mobile controls were what we feared most, and especially when one of us coming from the town had with him things that were not quite 'regulation.'

In the very first weeks we were obliged to send Rolf over into Sweden, partly because we needed a messenger just then, and partly because Rolf had done an excellent job and we did not want to run the risk of his being arrested in the last lap before the winter months. Rolf knew a great many people in the country round Oslo, and it was practically impossible for him to move about without meeting acquaintances. He had done his job whole-heartedly, and without his help from the very start the results the station had on its credit side would never have been secured.

As usual, the meteorological reports went at a regular time every morning and on special occasions both morning and evening; if 'big' events were to happen, in other words bombing in Europe on a large scale, weather reports were sent every other hour. This sending had now so got into our blood that the whole thing was done as a matter of routine. We often wondered, indeed, if the Germans did not sit every morning listening at the regular time and on the regular frequency we had now been using for a good six months. But the actual transmission was done in a few minutes, so that whatever they did they would not be much the wiser for it. But the other contacts now lasted over an hour or an hour and a half, as many as three or four times a day, and often more stuff had to be sent than was 'healthy' for the continued existence of the station.

The work itself could now be conducted on a far larger scale than down at Kristiansand. Oslo was a big place and things that happened in it were not nearly so obvious. Also people up in Lommedalen, as in other places round the city, were accustomed to seeing strangers at all times, so that if there were ten people living on one farm, that did not mean ten people getting a crick in the neck to see the passing stranger: 'Who can that be?—I don't like the look of him!' Nor did people down the valley know what those up at the other end were going to have for dinner before they knew it themselves.

This circumstance made the whole thing much easier. But it was sometimes rather awkward for Hjelm and me to go about the town in daylight. Certainly Oslo is a good-sized place; but it is queer how one tends to meet the people one would soonest avoid in the most undesirable places. Such a meeting could be very awkward if it took place where there were usually a lot of Germans and other undesirables, or in a crowded tram or train.

I did not visit my family for a good two months after I had tumbled into Norway; but later it proved to be necessary. In the meantime, before this emotional meeting took place, I was down at Majorstua one day waiting for the tram to Ris. While I stood waiting a number of acquaintances passed, and every time I had to hide behind a newspaper—wearing spectacles, I should say, and clothes rather different from what I used to have. Then a lady came along the platform, turned and placed herself beside me, leaning against the posts alongside the queue. I suddenly got busy blowing my nose and dropped my paper; at the same moment a tram came along which, by the way, was not going to Ris, but I jumped on to it. It was my youngest sister but one, whom I had not seen for more than three years. On the other side of me were three Germans, and a recognition on the platform could easily have been fatal.

My sister looked rather grim, and I heard the same day that the Germans had put mother and the rest of the family on to the street, as they were going to use the villa for a collection of 'office ladies and companions.'

While we were running the station in Lommedalen I made many journeys up to Ris by tram, and one day when the tram was crowded with people, including a fairly large percentage of German officers and other ranks, I could only find standing room in the rear car. I was reading a paper as usual, and preferably with my head turned the same way as most of the others. Then I suddenly had a feeling that someone was standing and staring at me—and I was right; in the front car stood a man of about my own age, staring his eyes out. He was a good old acquaintance of mine, with whom I had not had any contact whatever since I left Norway and who knew quite well that I was an airman and had 'cleared out' in 1940.

Now he was very slowly turning pale as he stood open-mouthed and staring. His thoughts were plainly written in his face. How long would he keep his mouth open without saying anything? I cautiously made my way forward to the other car.

'Hallo, it's you, is it? Well, how are you?'

I tried to speak in an everyday tone; but he, poor fellow, certainly thought he was seeing things. No reply—only an incomprehensible muttering. This could be dangerous—very dangerous for me.

'I suppose you're getting off at the next stop? We can get off together!' I continued in a rather dictatorial tone.

He only nodded, and in order not to attract more attention than we had done already, I went on chattering about one thing and another, about people who were mutual acquaintances of ours and who I knew were still at home. A stop at last. I simply shoved the fellow in front of me and out into the fresh air. The tram went on.

'But in Christ's name—have you gone crackers?'

It was a good thing these words, which I had feared, had not come earlier. We shook hands, and I gave him a short misleading explanation which had but little relation to the truth. Then followed my usual proviso: if anything should happen now to me or my family, we should know who it was who had been unable to hold his tongue. In that case he would simply be named as our nearest contact and would undoubtedly accompany us into eternity. . . . This usually proved effective.

We now had contacts in Oslo in several important organizations. One of the twins, Carl Sigurd, was employed in the Shipping Directorate and could give all reports of the whereabouts, sailings and arrivals of most of the vessels in which we were interested. We wanted the following information about ships: cargo, name, tonnage, where from, whither bound and approximately how many in the convoy. Under the existing system, with a messenger service between the town and the station usually taking about an hour, the advance reports of every single ship were a great advantage. If the advance reports came late, they went by telephone in a special code from boxes at different places in the town up to one of our contacts in the farms round Guriby.

Shipping reports from Oslo, however, now took a secondary place; more important things were happening. Hjelm had come into contact, through acquaintances, with the secretary to Riisnaes, 'Minister of Justice,' and thereby had been given quite free access to important political documents and 'juridical' developments in Norway, as well as the most secret agreements between 'the temporary custodians of law and order in the Great German Reich in process of development'! There were letters and orders from Quisling; there were replies, many pages long, with proposals for new and stricter ordinances to be imposed on the civil population of Norway; there were proposals for changes in the military disciplinary code—and there were plans for the future.

A great deal of this had to be sent out via Sweden by messenger, because it was simply too much to send out through one station; and in these cases the documents were microphotographed, one sheet being reduced to the size of a stamp, and sent out in the most incredible ways.

We had contacts with German drawing and engineering

offices which were improving the country's defences, and planning how the different central establishments should be located underground in 'most secret places' in the event of intensified attack from the air; there were plans for invasion which seemed never to have an end—or to be put into practice. There were contacts in mechanical workshops, which gave us access to secrets of German naval construction; there were drawings which were 'lent' for a day or two, so that we could get them microphotographed and sent over.

8 Nils Juelsgate, where the twins had their flat, became more or less the main base and central point of our activity at this time. The advantage was that their flat was in the town, and that it was in a big block of flats, where all kinds of people went in and out, from normal people to Nazis and Germans, and where loads of equipment and provisions for the various contacts did not attract much attention when a lorry stopped outside to be loaded or unloaded.

It was comparatively peaceful in Oslo at that time, apart from the usual raids in different districts. Of necessity both Hjelm and I had constantly to run into town, and not infrequently we came up against some kind of control on the way. But as a rule, if one's passport or papers were in order and one was not carrying too much in the way of parcels, this went off all right.

But as time passed, more transmitters began to work in Oslo for the different organizations. The Germans were quite aware of this, and sets were continually being seized. In October the Germans started a big sweep to stamp out this activity; things began to be quite lively also in the neighbourhood of Guriby and right into the area north-east of where we were. Reports came regularly that 'snoopers' had been seen in various places round about in Nordmarka, and one day during contact the two best known of these gentry passed the hut. Luckily we had then not a thing indoors; everything connected with our work was hidden round about in watertight containers.

Camouflaging the tent—First stage: The framework.

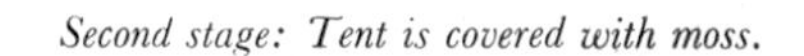

Second stage: Tent is covered with moss.

Third stage: Heather and trees are planted.

Fourth stage: Camouflaged tent complete.

CHAPTER XVIII

THE NET IS DRAWN CLOSER

None the less that day was the beginning of the end. As usual we were cycling past Grini on our way from town via Stenshögda to Lommedalen. For the third time I was stopped at the control point where the Grini area ran right down to the road. Three of the guards were leaning against the fence when I came. One of them shouted 'Halt!' as usual. I had a sack on the luggage carrier behind me with various unhealthy things in it, and was naturally not keen on a closer examination. Either the way I replied to questions, or my appearance, irritated the German; I cannot say. But at any rate he suddenly became interested in my sack; I therefore tried to distract his attention by smiling at the prisoners who were working on the land inside, ignoring his question as to what I had in the sack.

I have seldom seen a German lose his self-control so completely. He let out and caught me such a hard blow over the right ear that I saw stars for a moment. The devil! The two others smiled indulgently. Another stinging box on the ear, and another and another—I could not lift a finger in retaliation, for this would undoubtedly have caused three tommy-guns to go off. His face was simply ablaze with fury. 'I'll teach you to have some respect for us; there's to be no grinning at the prisoners here! Clear off!'

He had evidently forgotten his own question as to what was in the sack, so at any rate my object was attained. I was not slow to obey the order; a vibrator for a transmitter and a Sten gun would hardly make the three Germans more amiably disposed, and Grini so close!

Nor were things all that they should be up at the Holmevass cabin. Although it was now October and we had already had several falls of snow, there was nevertheless an increase of traffic in the woods round the station. Evidently other things were happening in those parts; other organizations had transferred their activities to our neighbourhood. D/F cars had repeatedly been seen at Guriby; the messengers up to the hut had continually been shadowed on the road by German and Norwegian cars.

Two days after the affair down the road past Grini, we received the alarming news that no less than three D/F cars had gone up the valley past the Baerum works. One remained standing by Guriby saw-mills, another a little farther down the road, and the third on the road leading through Krok Wood to Klevstua close to Middle Wood. When we opened contact we got a Junkers 52 as company in addition to these. It flew up and down the valley, over the station several times, circled round various farms on the edge of the woods, and we had long ago had to reduce volume and ask England to wait. The Junkers was about for over an hour, and there was no more transmission until later in the evening.

This happened again several times; very tiresome for us. At the same time more snow came; the D/F cars closed in on us.

It was about half-past eight on the morning of October 27. I had just sent the weather report and came sauntering down to the cabin and set about coding the day's telegrams.

A man came along the road below on a bicycle. I stopped as usual, and cautiously whispered a warning to Hjelm inside. It was Jan. When he was still a long way off it was clear that something serious had happened. It had been raining all the morning and Jan was soaking wet after his ride. He just flung himself down on the wooden bunk and began:

' "Uncle Hans" has been arrested—at four this morning—the twins have been warned and have taken cover.'

It was a bomb-shell; we just sat gaping. So that was how things were going. I should have been there at ten, at his house; but my trip had been postponed because of a supplement to the weather report. Jan knew this, and had leapt on to his bicycle the moment the news about 'Uncle Hans' came. It would have been fine if I had walked right into a big crowd of them. For the moment no one knew any details of what had happened, except the fact that he had been arrested. But the arrest had been made by Germans, which could mean several different things.

There was no time to be lost. It was not easy to say how long Hans would be able to keep silent as to where the station was. How much did the devils know? What had Hans actually been arrested for? . . . Hjelm and Jan immediately got to work packing up the station equipment, while I prepared to run into town. Every single thing was packed separately and placed in a watertight tin; these tins in turn were hidden in the woods round about in places long before prepared for this purpose. Within an hour everything had gone and all traces were removed; all that remained were the forestry pupils studying tree diseases and taking samples of soil.

Jan and I cycled down, keeping a good distance apart. We had to slow down round each bend, make a rapid survey of the next fifty yards, and continue, oppressed by doubt and anxiety. How many would there be this time? 'Uncle Hans'—one of the best contacts we had had during our work in 1943! It was heart-breaking!

Half-way between Guriby and Baerum works I started and made the prearranged signal to Jan, who was behind me. A D/F car was ascending slowly! For a moment I thought of turning, but it was clear that such a manœuvre would make the situation much more awkward than it was. We must just take our chance. When the driver caught sight of the bicycle and its rider, he stopped the car. 'Now you've had it once and for all,' I thought. I went on without changing speed—past the car where three men sat staring. Not a word, not a movement. It looked as if they were all interested in my reaction to their presence and nothing more.

Past—all well. Round the next bend I stopped and waited for Jan. He came. We went on—by Stenshögda, along the road past Grini. With rain falling it was unlikely that there would be a control at the usual spot, or guards either, as the prisoners would hardly be working at a place where the guards would have to stand and get wet. We approached Röa. When still some way off we caught sight of a man down at the bend before the bridge over the Lysaker river. It was Ottomar.

For nearly three hours he had been walking to and fro along the road between Röa and the river. Ottomar knew that I had an appointment with 'Uncle Hans' at his home. He had therefore come up to prevent me from walking straight into the trap.

We held a brief council of war. A number of our most important centres had been made unusable at one stroke. Hans knew 8 Nils Juelsgate. Jan's home at Ris had long ago been taken by the Germans. New places must be found. But, as we were to discover later, Hans held his tongue despite very rough treatment at 19 Victoria Terrace for months, and then in the worst prisoners' camp in Germany until the liberation. 'Uncle Hans' saved not only us and many others, but also the possibility of our continuing the work later.

About a week later Hjelm went to Sweden. He and his companions walked for many miles over the mountains in deep snow before they reached the frontier. On that day I myself made a trip to Kristiansand. There were still certain things not properly fixed up down there. We had not been able to obtain proof that the Germans had actually found *all* the hiding-places in which the food and clothes were. It would be extremely annoying if, say, 250 lbs. of chocolate or several thousand cigarettes were to lie rotting all the winter up on Svaland moor, when there was crying need of these things everywhere. Besides this, there was a lot of information I wanted to get; I was anxious, too, to fix up connections for a new man who might be sent to the district later, and a permanent connection to act as messenger-contact if this should come about.

I went north again by the road through Tveit to Birkenes and had a good meal with the Aabel family. Then a walk to Svaland moor in broad daylight, in long well-pressed trousers and wearing a hat. My frontier dweller's papers were this time made out for a 'commercial traveller' (in fox-skins). As I approached the edge of the moss where the stuff had been dropped, I nearly turned right about, and pretty sharply too. It was impossible to see anything; I only heard a rustling noise above me. Anxiously, and with the worst anticipations, I pushed my head just over the edge of a large rock. A cow elk and her calf were rooting calmly in the reindeer moss. Not a soul was to be seen, all was quiet—and everything had gone from the respective hiding-places; not even a scrap of cloth remained.

I went back to Aabel and on down into Kristiansand. Everything went according to plan, except that an 'old friend' up in Tveit recognized me in spite of my disguise. He was, however, one of the few who could hold their tongues on such occasions.

At Kristiansand all arrangements were made for the resumption of the work 'some time later on.' It was impossible to say then whether I should come back myself, or whether it would be a new man who was not so well acquainted with the police in those parts. And so back to Oslo.

A trip I made to Sweden went fairly well, even if the last lap was a bit hectic. We found that there was a new guard system along the frontier in the part where we were crossing. There were five of us; none of us knew very much about the others. As usual, everything was brilliantly organized as long as things went well, but on the morning of the second day, when we were getting near the actual frontier, some kind of obstacle was bound to crop up.

It was somewhere up in Austmarka: we had to go for some distance along a railway line. When we were about half-way along this stretch a queer buzzing noise from the rails became audible. 'Train,' someone suggested. 'No, it can't be,' the guide maintained. We did not want to leave the railway just at that spot: the line crossed a bridge there: there was plenty of water underneath, but a bath at five in the morning at the beginning of December, with nine degrees of frost, was a thing none of us was specially keen on!

We ran—but of course we did not get across before a German picket on a trolley had seen us. It was at fairly long range and not very dangerous, but it spoilt our otherwise pleasant moonlight walk. And more than that—it meant that we had to run during the last hours to the frontier.

It was only during this chase that we five really got to know one another.

I think we had all been in as tight places before; no one took the affair too seriously. We came to the lake where according to plan we were to find a boat with oars ready, unlocked, specially for this trip. But the boat was not there. The guide for the last lap cursed Norwegian refugees and everything connected with them. No doubt he did not mean it so very unkindly, but the fact was that his particular route carried only 'very important people,' as he put it. He himself had been at the lake the day before and had assured himself that everything was ready. Now—in the first place it looked as if we should have to walk nearly fourteen miles along the lakeside over the Swedish frontier and to the nearest inhabited house, when we could have had a pleasant row.

Then one of the others came forward. We had about five minutes' start of the Germans—five minutes in which to make up our minds. I cannot remember his fictitious name. But in the creek inside there lay two other boats—two boats fastened with chains and large padlocks round a big tree. The oars, too, were properly locked. According to the guide these boats were confiscated by the Germans and were sometimes used by them for patrol work.

The man from Stavanger was down by the first boat in a twinkling—and in less than a twinkling he had both locks unfastened, to the great astonishment of all present. Not till we were crossing the lake did I learn the secret: he was one of the most noted safe-breakers and burglars in Stavanger, and had spent the greater part of his life under lock and key! A very handy fellow to have with one under such circumstances. We could doubtless have unfastened the locks, but most probably it would have taken us a quarter or half an hour. It was high time now: when we were a hundred yards from land we heard the Germans cursing and swearing, using a varied store of the coarsest expressions in the language. They fired, but I doubt if they aimed.

Five hours later we were all sitting round a laid table in a Swedish farm. Such a reception and such food I had certainly never thought I should see.

It became a trifle awkward down in the magistrate's office, where one of the police officials was obviously a Nazi. He particularly wanted to know why we had left home, who had helped us and which way we had come. He got his answers all right, but whether they had much relation to the facts was another matter. I was, by the way, to meet this fellow later, so he was well worth remembering.

Kjeseter and Stockholm—the city where everything could be got for money, if only one had had a little more of it. I shall not go into details, but will only recount something that throws light on the much debated Swedish neutrality. The time I was then to spend in Stockholm as an ordinary Norwegian refugee under the name of Johansen, and also other visits to the same city under other names, I spent with a very good friend from pre-war days. His father was a judge of cases concerning Norwegian spies in British service and Norwegian messengers who had been arrested by Swedish soldiers or customs officials on the frontier. The father knew quite well who I really was, and had also a pretty good idea in what sort of work I was engaged, but he always received 'Herr Johansen' with the same cordiality. 'I hope we shall soon meet again,' he always said each time I was to set out on 'my travels,' 'but take care it isn't on the wrong side of the bar!'

CHAPTER XIX

A QUICK VISIT TO OSLO

I ONLY stayed a week in Sweden. I thought I had done with this wandering life for a time—indeed, for ever. I thought of going over to England—considered this, and more. There was someone waiting for me over in Canada, and to tell the truth, I had had some idea of getting married. But things were not to happen quite like that, at any rate not for the time being.

In short, I had to go back to Norway—to be more precise,

to Oslo. The reason was that the Germans were carrying out some special experiments at the Akers workshops in connection with a new mine-sweeper. We were interested not only in the craft itself, but also in the instruments. In addition to this I was to arrange for the sending of various articles of equipment to Mil. Org. and XU in Oslo for distribution. This included a quantity of explosives, arms and ammunition, in addition to wireless equipment and things which were sorely needed.

Christmas was drawing near, and as I had not a great deal to carry, I took with me a quantity of Christmas presents for the family. Silk stockings and underclothes, chocolate and marzipan were not just everyday things at home in those times.

The actual journey back to the frontier was quite simple. I was with a fellow from the district round Halden who had gone by that route himself countless times. From the last Swedish town we got a lift from some soldiers—to be more correct, the Swedish intelligence service, which co-operated as far as 'neutrality' allowed! Of course this was a profound secret at that time.

We approached the frontier in deep snow and came to quite a small farm on the Swedish side which was a 'station' on the route. Here I left everything which had to do with Sweden and Swedes, except a rucksack containing a lot of more or less dangerous things. I became 'Oscar Leonard Hansen, wood-cutter, resident at Idd, pr. Halden' (province of Halden).

Across the frontier in the middle of the night, starry and cold, the fir-branches weighed down by snow. There was little to suggest war—strange that that glade cut in the forest should signify the dividing line between two such utterly different worlds. For safety's sake we used the same path as the guards on each side; they did not use skis but had trodden a firm track. There was a guard hut on the Swedish side, and across the river, on the other side, was the Norwegian. There were people in the Swedish hut—customs officials, who were sitting playing cards when we passed. They did not hear a sound except at their regular patrol time every fourth hour.

The Norwegian customs men lived farther on, at a farm, and there was not a soul to be seen. About five we reached the first 'post' on the Norwegian side, lay up there till the evening and then went on towards Idd and Halden.

I had company only as far as Idd. At a farm there I made another complete change into town clothes, blue trousers and jacket, black tie, hat and an old light-coloured mackintosh—with a mourning band round my arm. It was Fru Hansen who had died; I had a letter from Oscar Leonard's sister with the melancholy intimation and a request to come into Oslo to attend the funeral, also a letter from the sheriff's office at Idd in reply to an application for a permit to travel, not only giving the permit, but condoling Oscar on his sad loss.

Yes, the papers were in order and were to stand me in good stead. A little way outside Halden, as I came cycling along with a suitcase containing my various belongings, four men sprang out of the ditch just after I had crossed a small bridge. 'Halt!' It was a German patrol. Papers? I produced the whole packet, and the senior of the four men took a quick look at them, while I tried in a melancholy voice to add a few supplementary remarks about my mother's death. Yes, the papers were in order, but—what had I got in the suitcase?

The three others stood with their tommy-guns, looking on. They did not seem to expect any great result. 'I had to start in such a hurry that I just snatched up a few clothes to have something to wear—but you can see for yourselves.' I leaned my bicycle up against the kerbstone, and slowly began to open the suitcase. Luckily it was dusk, nearly dark but yet not dark enough for the German to find it necessary to use a light. He lifted up with two fingers a dirty evil-smelling pair of drawers, which had not been washed for the last three months and which I had intentionally placed on the top of the suitcase with some other things of the kind. Then came a still more unsavoury pair of socks and another ragged pair of pants.

That was enough—the German let down the lid of the suitcase and shut it himself. 'It's sad to lose one's mother!' He saluted and let me proceed; he thus signified his deep sympathy with the Hansen family in the sorrow that had overtaken it.

There was, as I expected, a control on the train into Oslo. I sat in a compartment beside a Norwegian State policeman, and obviously neither the German nor the Norwegian police regarded all my false papers with the slightest suspicion. But this time too things could easily have gone wrong. There was not just one examination, but six on the way from Halden to Oslo. The system they used was one I had not encountered before; they took all those of the dangerous age in each compartment and asked about twenty different questions. The answers to each question were taken down on prepared forms. Half an hour later they came back to the same people, asked the same questions and compared the answers. The great thing was not to hesitate—and to give the same answer each time. A fellow in our compartment failed to answer a few of the questions the second time; he evidently had to reflect a little. When the German policeman flared up and began to be aggressive, the man grew rather angry and answered back. He ought not to have done that; the result was three resounding blows on the ear, and his removal, handcuffed, to a locked compartment farther back in the same carriage.

On our arrival at the East station two police buses stood ready at the end of the platform. One was filled, the other half-filled with young men who evidently had not answered questions correctly and were to undergo a 'closer examination.' I myself took the tram up to Skillebekk and let myself into the flat at 8 Nils Juelsgate, while one of the twins stood gaping at me like an animated question-mark: 'Shall we never be rid of you?'

This was a Thursday, and on the following Sunday a small cargo yacht under the Swedish flag was to lie to at the quay up in the Akers river to unload her very valuable cargo destined for Mil. Org. and XU.

On the very day on which I arrived I went, as ordered, to a certain place in the town where some posters had been affixed to a wall. I made a small pencil mark on a particular letter in a particular line from the top. Then I proceeded to the 'post-box,' which on this occasion had been put in a rather silly place—under the wooden bridge which crosses the Frogner stream between Madserud Allé and Halfdan Svartesgate just under the eyes of the new German wireless station! Of course there was a sentry up on the road, and it was a far from easy matter to jump over the railing, get under the bridge, and leave there a message naming the place where I would be glad to meet 'Herr X' for a conference about the unloading of the Swedish cargo yacht.

But it could be done if one man kept guard and could say each time the German turned his back or the coast was otherwise clear. . . . At half-past ten next morning I was walking up and down Thunesvei by the Ridehus, in the neighbourhood of Sköyen. I had a mourning band on my right arm, a distinguishing mark which, according to the message I had placed in the post-box, should cause 'Herr X' to address himself to me and at the same time use the agreed password.

But no 'Herr X' came. I walked up and down for about half an hour, and had the impression that people in the neighbourhood were beginning to be suspicious. At half-past two I was back in the same place. Not a soul seemed to be inclined to ask me for a match and receive the answer that 'unfortunately I did not smoke now that rationing had come in.'

Next day I was in Thunesvei again, only to obtain the same negative result. What had happened? Had the contact been arrested, and was there no one else to keep an eye on the place where the posters were? Had he not dared to look in the 'post-box' now that the Germans had mounted guard at the wireless station? I walked up under the bridge and had a look. The scrap of paper on which I had written still lay there.

We were in a fix. The boat was coming next day, and who was to unload her? Mil. Org. and XU were large organizations; who was to receive the things and how was one to get into touch with the right people? These were questions on which we had no time to meditate. Time was short.

The same evening we got hold of a lorry with a driver who was willing to undertake the dangerous task. This was 'Jonas,' a man who had done excellent jobs for us before and was up to his neck in illegal driving with the road authorities' lorry. On Sunday morning Ottomar was on board the yacht and had a talk with the skipper. I had the password, so that side of the business was all in order. We could come at five that (Sunday) afternoon. As a rule things were relatively quiet then. But there was a German sentry on the quay, so that side of the affair would have to be dealt with.

At exactly five minutes to five a man went up to the German sentry when he was at the point of his beat which was farthest from the yacht. The man had a number of questions to ask the sentry, and between these questions a very friendly discussion was carried on. Every time the German was about to go on a new question was asked. At exactly two minutes to five four men went on board the yacht and two minutes later came up on deck carrying a box. At five o'clock precisely Jonas drove up in his lorry; box after box was put into it; each man fetched a fresh load—seven boxes in all; two men flung themselves on to the deck of the lorry, where Sten guns lay ready for action under a tarpaulin; the two others disappeared up a back street; the lorry followed and was gone; the man who was talking to the German sentry said 'Thank you,' and the peace of Sunday reigned once more upon the quay.

The lorry proceeded up Karl Johan right under the noses of a heap of Germans, out to Sköyen and on to the road authorities' shed below Amalienborg. Here the boxes were hoisted up into a false roof.

On board the yacht down in the Akers river the Sunday peace was disturbed about an hour later. Of a sudden things grew lively on the quay; a number of policemen, mainly Germans, boarded the boat and searched her thoroughly. The skipper was arrested along with the remainder of the crew and the boat confiscated. Why? Not on account of any boxes, but because on his last trip he had taken a Norwegian girl over to Strömstad without permission; in other words, he had helped people to escape to Sweden. Not till some days later did we succeed in finding the people who were to receive the precious cargo.

We had two very good contacts in the Akers workshops who quickly secured the drawings and information that interested us. Some of the drawings were 'lent' for one night, microphotographed up at 8 Nils Juelsgate and returned; of others we were given a more or less spare copy.

I had a lady with me on my return journey to Sweden—my sister, who had been 'wanted' for over two months in connection with the affair for which 'Uncle Hans' had been arrested. We used the same route via Halden; this time there were two of us who had been to 'Fru Hansen's' funeral—it was remarkable how sympathetic people really were.

We crossed the frontier on December 19 after a splendid trip. Not one control, not one person who appeared to have the slightest suspicion of us. I had on me the case with the microphotographed drawings and the most detailed information, and when we reached Stockholm these were sent on to the head office in London.

Christmas and the New Year were celebrated in Stockholm, and on January 9, 1944, I went on to England by air. After a fortnight spent in conferring, writing reports, and participating in further plans for developments in Norway I received a provisional reward—two months' leave and a free journey wherever I liked. It can easily be understood that this was Canada—to be more precise, Toronto, after a splendid trip across the Atlantic in the *Queen Mary*. . . .

I was married ten days after I arrived.

CHAPTER XX

TO NORWAY WITH A NEW TASK

THE very day we returned from our honeymoon the telegraph office rang up: 'If willing new job report in London latest 22 April.' The significance of the telegram was clear—both for my own private plans now that I was married, and for the time which undeniably was coming. I could not say much to my wife—but there was no need to. She understood. We had both reckoned that I had done all my operational work in this war, and now it was more or less up to myself. A woman does not say as much as we men where such a personal sacrifice is required. Last time she had had to wait in uncertainty for nearly a year: how long would it be now?

On April 20, 1944, I reported at the headquarters of the British secret service.

The plans which had been drawn up for the impending return journey to occupied Norway were somewhat different from the previous ones. The objective was the same: nothing had been heard from the agent who had been sent to relieve me in Sörland—probably on account of the local conditions. But the main change was in the manner in which I should enter Norway, and I must say that I felt somewhat relieved at this, with that famous parachute jump in fresh remembrance. Moreover, I asked to have an extra operator sent with me this time, in order to obtain increased working capacity and, it might be hoped, a better result.

Instead of an air operation, as the first time, we were this time to be landed by a sea operation—to be precise, by a motor torpedo-boat on the west coast of Norway. Experience had shown that this method was a good deal safer for the agent entering the country; more uncertain, perhaps, as regards getting to the place where one was to be put ashore, but on the other hand more certain in that one then had both feet on the ground, and it was easier to calculate how things would develop from that point. Of course the local conditions had a great bearing on security; but it might be assumed that people in Norway had given sufficient information about these in advance.

Talking of security, I had a strange experience on my second day in London. While crossing the street by the Marble Arch, I suddenly caught sight of an airman from the 330th Squadron who had been one of my best comrades up in Iceland. When I approached him he just stood staring stupidly. I had not seen the fellow for a year and a half, and in such cases one expects, as a rule, a response to a polite greeting.

'What's the matter with you?' I asked. 'Have you lost your tongue?'

It came out at last: 'But in Christ's name—we thought you were dead and buried long ago—weren't you killed in a parachute jump in Norway? . . .'

After I had been dropped the year before the returning plane had reported that I had probably been killed in jumping in the conditions described earlier in this book. Of course this should never have come out; but, on the other hand, perhaps it was a good idea. The reports had reached the Shetlands, where the squadron then was; the boys had held a wake and made speeches and said a lot of nice things about the deceased which they certainly regretted bitterly later on. There was also a fellow there who had written condoling with my wife-to-be in Canada; thus the rumours arrived there well preserved and instilled doubt into her mind. Another man wrote to a friend of his in Sweden expressing regret at the accident; the friend had written home to Norway in so-called 'covered style,' so my friends had got hold of it, and through them I learnt in August 1943 of my death.

An agent had indeed been killed on the night of April 19-20, 1943, on which I myself had jumped. This was Evensen, who had started at the same time as myself but in a different plane. He was dropped on to a lake in the neighbourhood of Tinnsjö in Telemark; there too it was blowing pretty hard that night. The reception committee which was in readiness just saw a bundle come down from the plane; the parachute had not opened properly. Evensen was perhaps one of the best men the British secret service had at that time in Norway.

We were to be landed on an island a little to the north of Haugesund. Through contacts in Stavanger it had been planned that people from there should arrange for our reception. The torpedo-boat which was to land my assistant wireless operator and myself was also to have on board the agent for the Stavanger area. We both had over 2,500 lbs. of equipment which was to be packed in different ways on our arrival; some was to be sent by express steamer south to Stavanger, some right to Oslo via Stavanger, and some by fishing boat to Kristiansand. Every detail of the transport was left to the people on shore, who knew the local conditions.

An assistant wireless operator was really just as difficult to choose as a permanent colleague at home. Of course he was to be looked for in a narrower circle, in part known to me from earlier times, among the already trained 'agents' at the British secret service school in London.

But here, too, a number of important factors had to be taken into consideration besides the man's technical qualifications. Among other things, I wanted a man with local knowledge, preferably one from the Sörland countryside, a man who had not been too long away from the prevailing conditions and at the same time one who had not for a long time been in the limelight and who was not too well known to the Germans or to the civil population. A Kristiansand man, Lars Larsen ('Lasse') was chosen, a comparatively young fellow with a burning interest in the task entrusted to him, and, as events showed, a splendid operator. His personal acquaintances in the town of Kristiansand were to play a decisive part in the results that were attained.

We packed equipment for three days and the greater part of three nights. There was not much time in which to do it; on April 26 two planes were to take us and the whole of the equipment up to the Shetlands, and from there we were to go on by motor torpedo-boat on the evening of the 27th. According to wireless reports from the people who were to receive us on our landing north of Haugesund, everything was ready and conditions there were quiet. We were to land at 4 a.m. on April 28 on one of the outer islands, where two men were to be ready with a fishing boat to take us on to the main island inside. There all the equipment was to be unpacked and repacked for forwarding elsewhere. Before it was light again, the motor torpedo-boat would be a good way across the North Sea on her return journey to the Shetlands. This was the plan.

So once more we sat up in the little out-of-the-way flat where the 'chief' lived when he was in London, and went through the plans again over a cup of tea. The little thickset Englishman did not say any more than was necessary; but what he did say was worth stowing away in a safe place in one's head. This was on the evening of April 25. Early next morning we were off.

It was nearly twelve when we looked into the luggage room for a final check-up of the different packages. Then came a telephone call on the direct line from the War Office. It was the British liaison officer who was to accompany us on the flight to the Shetlands: 'The operation is called off!' I simply stood with the receiver to my ear looking foolish, until he repeated the words and asked if I had understood. Yes, there was no doubt about that; but what the devil had happened now?

We heard the reason when the English major arrived in a car a few minutes later. The War Office had just received a telegram from the people on the island north of Haugesund: 'CANCEL ALL OPERATIONS STOP ISLAND FULL OF GERMANS STOP CLOSING STATION STOP.' The telegram spoke clearly for itself, and there we sat on our boxes.

On few occasions earlier or later in the history of the war can the British have acted more quickly. The whole operation, which was then based on a landing from the sea, was in the course of two days changed to an air operation. That an uninitiated person may really understand what this meant, I will mention a few of the details which had to be arranged. Two four-engined Halifax aircraft were to be got ready, one for the Stavanger agent and one for us. Regarding us an express telegram was sent through a wireless station in the neighbourhood of Oslo to Jan, the shipbroker's son, with these orders: 'Be ready at place indicated with reception committee. Keep watch every night from 11 p.m. to 4 a.m. from April 29 to May 6. Prepare hiding-places for 1,800 lbs. of equipment. Plan transport into Oslo.' All the equipment was to be repacked into strong tin containers which would then be dropped by parachute. The containers were weighed and compared with the necessary sizes and types of parachute;

then Lars and I were weighed and each fitted with our parachute, etc. The reason for this haste was that after May 6 aircraft could not go farther north than 59° latitude, as it was too light at night.

So we were to have another little air trip! I cannot say I was particularly enthusiastic over the idea, and for Lars, who had only done five parachute jumps, it was not a welcome change either. But it had to be risked. . . . On April 27 we drove into the grounds of the old English country house I knew so well from earlier times.

Supper, April 28, 1944. Two poached eggs were carefully served on a plate to Lars, and two to me. I glanced quickly across the table. Lars just sat looking thoughtfully at the delicacy before him. It was our turn! But someone must have made a mistake. The telegram to the boys at home said they were to keep watch from the 29th, i.e. from to-morrow night. We got an explanation an hour and a half later down in the operations room of the airfield. The met. office had reported bad weather approaching; a front was moving south-east across the southern part of Norway, had reached Bergen and would probably give Oestlandet, with Oslo and the country where we were to land, bad weather in the coming week.

It was decided that we should take the chance that Jan and the reception committee would be on the spot a day before the time arranged. If the reception committee was not there, we were not to jump, as we could hardly manage all the equipment alone; moreover, it was not certain whether the country round 'pin-point' had yet thawed. But if we did not jump now we might not be able to jump until the autumn.

The four-engined Halifax aircraft stood ready, with nine full-packed containers securely fastened in the bomb-racks under its belly. Lars and I were ready in full jumping kit with our parachute harness on. A last good-bye to the British major, England and one's own ego. The door of the plane was slammed to. 'Contact!' The engines roared; we were airborne and on our way.

We were not the only people on the way to Norway that

night. A formation of American Flying Fortresses, over twenty aircraft strong, had started from another airfield in England a quarter of an hour earlier. In addition to these, six more Halifaxes were to start in the course of the next half-hour from the same airfield from which we had taken off. The task of these planes was to drop equipment for various groups which were distributed over an area from the neighbourhood of Trondheim southward to Stavanger. Most of them had the central part of southern Norway as their field of operations. As camouflage for these operations and our own flight the Allied Supreme Command had ordered the bombing of Kjeller airfield and the repair shops at Lilleström. The formation of Flying Fortresses was to attend to this side of the business. While these were attracting the Germans' attention, the Halifaxes were to go in quietly to their respective 'pin-points' and drop what they had on board.

There were variable cloud cover and winds on the trip across the North Sea. Lars and I sat on either side, as comfortable as possible in a corner. Now and then I glanced across at Lars, who also seemed to find it difficult to sleep. It was his first operation; it was my second; but I did not know if that really made much difference—at any rate not as regards the hole farther aft in the plane through which we both must go out!

The Norwegian coast! My pulse quickened. A few rounds were fired from below; but the explosions were absurdly far below us. Then we were on our way inland towards the Eiker forests.

'Twenty minutes to target!' The British skipper was speaking.

'O.K.—I'll be seeing you at Blom's!'* I tried a joke to keep up my own spirits. Lars had evidently understood already that it was just coming! I could just make out his face in the faint light of the roof lamp, and I did not fail to notice that it was a little paler than usual. I could not help smiling a little as I leaned over to him and spoke: 'Don't you be frightened—I'm frightened myself! But now comes the tug-

* Blom's is an Oslo 'pub,' popular among artists and students.

of-war, and the quicker you come out after me the better!'

The dispatcher signed to us that we could take our places on each side of the hole. The hatch which covered this was still down, as there was still very great doubt if the boys were on the spot. The plane slowed down, descended, and began to circle round. We were over 'pin-point.' The tension was great; I found it hard to sit still. The dispatcher on the after-edge of the hole stood talking ceaselessly over the intercom. It was he who was to give the sign for further action, and we both remained sitting and following his movements. The plane went on circling.

From time to time the dispatcher shook his head. This did not look promising. I relaxed a little; perhaps there would be no jumping after all. Suddenly the dispatcher took off the earphones and handed them to me. 'The skipper wants you!' he yelled across the hole. I took off my gloves and mittens, loosened my rubber helmet and put the receiver to my ear. 'Not a sign down there!' Not a sign of a light.

Then I had to unhook the parachute string, which had got caught up in the plane, and go to the skipper in the pilot's cockpit. There, down to the left, lay the Eiker bathed in moonlight. Right ahead lay Store Oeksne; 'pin-point' should be a little higher up to westward—but all was dark. The skipper did not want to circle round the place too much, and we made a little round trip up to the northward.

A good quarter of an hour had passed and there was still no sign of life below. 'Why not run over to Kjeller and have a look at the fun there, and then we can have a last try a bit later?' My proposal seemed to interest the skipper, and he nodded.

All the country round Kjeller was lit up, partly by a number of big fires below, partly by German anti-aircraft fire, which on this occasion seemed to be rather heavier than usual. The skipper throttled down and descended to a low altitude. Of course we kept well away from the place itself, but still we were near enough for some gun or other down there to have a try at us. There was no reason for taking any risks and, strictly speaking, it had little to do with our trip. But in addition to this the skipper took us on a little run down to Oslo and close by the Holmenkollen ridge below the level of the scaffolding on the ski jump.

Again we circled round 'pin-point,' again with negative result. The boys could not be there; they had been given rather short notice even for the following night. It turned out later that they were quite close by and could easily have received us where they were. As it was they had just pulled their boots on and stood outside the tent and watched the plane which went on circling round. But—they had an order, and this was to keep watch from the following night, so this plane must be meant for some other people who perhaps were in the same neighbourhood, or—it might only be on a reconnaissance flight. The possibility of our being Germans was also loudly discussed, as a German plane with lights had passed farther north a few hours earlier. So no one signalled.

We enjoyed excellent treatment in Britain for another week. Every evening we received the same negative information from the airfield: bad weather—no flight. May 3, 4 and 5 came; the next day, May 6, was the last opportunity for the operation, technically speaking. For the reception committee it would also be the last day and, according to plan, they would then leave the place and return to town. But we hoped that they too had had bad weather all the week, that it might have cleared up on this last day and that they would stay for another night in case something should happen.

May 6 dawned with thick fog and rain. This was damnable! But later in the afternoon it cleared a bit, and just a faint hope sprang up in us. 'Operational Eggs' for supper! It was said that the flight was only to be an experiment; but we learned that this time a Norwegian pilot was to fly the plane, and with him a good deal could be arranged.

The pilot, Arvid Piltingsrud, was an old friend of mine from before the war, and nothing was said about any 'experiment.' He had, indeed, returned from a flight over Holland a few days before in the most shot-up Halifax I ever saw; but this did not cool his martial ardour, and we started.

On the way over that night we agreed that the pilot

should let us know through the dispatcher if the boys were on the spot. It was further decided that we should jump whether the reception committee was there or not, and all nine containers would be dropped likewise. In this case Lasse and I were to assemble all the equipment as best we could, store it in different places, hope that no unauthorized person had seen the drop, hope that the ground was in a decent state; and then I was to go to Oslo to fetch the boys up again, leaving Lasse at 'pin-point.' Further, we and Piltingsrud had privately agreed that the minimum height for a drop, about 1,000 feet, should not be too literally observed on this occasion. The reason was that at 1,000 feet above 'pin-point' both plane and parachute could be seen a long way off if it was comparatively light. If one of us had an accident, which we did not expect, we were better dead than in the hands of the Gestapo; it was more important that the drop should not be seen now after all the difficulties we had had.

'Twenty minutes more!' That was 'Pilt's' voice over the intercom. All was ready; we were sitting there 'on the hole,' Lasse on one side and I on the other. A cold gust came up to us, and far below—hills and ridges, frozen lakes, boulders. I had ceased to think about anything but just this: on the red light and the word 'go' you *must* go out! Lasse, in a state of high nervous tension, sat on his side with his legs close up to me, ready to move up the moment I slung my legs into the hole.

I just sat and stared into the dispatcher's face. He was to nod if the reception committee was there. Not a movement—green light: 'Action station!' Legs into the hole—red light: 'Go!' The wind tore and pulled—the parachute was dragged out of the pack on my back, stiffened, a violent jerk and—the parachute opened easily. Without a hitch! The most important thing had happened! There came Lasse—a little to one side; but his parachute seemed to be all right too—and then, one, two, three, four . . . nine containers one after the other!

Hardly a breath of wind, and there—at my first glance down I saw what I had hoped to see—the triangle of lights!

So the boys were there after all. 'O.K., chaps, all lights out!' I shouted as I floated quietly and neatly down through the air. The whole thing was extraordinary—so utterly different from the first time, on the whole the easiest parachute jump I have ever made!

A quite gentle puff of wind from the north drove the parachute towards a big fir-top down in the swamp: 'Good,' I thought for a moment, 'a tree would suit me all right,' but no—just clear of it and down into a large clump of bilberry surrounded by hair-moss. Extraordinary! It was just as if a chair had been placed for me; I just sat down carefully as I should have done at home, about ten yards from the triangle of lights. I sent my best thanks to Piltingsrud, who had already disappeared over the ridges to westward. That fellow knew his job if anyone did!

'Hallo!' said two men in long trousers who approached me—the twins. If not embraces, there were handshakes. My parachute was wrenched off and rolled up under a fir for the time being. We sauntered over the swamp together and found Lasse with Jan. Lasse, to make things quite safe, had put both legs three feet deep in a boghole and could not possibly complain of a hard fall. The only comment he had to make was that instead of going out through the hole feet first he had gone almost head first. One of his legs had been caught in the loose string behind me; but nevertheless his jump had gone excellently after one or two somersaults as he came out.

In half an hour's time we were sitting round a small fire under some big trees, where the boys had their headquarters—an old army tent camouflaged with fir branches. They had kept watch all the last five nights, as ordered; every night they had had a kettle of hot water on the fire, ready to make a hot cup of tea for the two travellers from England. They had spent only one night in their sleeping-bags; then there was a heavy snowstorm and it was bitterly cold.

The worst part of it was that they had long ago consumed the ration of food they had brought with them, and for the last two days their menu had consisted of one cup of gruel three times a day. When the sixth day came, their spirits, as might be expected, were at zero. But the weather improved, and after a short discussion it was Jan who decided that they should stay one night longer—in case.

Our mutual joy was all the greater; questions were asked and news exchanged, and to go with the tea we produced the best kind of chocolate, cigarettes, and to wind up a little 'special toddy,' consisting of tea and good old English rum. I had letters with me for Jan from his fiancée in America, so he was put on guard for the next hour!

It was nearly two o'clock. There was plenty to do, and further jollification had to wait. Eighteen hundred pounds of equipment was to be unpacked from the containers, which still hung entangled in the trees. The first parachute was found, and then the work went quickly, for they had all fallen more or less in a straight line, and it was no trouble to find them in the light of the moon. The parachutes were unfastened, provisionally rolled up and placed in a hut of fir branches, which had been made for this purpose and at the same time had been used as a shelter for the men on watch; the advantage was that this hut was some way from the main tent, and in the event of anything unexpected happening both places would not be discovered at the same time.

The equipment was now unpacked and sorted into very important, less important and least important, and hidden in places as best suited the different classifications. At a quarter to five it was all finished—the equipment divided, the parachutes provisionally packed and the containers temporarily covered with fir boughs and everything hidden as well as possible under bushes and trees. Now time would show if the drop had been observed by anyone else. Two men crept into their sleeping-bags down in the main tent, two buried themselves in parachute silk up in the hut of fir branches, and one man was put on guard for two hours at a time. If anyone had observed the drop and reported it, we reckoned that the Germans could be on the spot at nine o'clock at the earliest. For the time being we could take it easy.

The day passed without anything happening. In the

evening we began to move the camp nearer the road by the dam on Store Oeksne. With the possibility still in view that we might be in danger of a visit, it was undoubtedly safer, both for the equipment and for ourselves, if we lay some way off. It was five miles down to this place, and it was far into the night before the camp was in order. A new tent we had with us was now used. The advantage of this was that it was a deep leaf-green in colour and was much easier to conceal. The same afternoon I sent one of the twins down to the village to go on to Oslo. We wanted more people to carry, if the whole job was to be done within a reasonable time; and further arrangements must be made for a lorry to take the stuff from the dam into Oslo or to Darbu, as conditions allowed.

We lay chatting for a time that evening round a small fire. It was nearly eleven when we all four simultaneously started, and in a moment were sitting with revolvers or Sten guns in our hands. Someone or something was coming up through the scrub in the gully which gave access to the camp. The kettle was poured over the remains of the fire, and we sat in darkness. It was obviously a human being—a few savage curses told us that; a twig cracked, and a whistle signal on four notes sounded through the silence of the night—our own signal. Five steps more, and Ottomar might have had a fine mixture of the best English lead pumped into him.

'Kalle' (Carl) replied with the same signal. 'What's up?' was the great question uttered by four men at once. 'The place is full of Germans!' was the simple, dry answer. Ottomar wrenched off his sack, dripping with perspiration after toiling up the long ascent from the village. The fire was blown up again; Ottomar had a cup of coffee and a bite of food, and we had his story.

All had gone well till he had cycled a good way along the main road. Then, at a bend, he had first met one lorry full of German mountain troops, then another, and finally, where the road ran through a little glen, six Germans had suddenly sprung out of the woods on each side, with tommy-guns and in full marching order, and shouted 'Halt!' 'The whole business was very awkward,' Ottomar told us in his quiet, unruffled manner, 'for I suddenly remembered that I had a box of English cigarettes and a packet of recently dated film in my sack—and I'd got brand-new English pants on as well.' I could not help laughing at the dry, detached manner in which he narrated the whole story. Yes, there had been a personal search and his sack had been examined; but what seemed especially to interest the Germans was the large reindeer-hide bag on the top of his sack. The cigarettes were packed away inside two smelly socks, the film in a ditto pair of pants, and the gentlemen did not seem to take much interest in these malodorous effects of a 'wood-cutter.' But they wanted the reindeer-hide bag, but as this did not appeal to Ottomar, they wanted at any rate to find out how they could get one like it.

Ottomar got a pass and went on through another control, for which his pass was good enough. From a peasant he learned what had happened. The sheriff's officer at Hokksund had shot a 'student' who was hiding in a hut up on the moor, and who had been down in the village to make purchases at the shop. Nine more of his comrades, who occupied two huts, had been arrested. This, at any rate, was the story the peasant had heard, and now all the moors round the Eiker and the Hokksund district were to be combed. Ottomar had the impression that the man added this last detail on his own account. But it would be extremely dangerous, in these conditions, to try to get a part of the more important stuff to Darbu, as we had planned, and Ottomar had therefore left his bicycle at a place near the road and made his way back to the camp through the woods to warn us.

This was a check to our plans; but of course it was not certain that these extraordinary conditions would last. On the other hand it was not impossible that a detachment of mountain troops might march up along the road to the dam, and conceivably patrol the country round. We must keep a sharper look-out from next day onwards.

We now began to move the equipment from 'pin-point' to new hiding-places quite near the dam. This was a tiresome job and took longer than we had reckoned. Each of us did two trips a day, each time carrying a sack weighing from 65 lbs. to 80 lbs. On May 10 I sent Ottomar and Kalle. If all was quiet in the district they were both to go on into Oslo; if not, one of them was to return and report. Of course neither of them had anything dangerous in his sack. All was quiet that evening, and Kalle did not return. We therefore assumed that all was well.

We three who remained went on carrying till May 12. Then I packed a sack with all the most important papers for the conduct of the wireless station, took Jan's bicycle and rode to Darbu. All was quiet and peaceful along the road; the only people I saw were two Germans on bicycles. One of them had a basket with what looked like black market goods more than anything else; otherwise they both appeared to be quite harmless. There was a happy but quiet reunion up at the railway station, and our man there was told all about the forthcoming transport. I went on into Oslo by train without any disagreeable interruptions, and there made my way up to 8 Nils Juelsgate.

CHAPTER XXI

TWO BITS OF LUCK

THE transport of the equipment from the Oeksne dam into Oslo was for some time an unsolved problem. The lorry-driver Jonas, who had worked for us earlier, was arrested in January when transporting refugees to the frontier, so there was little help to be had from that quarter. A lorry could no doubt be obtained through other contacts in Mil. Org. and XU; but at that time there was no one who would undertake to drive all the way from Darbu to Oslo. Nor would anyone undertake to drive to the region where the equipment was and drive it down to Darbu station. The reason was that at that time there was very strict control all along the road from Oslo to Drammen and likewise in the country round Hokksund. Moreover, a strange lorry going through Hakavik to the Oeksne dam would undoubtedly arouse suspicion, as only regular, well-known vehicles ran along this blind-alley road. We were in a fix. The one and only possible alternative was for a farmer, one of our contacts at Darbu, to drive with a horse and cart from Oeksne to the station. There was quite a lot to be arranged in the shortest possible time in Oslo, and as usual Kalle and Ottomar did a good job. Unfortunately Kalle had been pressed for time one evening when he was out on business; he rode into something or other on his bicycle in the dark and went head first over his handle-bars. He broke a kneecap and was kept in bed for two months.

Ottomar returned to the Oeksne dam and the camp on May 13; I went up on May 15, and on May 17 two more fellows, Morten and Botolf, arrived. On the afternoon of May 17 we tapped the electrical installation on the dam and opened contact with England. A new American transmitter was being tested—with excellent results. Twenty-two watts radiation on a Hertz aerial and a well-regulated, good receiver. After a minute's calling at contact time the station on the other side came in, clear and audible. There was a short and cheerful 'conversation'; I sent a telegram of about forty groups containing a short report that all was well, but that transport difficulties were causing a good deal of delay.

The transport was to be even more difficult than we had thought. The farmer on whom I had staked my last card could not undertake the driving. His two horses were commandeered for the time being; he did not want to borrow a horse from another farm, for everyone in Hakavik would undoubtedly begin to ask what this fellow was doing up in someone else's woods with a borrowed horse. We were in a fix again, and the only course remaining was to carry all the stuff to Darbu by night on bicycles. But what a job!

All the hiding-places were now emptied and the stuff carried down into a boat-house close to the dam and just beside the road. Here it was packed into cardboard boxes with glued paper round them and securely fastened with string. On each box a large red label was pasted: 'With care! Glass! Zoological specimens!'

While we were doing this, the man on guard suddenly gave the danger signal. All tracks outside the boat-house were rubbed out, the doors shut and locked, and we all retreated hurriedly across the dam and up the slope on the other side. Here we sat, each with his American tommy-gun and Sten gun ready. From the side of the ridge towards the village, where the road wound uphill towards the dam, came the sound of a big car in second gear. What could it be?

Orders were given in a low voice; it might be Germans; our rear was secure, and now as before there was to be no firing unless it was necessary. There came the vehicle round the first bend, a red lorry with tiles on its deck. But there was no immediate danger. But what the deuce was that lorry doing up here just now?

The lorry drove as far as it could towards the lowest sawing shed. A man got out—took a short walk round the shed, lit his pipe and sat down on the steps. After a few minutes he began to unload the tiles, which were obviously meant for the shed. Then I had an idea. While the other fellows sat where they were, covering me, I sauntered down towards the car in a leisurely manner.

The driver did not see me till I was quite close, stopped a moment with a few tiles in his hands, laid them down and took a long pull at his pipe. 'Morning,' I said, 'so you've got some tiles to put on.' Yes, he had. This shed was newly built and now tiles were to be put on it and on the two other sheds there before sawing began in a week's time. We went on talking about the weather, and about the affair of sheriff's officer Horgen who shot the 'student' down at Hokksund. (Horgen and his wife were subsequently 'liquidated' by the Home Front.)

During our conversation I put out a feeler here and there, and it was not long before the man had shown his colours. Naturally I replied on the same wave-length, and I gradually made him understand clearly where I stood politically.

I went on to talk about various happenings in recent times

of which the boys had told me in the evenings by the fire. The driver grew quite excited once or twice and was able to correct the story I was telling. It gradually became clear that this fellow knew more about the details than most people, and if I was not mistaken he belonged to one of the Mil. Org. teams. I do not mean to say that the man in any way talked carelessly—on the contrary he treated the subject of his conversation with remarkable skill. For anyone who knew the conditions it was just a matter of putting two and two together.

At last I decided to have a try. 'You say you're coming up to-morrow with another load; how about giving me a lift down to the village and to Darbu for that matter, if you're going that way?'

The man looked at me. 'Yes, I could manage that, but—how about the luggage?' It was my turn to give him a look; had he smelt powder already? Oh, the luggage was up in a hut farther on by Oeksne, which he certainly knew; and besides my own kit I had a quantity of zoological specimens. The fact was that I and two other zoologists had been up in the woods collecting various things which were to go down to the museum in Oslo. It had been intended that another lorry should drive for us; but now the driver had rung up and said that the lorry was smashed up and that we must wait a week. We had not time for that, so—if we possibly could get down now, as he was up here in any case, it would be fine.

The driver stood ruminating over the proposal; then he asked slowly: 'How many containers are there?' 'Nine,' I replied without winking an eyelid, 'about 1,800 lbs.—perhaps rather less.' As I spoke I took out a packet of 'Senior Service' cigarettes and offered him one. Yes, thanks, he had smoked that brand before!

The whole thing was fixed up—and we had got into touch with a Mil. Org. driver, whose like I never had the pleasure of meeting either before or since, a man who demanded only security and yielded a hundred per cent in return, Odvar Nyrud from Vestfossen. He was coming up with a load of tiles next day, and would take us and the whole collection of 'zoological specimens' down again and drive the whole lot up to Darbu. He was actually going to Vestfossen himself, but that did not matter.

Next day, at twelve o'clock exactly, the man on guard reported a motor vehicle on its way up the slopes towards the dam. The doors of the boat-house were shut, and we withdrew to the other side of the lake. It was the red lorry, and we soon saw Odvar jump out, sit down on the steps of the shed and light his pipe. To be on the safe side we waited a few minutes longer before one of use went down. All was quiet in the district, and the driver was willing to keep his word. I may remark that we had, very quietly, made a brief inquiry of our local contact regarding this driver Nyrud, but without saying anything about his having declared himself willing to drive. The recommendations he got were in complete agreement with the impression he had made.

Three men had already been sent to Oslo, taking with them, besides a wireless set and a few wireless parts, some other important things which we should be sorry to see in the hands of unauthorized persons in the event of anything going wrong with the transport. So there were only three of us to go down to Darbu station with the lorry and its load.

The whole transport went without a hitch. Lasse and Jan sat on the deck of the lorry, where the cardboard boxes were now well concealed by wood, and I sat in the driver's cabin with the driver. The fellows sitting on the load had their Sten guns ready for action; we in the driver's cabin sat with our revolvers on our knees. Fortunately there was no need to use either. Lasse and Jan jumped off, each at his appointed place, immediately before we came up to the main road at Darbu, while I continued with the lorry to a point where a short cut crossed a field to the station. The lorry had to go on rather farther down, where the actual station approach was.

Everything was quiet, and I signed to the driver to come on. Lasse and Jan in the meantime had gone to have a rest in the farmhouse where the farmer's son Arne, a year before, had played *God Bless our Good King* on a child's xylophone. There was still an hour and a half before the train left, and there was not much sense in the chaps showing themselves too much at the station. . . .

All the parcels, twenty-two in all, were marked with bogus addresses in Oslo, in case anything should have gone wrong with the transport by lorry. New labels had to be written; some of the boxes were to go to Kristiansand, some to Mosby, north of Kristiansand, some to Sköyen and some to Skarpsno, outside Oslo. Instead of sending the whole lot as express goods, we took luggage tickets for them all, and it was agreed with the station booking clerk that he should send two parcels by every train that went, so long as necessary. In case one of the parcels was discovered while being conveyed by train, we should not lose the whole cargo. All the parcels for Oslo were fetched by a forwarding firm in the usual way and driven to a cover address. Thence they were taken on to the different dumps.

While I was putting on the false labels, on which only the names of the places were right, I noticed an elderly man in a skin jacket and high black boots standing in the middle of the platform and following me with his eyes. I glanced at the man and continued the work I had begun. He was obviously from the wrong camp! Lasse and Jan, who had now been into the waiting-room and taken tickets, had noticed him earlier. As they were moving away from the booking office, they heard him ask to what place they had taken tickets.

Lasse and Jan had sat down on a bench behind the man as he stood staring at me. It had been agreed that from the moment we came into the station we did not know one another. Every time I looked in their direction, Jan pointed to the man. I could not nod, as the man stood staring at me all the time. When I had finished, I went into the waiting-room to say that I had put all the labels on the parcels. The moment I went in at the door the fellow made for the goods shed, and when I returned, apparently quite inadvertently, he was standing bent over one of the parcels, reading the label. He rose hurriedly and tried to smile.

'Where's all this stuff going, and what is it?'

I boiled inwardly. 'That's no business of yours!' I replied

curtly. 'But why do you ask, when you've just been standing here reading the labels?'

'As sheriff's officer here I have the right to ask!'

The sheriff's officer—an arch-Nazi if ever there was one! I stuck both hands in my pockets and went a step closer to him.

'Well, that's all the more reason for not poking your nose into other people's affairs, with conditions as they are nowadays. Your colleague Horgen was killed a few days ago, wasn't he?'

The sheriff's officer did not reply, and I continued:

'If those boxes had not contained zoological specimens, collected for a number of schools in this country, you might perhaps have accompanied your colleague into eternity, and if you want my opinion, I think you'd find it pretty hot there!'

The sheriff's officer stood for a moment looking at me contemplatively; then he turned his back on me and went up to his house above the station. Now we were in a hole! I walked along the platform, signed to the others to follow me, and went into the lavatory. The situation was discussed, and we agreed to take the chance of things going well and go into Skarpsno by train.

The train from Oslo to Kongsberg came into the station, and from the waiting-room we saw the sheriff's officer get in. Again we asked: 'What next?' An hour later the train from Kongsberg to Oslo came in. As we approached different carriages, carrying our rucksacks, I think we all saw the same sight simultaneously—the sheriff's officer. This time he got out of the train we were getting into.

What had he done on his lightning trip to Kongsberg? Did he realize fully what was happening, and had he great ideas of following up the matter himself through the addresses on the twenty-two boxes locked up in the goods shed? In that case he would be disappointed, even if we were to lose the greater part of the precious equipment. But had he reported the affair to Kongsberg? Had people been put on to the train to shadow us? Or should we get a visit on our arrival at Drammen?

With the American wireless box in my hand and wearing

my rucksack, I sauntered into a compartment in which sat a 'Norwegian soldier' from the 'Regiment Speer,' two Germans and two Norwegian civilians. The racks seemed to be pretty full, so the box containing the American wireless transmitter was the only one for which I could find room. I put the rucksack into the next compartment. The Germans talked quite freely, and we had quite a friendly conversation. The Norwegian from the 'Regiment Speer,' on the other hand, seemed rather sulky and sat buried in his paper, *Fritt Folk*. Just before Mjöndal, I walked along to the carriage into which Lasse and Jan had got: I nearly laughed when I saw them comfortably tucked away in a compartment along with two German S.S. officers.

When I returned to my own compartment the two civilians had left the train. Otherwise all was as quiet and peaceful as before. The Germans had settled themselves to go to sleep, so there was not much more conversation. 'Drammen!' Fresh tickets must be taken for Lasse and me, as neither of us had travel permits and had only taken tickets from Darbu to Drammen, which was within the three Norwegian (twenty-one English) miles allowed. Lasse's ticket was slipped carefully into his hand when we chanced to be standing side by side at a window.

I gave a start when I returned to the compartment. The Germans had got out, and only the Norwegian Nazi remained. He had left his place and, when I entered, was standing staring his eyes out at the box containing the American wireless transmitter which lay up on the rack. I grew hot; had he seen a box like that before? Was he suspicious about its contents? The question remained unanswered, thanks to the pipe of evil-smelling German tobacco he had lighted. An elderly man, a strong patriot, went for the Nazi and abused him roundly. 'Even if you are a blackguard, you've no right to smoke where smoking's not allowed!' The rest of the discussion is hardly suited for reproduction; the main thing was that the two disputants withdrew into the patriot's compartment. I took my box with the American transmitter, and my overcoat, and disappeared into the lavatory of the next carriage.

The journey to Skarpsno went quite well, even if I had to play hide-and-seek with the member of the 'Regiment Speer.' After all, one cannot stay in a lavatory the whole way from Drammen to Oslo without arousing suspicion.

The boxes of equipment began to arrive at Sköyen and Skarpsno stations in a steady stream. The West railway was banned, as on it there had been repeated examinations of luggage, express goods and ordinary goods. We had arranged it so that all our stuff had been unloaded from the fast train at Sandvika and sent on by the local goods train. A man at Sköyen let us know each time something had arrived; the parcels were fetched by lorry and the loading of the lorry watched in case other people should be showing an interest in the place, and in general the greatest care was observed.

The stuff was now repacked and distributed among different dumps. Conditions in Oslo at that time were rather insecure; continual house-to-house searches and arrests every single night. With things in that state there was always a danger of getting involved in difficulties, especially if one was out of doors much in the evening or at night. As a rule the streets were empty after eight o'clock.

Our greatest difficulty was moving the stuff from place to place, and I will say here that all our Oslo contacts did splendid work, from quite young girls and boys to elderly people. As time passed, the Germans noticed more and more that something big was brewing. The preparations which had clearly been going on for a long time over in England and Scotland could mean only one thing—invasion. But where? The German Supreme Command advanced the most improbable theories, and the German propaganda promised a reception such as the world did not dream of.

The propaganda conducted by the various belligerent Powers was most interesting to watch in these years, especially perhaps for us who had the opportunity of following both sides of it at regular intervals. But I must say that I had never thought the Germans could dish up what they did in that line. There was no doubt that it had an effect on a few mentally stunted individuals and uninformed people far out on the edge of what we call civilization. But it was surely a little too much to suppose that the mass of the people would allow themselves to be hoodwinked, as undoubtedly the plan was with all the occupied races. There was, however, one thing we could not help noticing in our contact with the different strata of society here and there in Norway. Right from the beginning of the war the Germans carried on an intense, fiery anti-Russian propaganda here, as in other countries. This propaganda left its trace and undoubtedly made a fairly deep impression all over the country. That it directly injured us I will not assert; but it did affect in a high degree the common effort which was to be expected in a country like Norway.

One was most afraid of one's own people; I think all agents, saboteurs and other 'visitors' in Norway during the war will agree that this was so. And there were many who stood aside, from hate and fear of Russia, when even the smallest contribution to the cause was asked of them, precisely because they considered the Allied cause to be too much affected by Communism. We did not notice this so much in Oslo, because everything was on a bigger scale; but it was all the more noticeable in the small towns and in the countryside.

As time passed, and the invasion fever of the German command rose higher, precautionary measures became sharper. The Gestapo and the police troops, both German and Norwegian, did their best to suppress the Norwegian underground movement. But the more they tried the more difficult it became. The more people they arrested, tortured and killed, the greater became the activity in the different areas, and the more stubbornly determined the people became to counter every ordinance issued by the *Herrenvolk* and its Norwegian Nazi helpers.

Many times the various men and women who ran the Oslo section were on the brink of disaster. I would make special mention of Wencke, Jan's sister, a lady aged twenty-two, who probably made the greatest contribution of our women helpers, both in 1943 and 1944.

This time we had decided that, so far as possible, we would take care of the parachutes in order to use their silk for various objects—especially camouflage suits for use in winter.

Ten parachutes were packed in paper bags, two in each bag, and were addressed from Darbu to Stabekk station. Here they were to be fetched by a farmer with horse and cart. This was Kaare Larsen of Muren in Baerum, one of our best contacts outside Oslo. Two of these bags were to come into Oslo, and this just in the worst days of this period.

Manus* had made a bit of a mess in Oslo harbour, so that the roads in and out of the town and the trains going both ways were under rigid control. My reason for using a lady on this occasion was that, in difficult conditions, a lady aroused less suspicion than a man. Ottomar was sent to shadow Wencke in case other people should show an interest in her.

At Stabekk station a good many German officers were assembled, probably some of those quartered in the school near by, and when Wencke came along carrying the two paper bags, one of the Germans, a major in the Air Force, immediately offered to help her. Ottomar nearly had a fit: if this came off, anything would! 'Yes, thank you, with pleasure,' Wencke replied. The major led the way with the English parachutes; Wencke followed him smiling. The train was overcrowded as usual, and the German major sat down on one bag and Wencke on the other out in the corridor. Ottomar had to be content with a standing place beside them and, on the journey into Skarpsno, listen to the most idiotic conversation he had ever heard (he declared later).

Lysaker station: passport examination by German and Norwegian police! Nor was that all; in several instances in compartments, where male travellers had big and heavy luggage, random examinations were made. Ottomar had meekly to show his passport and give an account of himself; Wencke sat absorbed in talk with the German major, who thought he had made a good catch—but only while the examination was going on. They were not disturbed—and the parachutes seemed to make excellent seats!

* One of the foremost leaders of sabotage groups in the Oslo area.

CHAPTER XXII

BACK TO KRISTIANSAND

WE HAD not much time. June, I had gathered, was to be the crucial month. The 'head office' was established in Oslo; all the parcels which had been sent from Darbu had arrived and been distributed; a regular messenger service to and from Kristiansand had been arranged through our earlier contacts on this route, also a messenger service to and from Sweden and a number of sources of information in the country about Oslo.

On May 28 I went to Kristiansand myself. All journeys over this route were to be made by night train. The reason was that most examinations hitherto had been made on the day trains. Only when something special had happened was there control on the night train as well. My journey down went off without disturbances; I got off next morning at a wayside station, and went on by train an hour later. All was quiet at Mosby, my destination, about seven miles from Kristiansand.

I then cycled up to the country round Oevrebö, where the proposed main station was to be established. I had a joyful reunion with Gunnar Upsahl, our main contact in those parts in earlier days, and there was no question of difficulties about starting a new season. The old hut was at our disposal, and father and son had worked out plans for great improvements since we were there last.

On the afternoon of May 29 I opened contact with England on the electrical circuit from the house itself, on the first floor. The station would start a full service as from the next day. Jan and Lasse came a few days later; they too had had an untroubled journey down. For Lasse this journey to Kristiansand perhaps involved some degree of special danger. It was not long since he had been obliged to leave the neighbourhood; if he met people he knew in the train, he might as well take the same train back, if the rumours had not already flown ahead of him. But he only *saw* acquaintances on the journey, he actually met no one.

Weather reports were then the most important thing. Our orders ran, 'if possible from June 1 at latest.' The material which was to be used in the first instance in Sörland had arrived at Mosby and Kristiansand in good condition, except the wireless equipment, which we had had with us in parcels when we travelled down. Gunnar now walked down to the railway station, collected the various parcels which had come, and took these up to Oevrebö openly by bus. The greater part of the things from Oslo were fetched in the same way on later occasions. If there was a control, we heard about it in good time, as Gunnar himself now and again drove the regular bus and knew the different drivers.

Now and again something unexpected might happen here as elsewhere; but Gunnar was always the man to get our things through. Now, when I think in retrospect of the different methods of transporting dangerous things from one place to another, I find it hard to understand how it always ended well. There were ceaseless controls, and our stuff usually lay quite unconcealed. As a rule, in fact, the Germans could both move the 'treasure-chest' and stand on it—even sit and rest on it after a tiring search, yet whole wireless sets, arms and ammunition, code-books and deciphered reports went through their hands daily.

We had several busy days digging hiding-places round about the hut; the order was that everything which could in any way betray the nature of our work—or that there was 'work' at all—was to be removed. Only the 'holy of holies,' the little bag containing the code-books, weather report tables, telegram books and all the other things that had to be used daily to draft each separate telegram, had to be in the hut for the greater part of the day. At night, when we had finished drafting the day's telegrams, this little bag, too, was hidden outside in a place used only for this purpose. Not infrequently it happened that we had contact in the course of the night; but the 'holy of holies' was then hidden immediately afterwards.

Over and above this preparatory work weather reports

went every morning at 8 a.m. G.M.T.: up at the observation post we noted the height and types of cloud, the force and direction of the wind, visibility, 'dry' and 'wet' temperature, relative moisture; we gave a general review of the weather in the last twelve hours and the level and tendencies of the barometer at the moment of observation, as well as a number of other conditions which were of interest to the compiler of a weather forecast across the sea.

To the best of my knowledge we were the only station in Norway which gave detailed weather reports, and these were of great importance for all operations from England over Europe as a whole.

These weather reports only very slightly increased the chance of the Germans locating the wireless station by direction-finding. It was impossible for us to vary the times of our met. messages much, as the observations had to be taken at a fixed time every day, and the reports had to be at the Air Ministry within the next hour and a half to be included in the morning weather charts which were sent out to all operational bases under Allied command. Further, every single met. message went on the same frequency and with the same call sign every day. But the messages went only in numbers; the frequency was the best we had; speed could be maintained at an average of seventy a minute. In these conditions, even if the German wireless stations did their best to locate the signals by D/F and, after a short period of activity, observed the met. message every morning, there was little chance of their being successful. Numbers are much more difficult to D/F than letters, as the message goes in a rapid staccato.

If 'big things' were brewing, we usually received a 'crack signal' after the morning met. report in the shape of a five-figure number. 'Big things' were, for example, large-scale bombings of Berlin or other places. The five-figure number meant that we were to send additional weather reports at two fixed times later in the same day: if there were two separate five-figure groups, we were to send weather reports every other hour throughout the twenty-four hours, until new instructions were received.

Thus we could not help listening eagerly to the next day's news report to learn where the operation had taken place and what result had been achieved—and in a modest way we liked to credit ourselves with just a small share in the result.

In the first week of June many of these 'crack signals' came. On June 5 reports were sent every other hour. June 6: invasion! What news! I shall not forget the faces of people in Kristiansand the day the news came, long before the Germans had pulled themselves together and realized what was happening. People stood in small groups eagerly discussing the news; the Germans who had suddenly had to get busy seemed just shabby little creatures scurrying along. But this impression did not last long; as the days passed and the Allied invasion gained more ground, our *Herrenvolk* became more and more hysterical and their actions more aggressive.

Our own work was to become more strenuous than ever. At this time there was a great change among our connections in Kristiansand itself. Special circumstances brought about a complete change of our sources and contacts in the sector. The change involved a complete recasting of our method of work, which required first and foremost a keen, reliable nucleus of people with only one aim—to work for the cause they had embraced, without regard to personal interests.

Our connections in Kristiansand had made a splendid contribution in the year 1943; I would emphasize in particular that of the railway guard up in Oesterveien, his son and the rest of his family. The guard's unfailing helpfulness on the Oslo–Kristiansand route and the reverse, towards both individuals and current messenger traffic, was wonderful. He was now transferred to the Kristiansand–Stavanger line and unfortunately could not be of the same use as earlier; but before he left his old position he had found first-class people to take over, and these were irreplaceable all through the 1944 season.

The contacts in the country districts, in Tveit, Birkenes and Oddernes, were still used as far as possible. But it was inevitable that individual members of the organization became a little too well known to the people in these parts. In the town, on the other hand, there was a complete change.

To deal with the shipping in the port of Kristiansand was still our most important task. But this was now to be attacked in quite a different way. Acquaintances were now to play a large part. Inquiries were set on foot about the position of individuals; the plan gradually took shape in collaboration with the British command. A man—let us call him Claus—was employed by the Norwegian harbour police and was on duty every night from 2000 to 0800 in that part of the Kristiansand quay system which most interested us. His work brought Claus into regular contact with warrant and petty officers and seamen of the German Navy under the orders of the *Hafenkapitän.*

Through the office of the *Hafenkapitän* went all information about every single ship arriving at or sailing from Kristiansand, and every single convoy; names, tonnage, cargo, armament, destination, escorts of convoys and their armament, the convoy's most secret call signs at the different times in the twenty-four hours, and a whole lot of other details which were of the greatest interest to us. The question now was: could Claus find, among his German connections, one or two who were willing to start work within the area of the German *Hafenkapitän*?

When the plan was first mooted the whole business seemed too risky, and we agreed to wait and see how things developed. It was obvious that Claus himself would run the greatest risk, so it was finally left to him to decide whether it was possible. There were two men in the harbour in particular, warrant officers, who seemed to have rather different political views from most of the Germans and a higher moral standard. As much attention as possible was therefore given to these two, but without the others getting wind of a developing 'friendship.'

It was the Germans themselves who made the first advance; their plan was not to carry out espionage, but to desert, steal the German harbour police's speed-boat, which lay moored every night where they could get at it, load it with food and equipment stolen from the naval depot close by—and set a course at full speed for England! Would Claus accompany them along the coast as a man with local knowledge? Despite the 'friendship' between the two parties, there was nevertheless marked suspicion on both sides, and on the first night Claus seemed very sceptical about the plan.

The possibilties were discussed next day in the attic of Claus's home. It was obviously a choice of risks. If the two Germans were told that Claus would have nothing to do with the plan, and further that he would report them if they put it into action—what then? Would not Claus, on the following nights, be in danger of getting a bullet in the back? It was easy for two Germans to fake up a story about sabotage or something of the kind. Perhaps, even, the whole thing was an *agent provocateur* business. If the Germans were to accept Claus's proposal that they should remain in their positions and start co-operation with an 'illegal organization,' what security had we that they would not give the whole thing away to the Gestapo? Also, what guarantee had we that the information they gave was correct? How could a security system be worked in the event of their accepting the plan? But if this co-operation was successful, it would undoubtedly give the best results we had had till now.

The plan was laid before both Germans at once, because we reckoned with another factor which made for safety. If there was only one man, he could easily change his mind after a time and withdraw; if there were two, this would be considerably more difficult. They accepted, and apparently with great enthusiasm, although it had been made quite clear to them that there could be no money reward. Our principle was work for a cause on idealistic grounds; if their efforts were inspired by a hankering after personal gain, the results would undoubtedly be proportionate. The guarantee we could offer was, in the event of anything going wrong, a 'free' journey to Sweden or straight to England; their reward would come after the war in the form of a secure future.

The Germans received their instructions through Claus on thin paper in newspapers, cigarettes, bread and similar ordinary articles of exchange. They learned about what interested us, how the reports should be compiled, and how often the regular harbour reports should be given. I will mention here that these two men had practically unlimited access to all secrets in the *Hafenkapitän's* offices.

For a month the work went full steam ahead. In addition to the station in Oevrebö we had for the second time an auxiliary station out in the country inside Augland bay, a mile or two outside the town. The information from our German friends was first-class. This is what we did: we asked questions to which we already had the right answers, and were thus able to check the value of their work and gradually establish their position. After a month's work they had the sinking of two German ships to their credit, and that settled matters. From then on they were entirely in our hands; if they tried trickery of any kind, it was quite a simple matter for us to put a nice collection of cigarette papers, on which their reports were written, in an envelope and send it anonymously to the Gestapo headquarters in Kristiansand. Claus above all was secure, at any rate so long as the Germans were at large, and our friends, too, were politely and cautiously made aware of the position. Any carelessness on their part could react first of all on themselves.

I have said that we set up an auxiliary station south-west of Kristiansand for the *second* time. The first occasion, some time before, deserves a brief mention. The main station in Oevrebö was at times rather a long way from the town. When the port was very busy and large convoys were leaving, the reports of these reached the station too late unless we had advance information. Several alternatives were explored with regard to the position of an auxiliary station, which must be only a mile or two from the town. That time we had brought with us from England a good 1,500 feet of insulated two-phase rubber cable. The intention was to use this for an auxiliary station on the 'Upturned Boat,' where we had a station the year before. The electric circuit which ran along the Södal road, where the current was 210 volts A.C., would be tapped with a free wire into a fixed watertight plug box, well hidden under the root of a tree or under a stone. From here the rubber cable, buried and screened, would run up the hillside to a ledge where I had reckoned on having a charging station for the batteries. This ledge was about sixty feet below the top, and was well covered by trees and bushes and very difficult to see from above or below. The station itself I had thought of placing where it was in 1943. From the ledge we had a splendid view over the whole harbour, over the whole approach from both west and east, and in clear weather for many miles west towards Mandal. A brief reconnaissance, however, was enough to make us reject this plan. The Germans had set up their big wireless station on Skraastadvarden, about three-quarters of a mile away, and a regular guard was mounted there; fifty yards below the top there was a German area, which was patrolled at regular intervals; at the farm below the cliff, where the path went up, a fine collection of German soldiers and horses were quartered; in short, on the whole the conditions were impossible.

The terrain on different sides of the town was combed without success. One cannot set up a wireless station just anywhere and start tapping. Hundreds of problems are involved, both technical and practical. Moreover, it seemed to be a regular thing that if we liked a place the Germans had already found it and installed something or other there or in the immediate neighbourhood.

So it happened that the country west of Augland bay was the only practicable ground left, in spite of its being completely surrounded by the strongest military installations in Kristiansand. There were in the first place the Mövig fortifications, which lay a short way outside. The road out to these we also were compelled to use. Then there were the great military constructions along the Rossevann to the south, the camp with the gigantic pill-boxes on the Brennas and along the road south towards the lake, and to the north the Mandal road and the large ammunition dumps. All these lay in a circle with a radius of two miles from Barlindal moor, where the auxiliary station was set up.

It will be understood, therefore, that every word while we were there had to be whispered; rubber shoes had to be used, wet or fine; in short, it was a game of hide-and-seek all the twenty-four hours of the day. But despite our disagreeable neighbours, the position had great possibilities.

We had one great, indispensable advantage: the ground round the station was very rough and people moving about in those parts were more or less confined to the regular paths. Our first camp was sited on the southern side of Barlindal moor itself. The main tent was well covered up with fresh conifer boughs and these reinforced with thick deciduous foliage. The camouflaged kitchen tent, a few yards away, was close up to a rock face and similarly covered; the wireless tent about ten yards from the main tent, quite hidden in a small depression in the ground.

We were to run this first auxiliary station for three weeks more or less in peace and with very good results. We received advance reports, as much as twenty-four hours beforehand, of every convoy that left Kristiansand harbour. From the top of Barlindal moor, in a patch of scrub, we had a first-class outlook over the whole harbour and exit, whence we could note precisely the sailing and arrival of every single ship, compare these with the advance reports from the Germans and give London exact information. It was no easy job being *Hafenkapitän*; such a distressing number of ships never reached their destinations.

The possibility of being located by D/F was considerable; we had Flekkeröy wireless station not far away, and in addition to this the Germans had every opportunity of taking cross-bearings from the various fortifications in the neighbourhood, and with D/F cars from all the roads round the area. Certainly we had Barlindal moor behind us with its south-westerly rock face, which gave a good deal of protection and served as a reflector for the station. But our only real security consisted in reports from a contact within the police, who was attached to the police wireless section. He was able to tell us now and again how far the Germans had got in locating by D/F the station which they had long known to exist somewhere in the immediate neighbourhood of Kristiansand. But of course it could happen that he did not every time get all the information we needed.

CHAPTER XXIII

EVEN THE BIRDS GIVE WARNING

WHILE running this first auxiliary station up in the Barlindal district we benefited greatly from a rather strange phenomenon. As we crept about in the area, or sat eating outside the main tent, or were busy with contact, coding or other work, we might suddenly begin to listen intently. One of the camp's two 'watch-dogs' was warning us; something was coming up the valley on one side or down the steep gully on the other. These 'watch-dogs' were two pairs of birds, blackbirds and stonechats respectively. The blackbirds were always in the narrow cleft that led up from the valley towards the camp, the stonechats in the gully down from the moor itself. If anything disturbed either of these two pairs of birds they uttered cries of a definite kind which after a short time could not be mistaken. It might be a sheep, or a hunting hawk, or a fox—or other wild creatures.

It could also be two-legged vermin. These often disturbed us; but every time without exception the visitors were 'announced' beforehand by one pair of birds or the other, so that we could take security measures. Yet the visitors always went past our door, sometimes a yard away from the main tent where we sat and could follow them with a tommy-gun or revolver.

By degrees a most amusing game developed between the German police wireless section and our station, sometimes very amusing indeed for us. I learned from our connection that the Germans had got so far as to suspect the district in which we were. The D/F cars began more concentrated work on the roads around. Lasse was now sent up to Oevrebö with the crystals or frequencies we had been working on for a long time. With the same call signs and at the same time of day he sent off the message from the main station, many miles from the district where the Germans were sure we lay. Suddenly, with only a day or two left before they began to go through the district with a fine comb, the signals came in from quite another quarter and also much weaker. So they were back where they began, and the only thing they could do was to start right from the beginning again. Lasse continued to send from Oevrebö for a week, while we at the auxiliary station had at the same time begun to work on quite different wave-lengths, at different times and with new call signs. We also reduced the traffic to the absolutely necessary minimum.

But unfortunately it was not only the Germans that caused us a good deal of worry. I was obliged to cycle into Kristiansand about every other day to work on plans and discuss their execution with the different connections. If the station got into contact while I was in the town, Lasse and Jan dealt with that side of the business. But I was involved in a lot of gadding about along the road from Augland to town, coming back the same day or the next. The people at the local shop had certainly already begun to wonder where we were, as from the things we bought they must have been able to guess that there were several of us. But there were many different strangers, both from Oestlandet and other places, working for the Germans at Mövig; we probably belonged to the same crowd. But we tried hard to turn up towards the moor at different points, so that the people who lived closest to us should not continually notice our movement to and fro.

Things went well, too, for a fairly long time—about a month the first time. Regular messengers came out from the town with the latest news and food; the food position was now considerably better. Three different 'barter centres' were in full swing; tobacco for butter, cheese or other foodstuffs. Some of this was sent in a special manner down to Kristiansand, collected by regular people and brought out to us; some was sent from stations up country direct into Oslo for distribution among the contacts there.

At the station we were unfortunately restricted to a very monotonous diet, as lighting a fire was forbidden. We used a Primus, and its hissing in the kitchen tent, which was well covered up, could be heard only with difficulty a few yards away. Only on very still evenings did we have to stop using it. Our menu, therefore, was very simple: bread and butter with something on it, oat gruel 'floating' in butter—three times a day, with tea or coffee. Very monotonous at times, but sufficient, when we hardly had time to eat anyway.

The station was run entirely on batteries. A regular contact down in Augland had undertaken this part of the work. The transformer was built into a small box on the wall of a garage, and the batteries placed for charging overnight and hidden next morning. It was Jan's job, at appointed times on regular days of the week, to carry the used batteries for a three-quarters of an hour's walk to a pre-arranged 'post office' in the woods. When he arrived there 'Battery Hansen' had been up earlier in the day with a set of fully charged batteries, and Jan had only to exchange them. The used batteries were collected later the same evening and placed for charging.

It was July 26; a steadily increasing stream of 'summer visitors' past the station had disturbed our idyll for the whole of the past week. We had had two visits from a Storch aircraft, and the last time we were convinced that it definitely suspected our position. For over an hour it circled round the top of Barlindal, swept over the station low down and came back the same way.

It was about nine in the morning. Tenvig was sitting in the main tent darning socks; Lasse was down in the valley fetching water, and I was sitting over in the wireless tent coding a report of one of the largest convoys we had had that summer. A really peaceful idyll. Then a branch cracked up in the gully, and a small stone slithered down into the scree. The stonechat began to chatter, followed by the blackbird in the cleft running down into the valley. I gave a start, stowed code-books and everything connected with them away in the bag, and fastened this round my waist. It could not be Lasse, as the stonechat up in the gully had given tongue first, and the noise came from there. It must be visitors.

A sudden thought came to me where I sat—the aerial! It had just been hung up, as we were to have contact in a quarter of an hour. Well, it was too late to start fiddling with that—people had walked right under it before now without seeing it. I crept over to the main tent, warned Jan, caught up a Sten gun and stood half outside, covered by the camouflage over the tent.

The man who was coming was obviously a practised woodsman; we could hardly hear him. There was a movement in the bushes fifteen yards away from the tent; the man was following the sheep-track which passed three yards away. He stopped—looked all round him as if searching for something or other—he had an axe under his arm. At any rate he was not a German—evidently the owner of the timber, or a workman in his employ.

He now stopped and began to fell trees ten or twelve yards away from the main tent. I remained standing where I was, bent forward, and tried to keep Jan posted on what was happening. The man was beginning to make a sheep fence on the side where the aerial was fastened! Row after row was felled; the man moved slowly but surely up towards the tree to which the aerial was fastened. Each time he felled a tree, he looked up to judge whether it was suitable. . . . There! he was standing upright with the axe half raised—he had seen the aerial! I cursed to myself; Jan grasped what had happened from my expression. 'Give me a pencil and a notebook!' I whispered to Jan.

'But in Christ's name, what's this?' . . . the fellow stood talking to himself for a minute or two; he looked up and along the aerial over towards the little hillock which concealed the wireless tent. He still did not see a thing in the direction of the main tent, two yards away from where I stood. His eyes flickered this way and that, and curiosity was written all over his face. Then I rose. The man literally jumped. My right hand was in my pocket round my revolver. There was no need to show our colours too much, if it could be avoided.

'Stop a moment, if you value your life!' were the words with which he was received. Jan remained under cover with a Sten gun in his hands; there was no need for the man to be able to describe more than one of us. 'What are you doing up here?' I asked.

'I own the timber!' he said meekly.

The man had to show his papers; as a precautionary

measure I checked the various data like an ordinary German control, and took notes. Not very polite towards a visitor, I willingly confess, and Jan had difficulty in keeping himself from laughing where he sat. I told the man to whom he was talking: students in hiding, with a wireless receiver to make the time go rather quicker while we were waiting for the invasion. I told him that if he valued his own life he should forget what he had seen, and keep away from the woods so long as conditions were as they were then.

But the fellow did not seem to have any great sympathy with students in hiding; he seemed to have his own view of the situation, without stating it. He was clearly nervous. At last I asked him to clear out in a 'fairly' polite manner, and he disappeared like lightning towards the valley, from which we were awaiting Lasse. But Lasse had overheard the conversation in broken sentences, and when the man came rushing downhill he hid behind some bushes to let him pass.

The whole thing was rather queer—the man's behaviour and appearance, and his obvious nervousness. This became clear when, instead of continuing up the valley, as he said he meant to do, he dashed down towards Stor Lake and took the shortest route to Augland. I followed hard on his heels right down to the next lake; he was running for his life. But he had a boat, and I came off worst, as I had to run the whole way round the lake while he rowed across at top speed. Instead of taking the road down to Augland, he went over the moor, so my plan of cutting him off lower down came to nothing.

The whole camp was struck in a quarter of an hour. All the wireless equipment was hidden in a place prepared long before, farther down the valley. Lasse went one way, Jan another, and I a third, each of us with full sacks. Not a thing was left but the remains of all the camouflage we had used.

Jan and Lasse did not arrive at the main station in Oevrebö till late the same evening; I took the road into Kristiansand and up to Eidet on the other side of the town, after making inquiries as to whom our uninvited guest really was. Our suspicions were justified; this timber-owner was the biggest Nazi in the neighbourhood.

I spent that night with the Mathisen family as usual. We had become acquainted with this family the year before when we were working up in Tveit and Birkenes. From the very first day we went in and bought our bottles of mineral water, we realized more and more that Eidet café held great possibilities: never so much as a hint of a question who we were, where we came from, or what kind of work we were doing, that we should be always drifting along the road on bicycles. The door was always open.

This place saved us in many a difficult situation in the autumn of 1943 and later. Once I came cycling along with a wireless transmitter in my bicycle bag, and had not stopped for a control. It consisted of two motor-cycles with three German police soldiers on each. I just got into the yard behind the café, knocked and asked if I could leave my bicycle bag while I was down at a hut, which through Arne had been placed at our disposal for use on occasions. Yes, certainly, I could leave it either in the house or under the steps. I chose the latter, laid an old tarpaulin over it, and went down towards the hut just as the motor-cycles swung into the yard. The Germans followed me; but instead of going down to the hut I just went for a stroll in the neighbourhood with three Germans fifteen yards behind me all the time.

None of them made any approach to me; they probably only wanted to see what I was like and if I was doing anything in particular. They evidently thought I had not heard them; but when I turned suddenly they were standing chatting as if my person did not interest them at all. Instead of giving them a wide berth, I went up to them, greeted them politely, and asked if they could sell me a cigarette. Yes, they could; one of them even gave me a light. I do not know which of us was most surprised at this mutual courtesy.

I took my bicycle and rode into the town. The wireless transmitter remained at the café for the night; but the woman of the house had taken the bag into the kitchen as a precaution against its disappearance.

It was as a student for a forestry degree or wood-cutter that I now took a room on the first floor at Eidet, and 'a thousand

and one' tall stories indeed were told by forestry pupil Oeyvind Fredriksen in the course of the many pleasant hours spent with the Mathisen family there. Whether the two heads of the family were deceived was quite another matter; but despite warnings from various quarters against giving a lodging to 'this strange man who was obviously up to something shady,' no question of a personal nature was ever asked; nor was the door ever shut upon the said Fredriksen.

The day after we had been visited in our camp up on Barlindal moor, I walked back to those parts to find out if anything had happened in the meantime. This was of the greatest importance because the Nazi might by now have given a very exact description of me, and in that case it might be a good idea to alter the façade a little.

The rain poured down; not a soul was to be seen, either on the way to our old camp or up there. The rain had washed out every footmark. So possibly our reference to what had happened to other talkers had had some effect after all. With the wireless equipment in my sack I made a detour down to Augland and looked in on our contact there. Yes, there had been two cars with German police out there the same morning, and they had made a number of inquiries in the houses along the edge of the wood. He could not say what the reason was, but the probability was that the Nazi had been talking.

Well, the Germans knew. I took my bicycle and rode over the Brennaas up to Oevrebö, and none of the many Germans I met on the road seemed to take the least interest either in me or in my fair-sized package. Jan and Lasse had gone by the same road, and they had had no trouble either.

Up in Oevrebö our work was continued at full speed. We were obliged to return to the messenger system; but it was now developed to such an extent that all advance reports of convoys and movements in the port came in good time. The actual sailing of the convoys was telephoned up to the village shop, whose owner, Ilebaek, and his family did excellent work throughout the summer and autumn of 1944. The so-called 'vegetable code' was used.

The wireless station itself was now sited about 200 yards

from Upsahl farm, partly buried in the ground and covered by a large boulder. The current was tapped by a rather ingenious installation down in the barn, connected with a fixed rubber cable which was buried in the ground and ran to a junction box under the root of a tree about twenty yards from the wireless hut. At contact times we had to run an extra cable to the apparatus, which, when not in use, lay hidden in a watertight hiding-place a short way below in the wood.

The amusing thing about this main station was that from where the man on duty sat during contact he could follow all traffic on the road and also keep an eye on the large German camp which lay a couple of hundred yards above Upsahl farm. An officer from the camp had been to Upsahl and asked if he could buy milk. This was the reason why we preferred not to establish contact from the farm itself. We were, indeed, compelled to do this when time was short; but it would be very unfortunate if this visit were repeated.

A little after six every evening was also a very unfavourable time. You could sit on the rock above the farm and observe one person after another coming with a milk-pail, as we used to do to conceal our activity from people interested in it. One man after another came loafing along, went through the door into the farm, but did not come out again. At twenty-five minutes past six a man came out, one of the two sons of the house, sauntered over to the barn, and returned in a minute or two carrying a large box. If you then paid a visit to a small room upstairs, you found it crowded—the whole family and a few near neighbours sitting absorbed round the wireless—the London news—while one of the members of the family sat keeping watch at the window which looked towards the road and the German camp.

Continual series of questions streamed in to the station from the Allied Supreme Command, questions which set our imaginations working with regard to their purpose. They were all connected with the invasion, which was now in full swing, and all touched upon the possibility of which we were all thinking in those days—would there be an invasion of Norway?

One telegram was as follows:

1. Is there a divisional staff in Arendal? Give number, H.Q. and name of C.O.

2. Is there a Grenadier regiment's H.Q. in Kristiansand South, and/or in Lyngdal? Give number, location of H.Q. and name of C.O.

3. Are the Army troops in Mandal subordinated to Lyngdal or Kristiansand?

4. Is there an Army Coastal Artillery regiment's H.Q. in Kristiansand? Give location and name of C.O.

5. Command of coast defences:

(*a*) Are coast defences within the Naval Commandant's area divided into operational groups, with, for example, one in Kristiansand, one in Arendal, etc.?

(*b*) Are any of the Army Coastal Artillery troops subordinated to the Naval Commandant for operational purposes?

(*c*) Are any of the Army Coastal Artillery troops under command of O.C. Battle Group?

(*d*) Give liaison centres for coast defence.

6. Try to get a list of all vessels under the orders of the Naval Commandant.

7. Get the number of the regimental staff at Borgestad, near Porsgrunn, and name of C.O.

8. Give location of battalion H.Q.s in division. Are there battalion H.Q.s in Kristiansand, Evjemoen, Birkeland and Arendal?

9. How are the divisional field artillery, A/Tk artillery, and recce battalion disposed?

This was only one series of questions, and it will to some extent make the reader understand what kind of extra work was required besides the ordinary information which was sent about shipping movements in the district, and which undoubtedly gave the most visible results. Thanks to indefatigable connections and our German friends, every single question contained in the above telegram was answered in a comparatively short time.

Our two principal German connections met when off duty

a number of officers, N.C.O.s and men from other detachments and regiments, and sailors from the different ships. It is strange how much discussion of military dispositions and plans there is in Service circles, and naturally our German friends kept their ears open. They had, moreover, allied themselves with other Germans over whom they had complete control. Every normal person will ask why these two were willing to give this information, as did other individual Germans during the last stage of the war. The answer was: personal gain, and the desire to get ashore from the ship they themselves had helped to sink. Yet I maintain that our German 'friends,' acting as traitors to their own side, were a good deal better than most others of that kind—without a penny by way of reward and with their lives at stake every minute. Otherwise, I would say what a German once said to me a short time after the invasion: 'We hate traitors, but they can be useful now and again!'

For a few weeks we were to be able to 'take it easy' up in Oevrebö. That is to say, in comparison with the life we were compelled to lead on Barlindal moor. It was something to be able to talk loudly and not to have to go about whispering to one another all day, not to sleep uneasily every night, always revolver in hand, not to have to wake Lasse every time he began to snore or shake Jan whenever he talked in his sleep or dreamed that he was fighting twenty-five Germans at once!

At the main station we were able to establish a very dependable warning system in case of suspicious traffic on the road. People up there had begun to grow accustomed to the three townsmen who lived in the hut up by Stoess Lake. Why, a leading Nazi lived opposite, so despite all evil reports they could not be such 'dangerous fellows' after all. People from the district were constantly up there bathing, and we joined them with pleasure when convenient.

Meanwhile the road between Kristiansand and Oevrebö was beginning to be less pleasant. As the invasion of France steadily progressed, we had the impression that the Germans were becoming more and more savage; there was always a control on the road, and especially at the outskirts of the town. We particularly disliked the main road past Mosby, and therefore used the Södal road on the other side of the river. The Germans had undoubtedly discovered that it was safer to live outside the town, and had evacuated all the larger camps and were quartering their men and equipment outside, in the various farms up the valley. As the result of this practically all the farms up in the Södal country were occupied. But for ourselves this was just as great an advantage, as the Germans thus felt less anxiety about illegal traffic along these roads.

CHAPTER XXIV

NO PEACE

We were again packing equipment for the auxiliary station, and Barlindal moor was proposed. Idiotic? Really not so silly as it sounds. The Germans, having carried out a search when we were reported by the Nazi who owned the timber, would probably assume that we should in no circumstances return to the same district. So we were going back to the same country, after a little reconnaissance.

The transfer went off excellently; at this time others besides ourselves were cycling about with large parcels. The holiday-makers' summer traffic had started a long time before. But it was not exactly the same place as the first time. A little farther west, about two hundred yards away, there was another hill-top at about the same level as the highest point of Barlindal, and from it we had quite a good view. The camp itself was this time placed on a quite dry swamp, another inaccessible place. But it was not quite as good as the previous camp, for which reason all the tents were built in, covered with twisted boughs, moss and dry trees, and the whole thing so arranged that it all blended with the surrounding swamp. Each tent looked like a large overgrown rock.

We were to receive another series of questions which was

to give us an extra 'headache.' The questions referred in the first place to the submarine base at Marvika, on the fjord above Kristiansand, and after that to possible submarine bases at Arendal and Flekkefjord. The details required were:

1. *Repairs*
   (*a*) Are there welding apparatus? Are these electrical or acetylene?
   (*b*) Are there shops for repair of electrical apparatus?
   (*c*) Are there stores of electrical apparatus? What apparatus?
   (*d*) Are there stores of machinery spare parts?
2. *Batteries*
   (*a*) Are there charging apparatus?
   (*b*) Are there stores of acid?
   (*c*) Is there distilled water?
3. *Torpedoes*
   (*a*) Are there permanent torpedo stores?
   (*b*) Can torpedoes be repaired?
   (*c*) Can they be trimmed?
   (*d*) Can they be loaded?
4. *Depot Ship*
   Are any of the following always present:
   (*a*) Mother ship—repair ship?
   (*b*) Oiler or floating tanks?
   (*c*) General supply ship?
   (*d*) Torpedo supply ship?
   (*e*) Quarters ship?
5. Is the submarine base being extended? How?
6. Give maximum capacity of base—possible capacity in connection with possible development.

Besides these questions there were a number of others to be answered in respect of Kristiansand, Arendal and Flekkefjord.

Kristiansand was an easy job, and the answers were given within three days, thanks to an admirable contribution from our German connections and our friend the customs official. Arendal was little trouble, as submarines had only called there now and again and, as far as our authorities knew, there were no plans. With regard to Flekkefjord the situation was rather different; there were plans enough, but no one could say exactly how far advanced they were.

So I should have to make a short trip to Flekkefjord. But —one thing struck us before I started: Flekkefjord was not really in our area; it was under the agent in Stavanger. So why had the questions about that harbour come to us? Something must have happened over there, where one of the best agents was at work.

During the last journeys to and from Stavanger there had been controls; something had happened over there, causing the Germans and Norwegian police to be specially on the alert. Stavanger was full of rumours; but it had not been possible to get hold of any connected information.

Our old friend the railway guard was again to give a helping hand. He was not on duty himself the day I had to make the journey, but one of his friends, who was briefly notified of an extra passenger who had no travel permit and would take his ticket on the train.

All went well, although I was in company with several plain-clothes policemen from Stavanger on their way back from the hearing of a big case in Kristiansand—quite decent fellows, by the way, who seemed to have sound ideas about the whole situation. They did not seem to be in any doubt as to who would win the fight in the last round; but having taken part in it for so long, they would do their best to make the Norwegian people suffer for its antipathies to the last.

I was travelling in the capacity of 'adviser' to the N.S. (Quisling) publishing firm Blix, and I cannot help saying that their bearing and their frankness astonished me.

On my arrival at Flekkefjord I unluckily came up against an examination of passports and luggage by ordinary German police soldiers; but my passport was in order and my luggage insignificant, so this little episode caused no trouble.

The district doctor at Flekkefjord was the man on whom I called, and he was able to give a good deal of information supplementary to what we knew already. He was also commissioned to furnish in future regular weekly reports on shipping movements of any kind which could in any way be connected with possible large-scale submarine plans in Flekkefjord.

'The whole people in illegal work' was our watchword through these years under German occupation. The district doctor and his family set a good example. From where we sat in their living-room we could see down into the exercise yard behind Flekkefjord police station. The son of the house was not more than eight years old, but none the less he did his bit. At a fixed time each day this little boy crept in through the opening where the tubs from the prison's old-fashioned closets were taken out for emptying. He crawled along on the planks under the row of holes till he reached a particular hole. There he was able to sit huddled up till a particular person came and sat down in the ordinary way, tore off toilet paper and let it fall after use. Among this paper the daily post was inserted, and this was now fished up and brought out by the same route. This boy was never caught—at any rate not for that. But he and some of his young friends were fond of unscrewing the caps of the petrol tanks on German cars and dropping in lumps of sugar, or of putting sand into the oil. He was arrested along with a few other small boys, but was released with his father's help, the offence being treated as a boyish prank and the punishment left to his father.

The information sent out of the prison in the manner described consisted as a rule of results of interrogations; prisoners who had been obliged under torture, or for other reasons, to give the names of fellow-workers who were still at large, thus warned them through the boy and his father. Many were certainly saved in this way from a cruel fate.

The return journey to Kristiansand went smoothly. But conditions there had again become rather different. In the last fortnight it had rained the whole time, night and day. The camp of three tents was, as I mentioned earlier, sited on a dried-up swamp in a little hollow. When I came back I found that Jan and Lasse had had to move the main tent. They had wakened one night and found water standing several inches high on the 'floor'; all their clothes and equipment were soaking wet, and they were wading among the tents in water and slush.

In addition to this there had been a visit from a German patrol; it had practically walked between the tents when only one man was there. But they had not seen a thing—thanks to the most accurate camouflage work. Why this patrol? Were they just a party out for fresh air, or had they other reasons?

The wireless apparatus, too, had been in the rain, and there was continual short-circuiting during contact, without our being able to do anything of much use. The Germans had probably got to work with a new system to defeat the station. For the first time we had the impression that they now had complete knowledge of the wave-lengths the English station most often used, and were trying to make as much disturbance on them as possible. We might begin to send our messages in excellent wireless conditions; but it was not very long before they came in with howling and false signals to spoil communication as best they could. We had to play hide-and-seek on different wave-lengths, continually asking Central to change over to another.

One morning, during an early contact, we had a very curious experience, which was to be repeated later. As usual, I called up exactly on time—and got the correct signal in reply. I sent RR and started on a telegram of about sixty groups. We were very busy that day and had distributed fifteen telegrams over three different contacts. As usual I sent twenty groups, went over, and asked Central if it had got all correctly. 'Central' asked me to repeat a series of groups before group fifteen. I repeated, quite slowly so that the signals might be understood this time. RR was sent in reply. So I went on again with the next twenty, and asked again. Repetition, this time first of a few groups between twenty and thirty. As soon as this was cleared up, there came another request for groups between one and ten, groups which I had repeated before. This was very queer—the people sitting at the receiving end were supposed to be experts. But I repeated afresh and got RR again.

But when I had finished these groups, we were asked for

the groups between twenty and thirty which I had repeated earlier. Then we became suspicious and moved the knob of the receiver a few hair-breadths to one side. There was the real Central calling wildly. So it must have been a German station we had now been talking to for over a quarter of an hour—most likely the police wireless station in Kristiansand.

The swine had pulled our legs pretty effectually. By some means or other they had now been listening to our messages for a fairly long time, and as we had kept a regular system of changing call signs and the Germans in all probability had kept track of the call-signs that Central used, they had been able to reply to our signals. That they could have been able to interpret the messages we sent was out of the question. But their object in continually putting queries and asking us to repeat groups was to have a better opportunity and more time to locate the station by D/F. They had found out the wave-lengths that Central used, and had got as near there as possible. Meanwhile, in a fury, I sent 'Heil Hitler' in clear. There was a sudden silence!

I must say that we began to feel they were getting warm again. Our connection at the police station had given us no information of any significance; it looked as if the police, too, realized the possibility of there being spies in their own ranks. We moved from those parts—this time at a more placid tempo than the last—along the road from the southern end of Stor Lake. Lasse went up to Oevrebö the very same evening. Jan and I took the last part of the equipment with us the morning after; we crossed the moor to the other side of Stor Lake and went down to the dam.

We went pretty slowly, as each of us was carrying packages weighing about 80 lbs.; we looked more like pack donkeys than anything. It can easily be understood that two Germans who came round a bend in the road rather suddenly, before we had a chance of getting out of the way, were somewhat astonished and interested. One talked quite good Norwegian. They both had fishing rods and were probably going up to Stor Lake to try their luck.

'Guten Morgen!' It was Jan who opened the conversation —for safety's sake. Had we been walking? Yes, we had—to

some extent at any rate. We told the usual timber-felling story and added a short fishing story. Were there any fair-sized fish up in Stor Lake? 'Yes,' Jan replied, 'but it all depends on what you call fish!'

The Germans evidently did not grasp the meaning of the last remark, but were very pleasant and chatty all the time, with their eyes on the large packages. After a final remark about the weather we continued downhill.

Apart from two D/F cars, which seemed to be ready for action at any moment, and one patrol on the road, all was peaceful; no one seemed to take much interest in us or our packages, and we crept once more into the hut up in Oevrebö and were happy. The main station was hard at work again, with as many as four contacts a day.

CHAPTER XXV

AN INCH OR TWO FROM THE 'ARCHIVES'

ON SUNDAY, September 17, we really had a narrow shave. As I have said before, in the last few months the controls had steadily grown more severe. The controls in themselves were usually plain sailing, so long as one had not a sack full of things which could not bear the light of day. But even if all was in order to that extent, and even if one had no parcels at all, it was not uncommon for someone to be detained for 'closer examination.'

On this account we chose Sunday by preference for the transport of 'stuff' from one place to another. People were out for walks, and most of them carried large or small parcels; one more or less would make no difference.

It was necessary that a few spare parts for the American transmitter we were now using should be fetched from a little dump we had up at Eidet. Along with these there was a quantity of clothes and some tobacco that I would have liked to get up to Oevrebö. On the way into the town there was the usual control at Mosby, but as a rule this was quite harmless. Nor should the control down the Södal road cause any difficulties, if previous experience went for anything. I now knew the men who were usually on duty there fairly well, and as a rule they waved me on without my needing to stop, whether I had a package or not. They had too often had to listen to the long string of dates, names, and all the German local commands I had worked for in the last year. Up at the crossroads, where the Sörland road comes into Kongsgaard Allé, there was not the least sign of a control.

As usual I spent the greater part of the day up at Eidet, bathed with some of the young people from the country round, and heard of the latest current rumours and facts. The Mathisen family were able to tell me about the traffic along the Sörland road, and of what kind it was, and even give me quite accurate information as to the number of vehicles in military convoys. All naturally, in the course of a general conversation, in which neither of the parties displayed open interest.

It happened on the way home. I took the road towards the town along with the stream of other cyclists who had been out after black market food up the valley. I had a rucksack, not conspicuously large, like all the others. I rode at a fair speed past Volle Lake and down the slope towards the crossroads where the Kongsgaard Allé began.

Then—I went cold for a moment—control! Not an ordinary control, but at least twelve or fifteen men wearing helmets, with tommy-guns and in full marching order. This would never do! For a moment I thought of braking, turning off the road and attempting to escape, but there was a barbed-wire fence and a long field without a scrap of cover. It was too late anyhow—only another fifteen or twenty yards. I would try to ride through without slowing down—pretend not to hear—no, there were German police soldiers a good way lower down.

'Halt! halt! Pass control! Halt, there!' A German *Obersturmführer*, brandishing a tommy-gun, nearly hurled me off as I braked as hard as I could, skidded past and did not stop till I ran into a tree ten yards lower down, after nearly knocking another soldier off his legs. The *Obersturmführer* raged—the soldier abused me roundly—a hundred times I begged for '*Verzeihung*.'

Was I trying to dodge the control? Did I not understand German? Didn't I understand what halt meant? Bad brakes—had not noticed the control till I was right into it—again a hundred times '*Verzeihung, Herr Oberleutnant!*' (It was very curious how most Germans rose in self-esteem when one added a few ranks in addressing them!)

My flow of speech was suddenly checked; three Norwegians with bicycles and large packages were standing with their hands up by the roadside; one man, also with a large package and a bicycle, was standing in the middle of the road, while two Germans were spreading out the contents of his sack. Another German was about to search him. There was certainly little chance this time—nor later, if I was arrested now.

The '*Herr Oberleutnant*' stood for a moment looking at the men who were being searched; then he turned to me. 'Passport!' There was no 'please' this time. Name, age, residence, profession, where I had been, where I was going, etc.—the usual catechism. Yes, that side of the business was certainly in order, but—'hands up' and personal search!

I grew cold—the revolver! It was in the shoulder-holster that was now stretched round my waist, so that the revolver itself lay in the top of my fork. Pockets—under my arms—round my belt and along the outside of my thighs—off with my rubber boots, and—up the inside of my trouser-leg—thorough search round the lower edge of my drawers. . . . At that moment another man with a full rucksack bore down on us, and he also seemed to have difficulty in stopping. The *Obersturmführer* rose suddenly when only a few inches from the critical point, and yelled curses at the new arrival.

I remained standing with my hands up, while the German almost exploded with rage. Then he turned to me again—he could not remember for the moment how far he had got—yes—his thoughts were written plainly in the wrinkles on his forehead. It looked as if he had finished!

Then the rucksack! A cold sweat once more began to run

down my back. It was inevitable! The man in charge of the control stood looking at the Germans who had now set to work examining the next man's luggage. Yes, it looked as if they had enough to do. I was still standing with my hands up, trying to seem uninterested despite my nervousness. The German took three long steps, grasped the bicycle from behind and lifted it up. Weight in proportion to size was evidently what interested him. He dropped the back part on to the road from eighteen inches above the ground, listening as he did so . . . no, there were no weapons there at any rate.

It was quite natural that his questioning, searching eyes should all the time be fixed on mine, but why crawl through purgatory instead of leaping through? He pressed the sack and its pockets, and then asked: 'What have you got here?' 'Apples, working clothes,' and then came the usual story about the 'forestry pupil'!

The *Obersturmführer* looked at the others again; could they take the next man? No, they were just where they were —he came back to me again, just looked me hard in the eyes for a few agitating seconds, and then came the word which almost made me burst into hysterical laughter: 'Pass along!' He continued to stare, probably to ascertain the effect on me.

I felt that I was shaking like an aspen leaf, but it cannot have been so. I let my arms fall slowly, bowed and repeated my apology, and—asked if he had a cigarette. 'Pass along!!' —he literally hissed out the words, and went on to the next man before I had so much as remounted my rolling Pegasus.

The control on the Södal road did not seem much interested to-day, when I rode past with evil forebodings, nor did the usual post at Mosby, nor a cyclist patrol I met up among the cliffs. But I breathed a little easier when I arrived at the hut that evening, and especially as all was still going well there.

The main station in Oevrebö was now working at full pressure, really too vigorously at times, considering the local conditions. There were always more controls, always more 'strange' or 'mysterious' persons reported in the district. The Germans seemed to be quite determined that illegal work should be stopped at any price, especially now when there was no guarantee that the Allies would not attempt a new invasion.

The arrest of many agents in recent times had undoubtedly had important results; the Germans were obviously beginning to get a grasp of a number of systems which were commonly used and to know the different kinds of equipment, for wireless and for other things, which agents were obliged to carry with them from place to place. As I mentioned earlier, we had been pretty well off for food all that summer, although we were restricted to rather monotonous diet while running the reserve station out on Barlindal moor. But the contacts in Oslo had to have food, as well as the stations and contacts in Sörland.

But nevertheless we got what we wanted—through our contacts up-country and a previously mentioned contact in Oslo, Preben. The last-named supplied us with 'Danish parcels,' or 'gifts from the Danish Red Cross to the sick and old.' An excellent and most valuable system, which helped not only us, but many others in a similar position.

CHAPTER XXVI

FRESH SUPPLIES

IT WAS now time to prepare for a new drop of equipment by parachute from the other side. 'Pin-point' had already been fixed for the same area as the earlier drop, namely the Eiker forest, south of Darbu railway station and north-west of Drammen.

Lasse now took over the running of the station, and Jan attended to the most general meteorological observations for the met. reports, so that this should not stop either. I myself took one of the wireless sets and two crystals for use in correspondence, arranged on a provisional basis, between 'pin-point' and London during the period in which the stuff might be dropped.

Before our friend the railway guard left the Oslo–Kristiansand line, he had initiated his successors into the work for us and the others for whom he had done services. The guards who had taken over from him were called Tveit and Ovesen, and they were to keep things going to the very end, even in the most difficult conditions. Not only were people to be 'carried,' but there was also to be a regular delivery of messenger post—and parcels. That all went well so many times in the course of that season, with controls all the time and snoopers among the passengers and at the stations, is due entirely to the splendid work of these two men.

Kristiansand railway station had long ago been put out of bounds for us, so we had to take the local up to Grovane station and get into the ordinary Sörland train there. The morning I was to go to Oslo the same thing happened as on one earlier occasion. When the train stopped at Grovane, no less than six German police soldiers and one Norwegian State policeman got off. There had been a control on the way from Kristiansand to Grovane. Tveit, who was standing on the step of the guard's van at the back of the train, nodded cautiously as I went past and got into the next carriage in front.

We usually travelled to Oslo, or the reverse, by the night train, because as a rule there was less risk of a control on this. But on this occasion I had not time to wait. As far as Kongsberg everything was normal. But we received from the stationmaster there the most unpleasant news that there was a state of emergency at Vestfossen and Mjöndal; consequently, the danger of a thorough examination was very great. No passenger was allowed to get off the train at these two stations, where German patrols had taken up their positions with machine-guns, tommy-guns and complete fighting equipment.

The train should really have stopped, but this time it went at a slow speed through both stations—by agreement between the engine-driver and the guard in charge. Passengers for those stations had to take the first train back next morning—whilst I arrived in Oslo safe and sound without any further setbacks.

In Oslo the 'head office' had been informed of the time of

the drop. All preparations had been made. Four men—the twins, Morten and Botolf—were again sent up. But because of the state of emergency, which had just been cancelled, I made a trip up to Darbu for safety's sake to investigate the conditions a little more closely. We should not be very popular if we came down with a whole drop and handed it straight over to the Germans.

Unfortunately all was not as it ought to be either up-country or along the roads down to Hakavik. There had been raids on the farms along this blind-alley road, usually so quiet and peaceful; there had been searches at the Hakavik electricity works, which had yielded as booty only a hidden Opel saloon car. But—according to the farmer at Darbu—a whole gang of the 'men in green' had gone into these parts the same day. Exactly why it was hard to say, but according to rumour it was arms the Germans were after.

Then I looked up the Mil. Org. driver. I took the train down to Vestfossen, where to all appearances everything was quiet now, and walked for half an hour up to the houses where Nyrud lived. Last time, when we had met in such a queer manner up at Store Oeksne, we had arranged that he should drive again later if it was convenient. Yes, Nyrud was at home, but—a few changes had taken place since we last saw one another.

He had ceased to work for Mastebogen; he was no longer driving along the road between the Store Oeksne dam and Vestfossen, and he was no longer driving an ordinary lorry, but a timber lorry without a deck; in short, his field of activity lay in quite other quarters than those in which we were interested. This was a setback. I have seldom met a man who racked his brains as Nyrud did to find the best solution of a problem, no matter whether the result might mean certain death to himself. On the following Sunday he would, as usual, not be working; he might perhaps be able to 'borrow' a lorry; if he could he would come up, if we could let him know that the drop had taken place before that day. If not, he thought he could get another man whom he could induce to drive, in spite of the rather risky conditions.

That was fixed up. I returned to Oslo, and our further

plans were gone through for the last time during the night. Next morning two of us went to Darbu, put up with our friend the farmer and stayed the night there. The report from Hakavik was better, but not altogether good. Early the same morning a large German lorry had driven past and taken the road to the electricity works, where the road up to Store Oeksne begins to wind up the side of the ridge. The lorry had not come back yet. We must wait till next day.

At half-past seven in the morning the lorry came along—with the confiscated Opel car in tow. So that was all! We hoped so. We went down on our bicycles and looked up another farmer, who lived close to the road and had done us services in the past. Yes, he could tell us a certain amount about the investigations that had been made; but I cannot say that it added much to our knowledge.

Instead of passing Hakavik ourselves, we turned off from the main road some way short of it. There was no need to put people's imaginations to a still severer test; when the reception committee had passed the place last spring, carrying heavy packages, on their way to meet us, rumours had at once begun to circulate. The electricity works watchman up at the Store Oeksne dam had received special orders to look out for saboteurs. A repetition of this on a larger scale would undoubtedly be unfortunate.

We slept that night on the old camping-ground near the dam, and next morning at the appointed time we opened contact with London. The watch-keeping at 'pin-point' had been postponed one day and would now be from September 27 inclusive.

Before we went into the woods this time, we had thoroughly examined the dam watchman, who lived ten minutes away from the dam itself. He was evidently O.K. He was, however, extremely astonished when we quite frankly laid our cards on the table. We told him we were waiting for a parachute drop; he would undoubtedly hear the plane when it came. We did not want any official announcement, only his support in arranging an efficient warning system.

The dam watchman was in telephonic communication

with the works down at Hakavik; there was also a telephone at the dam itself. Both telephones were on the same line; two rings for the dam, one for the watchman's dwelling. Yes, the dam watchman said, he had a very good fellow down at the works, with whom he had had various dealings before. The arrangement was quite clear. In the event of outside persons arriving immediately after the drop, the man down at the works would ring up the dam watchman. We would station one of our men at the dam watchman's, and if a telephone message came our man would hurry along to 'pin-point' and warn us. Then we could leave all the things in the hiding-places and take the road down towards Sandsvaer or the Eidfoss mills with a start of at least three-quarters of an hour.

When I think of the dam watchman now, I cannot help feeling rather sorry for him. He had not been sounded, but practically given orders. He did not have much chance of protesting. Nor did his wife make any objections, realizing that it was useless. The dam watchman threw himself into his job heart and soul, although he was obviously uncertain whether he was dealing with the right sort of people.

In the course of the evening, Ottomar and Kalle arrived, and about eleven Botolf came. He brought an unpleasant little piece of news: on the same day twelve German soldiers and three officers had come to the Hakavik electricity works and demanded quarters. They were 'timber-fellers,' it was stated, and they were to cut wood for a large German camp near Vestfossen.

Awkard—very awkward. What did it mean? Germans felling timber for themselves! I did not think I had heard of such a thing before. And why just now? For a moment my thoughts went back to the life and death chase all over Svaland moor a year before; a repetition of that was not desirable. Should we be compelled to call off the drop altogether, wait for the next period and move 'pin-point' to different country?

The possibilities were most carefully weighed, and the end of the discussion was that we continued as we had begun. The next day was spent in combing the ground round 'pin-point' to examine the possibility of 'tourists' appearing. Unfortunately there were two men living in a hut a few hundred yards from the place where we had previously been dropped. This place, therefore, could not be used. We moved down to a rather larger stretch of moss, nearer to the Oeksne and nearer to the dam, to which the stuff had to be carried anyway. At the same time it was not far from the hut where the two linesmen were living. They were inspecting the power line over to Sandsvaer.

To be on the safe side we took a little walk that way and started a chat to find out what sort of people they were. I have never seen two fellows more furious than they when I told them that we belonged to the State police and asked them if they had seen anything of some 'students' whom we knew to be in those parts. If there had not been three of us, I hardly think we should have got out of that hut with whole skins! Well, they seemed to be all right, so no further steps were necessary.

Carl Sigurd Elligers really ought not to have come on this trip. As I have said, he had damaged his knee badly, and he was still not quite fit. But Kalle was one of those fellows who would never stay at home when anything special was brewing. This time, too, it had been impossible to keep him at home. He was now to have the job of sitting at the dam watchman's in case anything unforeseen should happen.

With the carrying of all the equipment last time fresh in our memory, we had arranged this time to have a boat—the dam watchman's barge, which was supposed to be used only on duty. To cover the dam watchman we went through the form of 'stealing' the barge by breaking the lock. It was pure chance that the oars were hidden in a place where they were easy to find. On the evening of the 27th two of us walked down to the dam watchman's, as usual, to get into contact with London and find out whether anything was going to happen or not. As soon as the dam watchman appeared at the door we could both see that something was wrong. Two German N.C.O.s had been in only twenty minutes earlier. Timber-fellers! This was very queer—had one of our own people not been able to hold his tongue? But who on earth could it have been? Had the Germans full information about what was going to happen?

We must make contact. While the dam watchman was sitting on the steps outside having a smoke, a message came over the wireless: 'We are coming to-night!' Things began to move; the wireless set was securely packed and hidden in a particular spot behind the dam watchman's house. Kalle stayed there, whilst I went up to the dam, took the boat and rowed three-quarters of the way up to the north-west end of Store Oeksne. Thence it was only a quarter of an hour's walk to the camp at 'pin-point.'

Everything was packed up; only the tent remained so that we might have something to creep into while we waited. Screened lights were got ready, and from 11.15 p.m. we kept watch.

It was brilliant weather, starry and cold with a light northerly breeze. The moon was just about to creep up over the ridges to eastward; all was as though specially ordered for a successful operation. Time passed. Now and again we sprang up, hearing the noise of aircraft. But it was only a false alarm; the noise came from far away to the south—a big raid somewhere or other. We sank back into the heather, where we lay behind a big stone the better to keep ourselves warm.

It was 12.40 a.m. Then came the noise of a plane again, this time from the south-west, and soon the silhouette of a Halifax appeared, faint against the starry sky. It drew nearer—there was no doubt it was ours. Light! I sent the call-sign, a series of D's. The plane passed over 'pin-point,' swung farther north and came in at a lower height straight towards the moss where we stood ready.

Then suddenly, several hundred yards before it got right over us, it swung out to the side and dropped sharply to a lower height. I stopped flashing. The aircraft passed—and seven parachutes opened up, one close after the other, silhouetted against the full moon!

Here was trouble—at least a mile and a quarter from where we stood. What in all the world had happened? We stood staring hard at the parachutes so as not to lose the direction, till they disappeared into the darkness and among the trees. Then we started running.

We searched for an hour in the depths of the fir-woods before we found all the containers: every single parachute was entangled in the tree-tops. It was after five in the morning before everything was more or less unpacked. The parachute harness was distributed in various hiding-places; some of the containers were sunk in a small pond, while others were covered up where they lay. However bad the drop may have been, it had one advantage. The way down to the Oeksne, where the boat lay ready, was shortened by about a mile and a quarter, so that there would be only five hundred yards of carrying when we began the transport. But all the same—why had the pilot so suddenly altered course but dropped the containers nevertheless?

I did not learn this until months afterwards, when I met the pilot in a London club. As he was coming in for the drop, he had suddenly seen a light turned on about a mile and a quarter beyond 'pin-point.' He assumed that unauthorized persons were there, and thought it best that these should not see too much of the whole performance, although he fully realized that the whole plan might be a failure. A slightly stronger wind could have sent the whole cargo down into the Oeksne. The light he had seen could not have come from any place but the hut where the two linesmen were staying.

The others crept into their bags and I took the first watch. It had become light, the sky had clouded over a good deal, and it looked as if we should have rain. Well, there could be nothing better. For the present all was quiet, and we could hardly expect anything before the day was well advanced. It would take the Germans a fairly long time to come up from Hakavik, and it would be very difficult to find out approximately where the drop had been, if anyone had suspected it. All we could do was to wait and see what happened, and hope that we should not have a visit from Kalle before the time fixed.

The whole day passed without anything abnormal happening. Kalle came up at 6 p.m. as arranged, and could only report that all was well. We began to move the containers, one after another, down to the place where the boat lay well camouflaged with boughs. About eight in the evening we had a visit from a Storch, but it disappeared northward after fussing about a little in the country above the Eiker.

On Saturday the 30th everything was still quiet. Botolf was now sent to Oslo to arrange matters in the town and get everything ready for the reception of the stuff. Ottomar was sent down to Darbu for cardboard boxes which were to be dispatched from Oslo in the meantime. At the same time he would look in on Nyrud and find out whether he could drive as agreed. Ottomar came back in the course of the afternoon and brought the good news that all was quiet in the valley and that Nyrud had 'arranged' to get another lorry and would be at the dam as agreed at twelve o'clock on Sunday, i.e. next day.

At 21.30 three men went on board the fully loaded barge. We only just kept afloat, although the barge was unusually large and solid. It was pitch dark as, with a fresh breeze behind us, we rowed the whole of the stuff to the dam in three-quarters of an hour. Not a sound was to be heard apart from the sighing of the wind and the splashing of the water. A light rain was falling. One after another the containers were moved into the boat-house, the contents repacked in cardboard boxes and the containers taken out in the barge and sunk in the Oeksne. We went on till midnight, packed and closed the boxes and labelled them WITH CARE—GLASS! Tired and exhausted we lay down in the sawdust under the floor of the saw-mills; if anyone came, the dam watchman had promised to let us know as soon as he received a warning from below by telephone. It was cold; the thermometer showed $-4°$ F.

At 5 a.m. we were at it again, packing boxes. We had posted a sentry now to be on the safe side. All was still quiet, and remained so till ten minutes to eleven, when there was a sudden excitement; the dam watchman came puffing and blowing up on his bicycle and told us that a German had rung up from the works and asked if he had seen anything of two soldiers who had disappeared while at work and were presumed to have deserted.

The dam watchman was strongly of the opinion that the Germans would come up to look for the 'deserters.' Our view was that the reason for their ringing up was quite a different one, and that the story about the 'deserters' was only a pretext. The dam watchman was in no doubt that things were all wrong; he vanished downhill on his bicycle like greased lightning the same way he had come, after having received precise instructions how to act in the event of the Germans arriving.

Practically everything was now repacked in cardboard boxes, ten large and six smaller ones, plus three paper bags containing parachutes. We worked till the sweat streamed down us to remove all outward traces. Not more than five minutes after the dam watchman had vanished downhill the sentry reported a horse and cart on the road to the dam. More people were coming. The doors of the boat-house were shut in an instant; Ottomar and Kalle disappeared across the dam and up the slope on the other side; I myself remained sitting on the planks down by the saw-mills. It was one of the peasants from the valley; he was coming up to fetch a quantity of fir planks to build a boat with.

To be on the safe side I helped the man to load up the planks, and hoped that this might make things go a bit quicker. But the fellow seemed to have plenty of time to spare! I could not really drive him away either, or tell him that we had the contents of a parachute drop lying in the shed waiting to be collected at twelve o'clock. He talked and talked, made me smoke a pipe of home-made tobacco, held forth about conditions here and there. At last—at five minutes to twelve—he turned his horse and set off. But the load was too heavy; the horse could not pull it up the short slope above the dam. The man had to unload half of it, take the cart over the crucial point, and then carry one plank at a time up to where it now stood.

It can easily be understood that he was much astonished at the energetic help I gave him, and perhaps still more astonished at the unfriendly tone I had assumed. He did not tumble to anything even when I practically told him to clear off!

Morten was now sent down; it was better that we were not too many if anything should happen, and we were, moreover, interested in getting Morten to Oslo as quickly as possible. He was to arrange for the transport by lorry of all the stuff that had been sent to Skarpsno and Sköyen railway stations. . . . Ottomar, Kalle and I sat waiting up on the hillside.

Not many minutes had passed after the peasant's departure when the sound of a car on its way up the rocky ascent to the dam reached us where we sat holding our Sten guns. Now the great question was: were the Germans coming to look for 'deserters,' or was it Nyrud?

An ordinary Norwegian motor lorry with a generator came in sight at the bend; it must be Odvar. As a precaution Ottomar and Kalle remained sitting where they were, while I sauntered down, only to be able to give the signal a moment later. It was Odvar. And now we had something to worry about: on the road from Vestfossen to Hakavik he had driven past not less than two closed German cars, and on the road into the works he had seen several 'greens' standing talking together. There was no doubt that something was happening. Should we take the chance? Was Nyrud willing to drive—to have a try?

As usual, the fellow would not say no, if only he could have something to shoot with. The cardboard boxes were hoisted on to the deck of the lorry in a few minutes; all the time we were waiting to hear the telephone at the dam ring twice, as we had agreed. But nothing happened—for the time being.

Everything was ready; Ottomar and Kalle took their sacks and went off across the dam and up the ridge on the other side. The plan was that they should go by the 'back way' down to the village, where they had hidden their bicycles, and then cycle to Drammen and take the train from there. There were thus only two of us in the lorry: Odvar Nyrud and I. In case things went wrong and I had not reached Oslo the same evening, everyone was to go into hiding and wait upon events.

We started, with our revolvers on our knees. Scarcely fifty yards from where we had started Nyrud stopped abruptly, and at the same time we both jumped in our seats: a motor-cycle and side-car, with two German police soldiers and an officer, swung over the brow of the hill and braked sharply.

'Shoot!' whispered Nyrud. 'Let's get them!'

'No, hold on for a moment—don't shoot till I tell you! There are sure to be more of the same sort farther down!'

The officer in the side-car had risen with one hand on his revolver holster and the other in the air. 'Halt!'

I opened the door and got half-way out on to the step; with one hand I kept a tight hold of the revolver, which was hidden by the front of the lorry. The German on the pillion had a tommy-gun and had only to pull the trigger in the event of protest from our side.

'Back a little, so as to get them alongside us!'

Nyrud backed with one hand on the wheel; he had his revolver in the other. The word bloodthirsty does not describe the expression of his face.

'Come up alongside!' I called to the Germans, beckoning to them. They came—quite slowly, with the officer still standing up in the side-car.

'Halt, and stop your engine!' He repeated his order in German, a language we naturally did not understand on this occasion.

'Shall I step on the gas?' from Nyrud again. I had no time to answer; he was leaning out towards the Germans, who had now stopped beside us, while the officer regarded with interest the large covered pile of cardboard boxes on the deck of the lorry.

'Stop the engine!'

'Wait till they've stopped their own engine!' I whispered to Odvar. He waited. At the same moment the officer got out of the side-car, while the driver of the motor-cycle closed his throttle and turned off the ignition.

'Now!' Odvar had long before changed over from generator to petrol, and he 'stepped on the gas' in the fullest sense of the word! What actually happened I still find it hard to understand, but the fact is that we were round the bend

before the first shot was fired. We both sat automatically huddled up in the driver's seat and expected a charge from behind every moment. But it did not come!

How we drove! Not for nothing had Nyrud driven along this stretch of the narrow stony forest road to Hakavik for several years with heavy loads of timber and planks; he knew every bend and every big stone. He still kept a tight hold of his revolver. We slid round one bend after another at break-neck speed; every moment I expected a limb of a fir-tree in the driver's cabin.

I myself sat looking ahead and behind alternately. Then, as we slid round a rather sharp bend and bumped over a large stone at the same time, one of the paper bags tumbled off the deck. Was it one of the parachute bags?

'Go on down and try to push through!' I shouted to Odvar. 'If it gets too hot, you'll have to stop and get into the woods; I'll clear the bag out of the way and at any rate try to hold the Germans up for a few minutes, so as to give you a longer start. We must warn Ottomar and Kalle!'

Odvar slowed down a little to let me jump off. In a few seconds the lorry had disappeared round the next bend; I ran back and cleared the paper bag out of the way, scrambled up the slope at the side of the road and lay down. Not a sound was to be heard. What had happened to the Germans —had they had a breakdown? Or had they not pursued us because they knew that there were many more Germans farther down, ready to capture the lorry?

I lay waiting for a quarter of an hour. All was still quiet. But Ottomar and Kalle were on their way down with various things in their sacks which would be fatal if they came up against a control. I went down across the valley and up on the other side as fast as I could; if I could reach the path where it approached the main road before the boys got so far the situation would be saved.

I arrived quite breathless, lay down behind a fir and waited. Ten minutes passed, and I cautiously drew back under cover; someone was coming from above. It was Ottomar and Kalle, whistling and singing, without a notion of what had happened in the meantime. The sacks were cleared of all that had to do with the job, and they went on down to carry out the original plan.

I myself took the road back to the dam, first and foremost to fetch my sack, which was still lying up there with all the most important papers, well hidden under the root of a tree on the west side of the dam, where we had lately been.

At the dam all was comparatively quiet; there was not a sign of the motor-cycle. Perhaps it was lying somewhere lower down along the forest track after having tried to keep pace with Nyrud. I took my sack and set off downhill, took with me all the stuff which had been removed from Ottomar's and Kalle's sacks, and went on down to the place where the bicycle lay hidden.

For an hour I remained lying behind a tree with a good view over the road. Five German cars had passed. Yes, there was something happening somewhere! But what was it? It was quite unnecessary to run the risk of a control with that sack; so without luggage, and without a thing which had any connection with illegal work, I took the bicycle and went off towards Darbu. Three German cars passed, but not one seemed to be interested. They were all going at high speed.

It could only be Nyrud who had caused all this traffic; in any case it was at the moment impossible to find any other solution. I learned something else, however, from a contact along the road. There was then a 'celebrity' in the Norwegian criminal world who was nicknamed 'Rottenikken,' and the whole thing was his fault from beginning to end. He had murdered the sheriff's officer at Sem, kidnapped his wife, plundered a number of houses and taken to the woods.

The last traces of him were in the neighbourhood of the Hakavik works, and the general opinion was that he had taken the road up towards the Oeksne and the country behind it. Thirty Norwegian State police and more than twenty Germans had gone in to search for him. And—the farmer was also able to tell me that a motor lorry belonging to a firm at Vestfossen had come at breakneck speed down the road from the Oeksne dam, and two men in the driver's seat had fired at random when German policemen had tried to stop the lorry, both by the dam watchman's cabin and down at the crossroads where the forest road from above runs into the main road to Darbu and Vestfossen.

After that the driver had driven right through a tree with which the Germans had tried to block the road, had run over at least three Germans and shot one, got through and continued along the road towards Vestfossen. The farmer was able to tell me that he himself had stood and watched the lorry rush past with two German cars just behind it, and how the Germans were firing as hard as they could. What had happened afterwards he did not know; but it was assumed that 'Rottenikken' had had some accomplice, or that he had compelled the driver to drive him.

I saw from the farmer's manner of speech, and his excitement, that this story was certainly exaggerated; but probably most of it was true. What had happened later?

The road became quieter; just a man or two walked quickly past. I went on to the crossroads, where one road goes to Darbu and one to Vestfossen, and along the same road back to the spot where I had hidden the package. Not a car was to be seen on the way back. At about eight I chanced it, and strange to say my walk up to Darbu met with no interruptions. Every time a car or motor-cycle came along I laid my bicycle down in the ditch and skipped into the woods.

Darbu railway station—the platform! I nearly fell flat when I saw all the cardboard boxes stacked up along the wall of the luggage room with a large tarpaulin over them! So Nyrud had brought it off! Or—had the Germans themselves placed them there after capturing Nyrud, and were just waiting for the person who would come to dispatch them? I retreated cautiously into the waiting-room, with a feeling all the time that fifty pairs of eyes were following every movement. But no, all was quiet; the booking clerk, who was one of our people, was able to tell me that the lorry had brought it off by 'taking a few short cuts' over a field or two and along some farm tracks, and at last getting back to the main road. Marvellous!

All the cardboard boxes were now to be sent into Oslo, in pairs, as luggage, each pair by different trains on the first five days. The plan was altered, however, as a large quantity of dynamite and explosives had been stolen at Hönefoss. There was a state of emergency there, and a number of railway stations, as well as the express goods office in Oslo, were being systematically searched. All our goods were sent by three different trains as luggage to Sköyen, where it was fetched by lorry and driven to 8 Nils Juelsgate for distribution!

What had happened to Odvar Nyrud? We did not care to make any direct inquiries at his home, for fear of walking straight into the hands of the Gestapo. But it was evident that the affair must result in complications for Nyrud; the lorry he had used had the firm's name on its side; it would be the easiest thing in the world to find out who had driven it. But Odvar had vanished; no one knew where he had gone. We assumed that he had made his way to a training camp which Mil. Org. had somewhere up-country. One might search for a long time without finding a driver like him.

CHAPTER XXVII

SECRET WEAPONS

For me it was now back to Kristiansand, after everything had been fixed up in Oslo. It was now the middle of October. The station in Oevrebö had been going under full steam while I had been away, although the conditions had become quite considerably worse. Jan and Lasse had actually thought of closing the station altogether for a week, in the hope that the control of the roads and the activity in the country round the station might be relaxed a little. But in the meantime great things had happened.

A little scrap of tissue paper had come by special messenger from our German friends; the ship *Moltkefels* had arrived from Germany with a cargo of curious large cases. They thought this was a new secret weapon. The reason for this supposition was that when the *Moltkefels* was reported off Oddernes, about to enter the harbour, the air raid sirens were sounded in Kristiansand. All who were on the quays were made to go down into the shelters; even the German soldiers were chased down. But here the authorities made a very bad slip; they employed a few chosen members of the Norwegian harbour police to drive the Germans away, and one of those who showed the greatest zeal in performing this duty was our own highly efficient principal contact!

When all unauthorized persons had been removed to a distance, he was standing quite near the spot where the *Moltkefels* had come alongside; our two German friends were the first to go on board to fetch the ship's papers for the *Hafenkapitän*. But this time the ordinary routine was not followed; they were not allowed to break the seal, and there were obviously good reasons for this.

Great things were brewing. Our people worked day and night to get more detailed information. But the Germans had taken precautions, and the work was very difficult. The slightest mistake now, and we should suffer for it. Our German connections were enjoined to show the greatest caution. Detail after detail came to light, and at last the whole thing could be pieced together with reasonable certainty.

The Germans learnt through the crew of the *Moltkefels* that the ship had for some time been lying in a port in France as a quarters ship, and at the same time had been concerned in a plan for rapid evacuation. Without any warning the whole crew had been changed, the officers as well, and one night orders came to sail for a destination in Germany. She lay there for ten days loading the 'new secret weapon' under very close guard. Thence she had come to Kristiansand. The Germans' confidant on board was also able to tell them that the *Moltkefels* was to make another voyage to fetch a new cargo.

The crew of the ship did not know what the mysterious cases contained. There was something like a tacit competition as to who had found out most. We obtained some details—enough to be able to establish that the cases contained a new rocket weapon, the weapon which was later called V3. Obviously experiments were to be carried out in Norway. But from what place?

The cases were taken up to Gimlemoen on specially constructed trailers. A contact hastily established in that region, who had been working for the Germans for some time past, was able to tell us that the very next night the cases were to be taken to an unknown place along the road eastwards to Arendal.

The same evening I cycled down the Södal road to go up to Eidet café. If the convoy was taking that road, perhaps it would be possible to follow it and find out where it was going. But the Germans had evidently taken precautions. In my bicycle bag I had a rectifier and a few other wireless parts, as I had thought of using a transmitter we had lying under the floor of one of the huts at Eidet. The transmitter, however, lacked rectifier and wire, which we had been obliged to use earlier at the main station.

Besides these things, I had with me the usual quantity of food and clothes. I took it as a matter of course that there would be a control down on the Södal road; it was only to be hoped that it would be as slack as usual. It was drizzling, and I went at a good pace round the last bend before the control. But—this was different from what I had expected. Instead of two men there were four; instead of ordinary equipment they had tommy-guns and hand-grenades in their belts. Nor were they the men who were usually on that control.

I braked automatically, measuring the distance down to the river. Not a chance! 'Halt!' and then the usual rigmarole over my passport. But not the usual politeness; it would not do for me to stand with one leg on each side of the bar and the bicycle under me; no, I must get off altogether. Then, while one man checked the various items on the passport, and another stood with a tommy-gun insolently pointed at me, the other two walked slowly round the bicycle.

I was in a cold sweat. It was the outer covers they were interested in; one was of English manufacture, the other French—both had come with the last drop from England! I glanced down at the front wheel; it was covered with dirt after being wheeled through the slush out of the hut up in Oevrebö. One of the Germans bent down and was evidently trying to read the maker's name. The name 'Michelin' had a good coating of dirt on it, and it looked as if he was afraid of getting the dirt on his hands, as he took a piece of stick and tried to scrape some of the dirt off. *'In Ordnung!'* he then said curtly.

But what had I got in my bicycle bag? The same business with some additions. The fellow who seemed to be in charge of the control went over to the bicycle bag and squeezed it. 'Please remember the eggs!' I begged him as prettily as I could. 'If you don't believe me, I'll lay out everything on the road—but just spare the eggs!'

The Germans did not say a word, but only nodded; and I began to unfasten the straps which held down the lid. It went all right with one; but the other had got caught in some way. The Germans followed my movements with interest. I had difficulty in standing still; I tried in vain to find a way out.

'Yes, that'll do!' The man in charge turned his back and sat down on a roadside stone. 'Go on!' I took it quietly, tried to seem indifferent, shut the bicycle bag again, took out a ragged handkerchief and wiped my nose before getting on to my bicycle and giving them a 'thanks' and an *'Auf Wiedersehen!'*

I had gone ten yards when the man in charge called after me 'Come here!' I turned cold again; talk about a cat-and-mouse game! This was a little too much for a normal human being. I stopped and turned round. One of the Germans was standing with his tommy-gun pointed at me — most unpleasant. I wheeled the bicycle back. It was the outer covers again. 'But I've been examined!' The German who seemed to be afraid of getting his fingers dirty said a word or two to his superior. Yes, it was all right, I could go on!

For safety's sake I left everything I had with me in the cellar of a friend on the Lund side, took the road into the town and got hold of one of the other boys. He took his own bicycle and rode up Kongsgaard Allé to Volle Lake and back to see that there was no control on that stretch of road. No, it was all right there. But if I was to get to Eidet Café before it grew dark I should have to hurry. Only the day before the Germans had issued a warning through the newspapers that anyone cycling after dark without a light would be shot. Unfortunately I had no light.

Back for the bicycle and my belongings and on up the Kongsgaard Allé-Volle Lake-Blege and down the hill towards Eidet. It was dark already. As I swung in from the road across the yard and up to the back of the café, I noticed that a number of people were standing in front. But it was quite common for people to collect there of an evening, and I attached no great importance to it.

As usual when I had dangerous things in the bag, I took it off the bicycle first. But I had only just got the bag off and stood the machine up against the rocks behind the café, when two Germans came drifting round the corner of the house. Was I trying to escape the control? I just stood gaping at them; control? I had not seen any control—it was dark, and moreover I rented a room at the café, lived there! Passport—thank you! Yes, that was all right, but had I any luggage? No, of course not. . . . A very delicate situation; the passport I was using at the time was made out in the name of 'Claussen, Olav, commercial traveller,' while the people at the café knew me only by the name of 'Oeyvind Fredriksen.' Complications could easily arise.

I stood for a while chatting with the men on the control. They had tried to 'take' the room I had; but the proprietor, who saw red whenever a German showed himself, refused. . . . 'Now you can sleep well,' said the man in charge, when I bade him goodnight. 'We shall keep a good watch!' he added.

The boys from the neighbourhood had repeatedly called me Oeyvind; but the German had certainly long forgotten what was on the passport. Nor when, somewhat later, he burst into the Mathisens' sitting-room, where we were sitting talking, and 'Oeyvind' was said several times, did this have any noticeable effect on him.

The convoy came at half-past three in the morning. I was wakened by the racket long before it reached the bridge. My room looked on to the road: a stall ten yards from the stage!

First came a string of motor-cycles with side-cars, three police soldiers fully equipped in each. Before the transport reached the bridge, they had looked underneath it with lights. Then there was a short conference with the four guards who were permanently stationed outside the café. Three large tank wagons came first, after them motor lorries of the largest type the Germans had, with the specially built trailers and the mysterious cases.

It was not difficult to see, despite the darkness; the cases on the trailers were furthermore lit by the lights of the lorry behind, so that all the cases except the last were fully visible. One thing could be established at any rate: they were not one-man submarines, as had at first been supposed. The dimensions of the cases showed that plainly.

All was quiet again. To try to shadow the convoy would be hopeless; the guards outside would become suspicious at once if a man set out northward at this time in the morning. One could only hope that the contacts up in Tveit would be wakeful enough.

There was a control on the Lund bridge next day, when I had meant to have a run into the town first and then up to Oevrebö. The control was of the usual kind and caused no difficulties. I reached the hut in the course of the evening. Here, too, things were lively, rather more so than usual. That day the station had had its closest shave hitherto. In the middle of contact a patrol of seven Germans had passed two hundred yards away. Jan and Lasse were fully aware that the moor was full of these green-clad devils; reports from our connections in the neighbourhood had come in steadily. There began to be an atmosphere of panic in the district; farm after farm was searched and arrests made. The traffic being carried on by the station was extremely important, and it could not stop at that moment.

But things grew worse and worse; the roads more and more closely watched. The messengers from the town were regularly shadowed and had great difficulty in shaking off their pursuers. It was evident that the Germans' D/F had brought them closer, and that they had a fairly good idea where the station must be. Also, the season for elk-hunting had arrived; and even if the regulations were not very strictly obeyed by all those who had no shooting licences, it was only the Nazis who could indulge in it openly and unhindered—and they caused us a good deal of worry.

A fresh transport of V3 was reported from Gimlemoen; again I was to make an expedition up through familiar country to find out, if possible, where the transport was going. It meant a trip right up to Birkenes, and—one I did not want to make on a bicycle again. Six controls and four personal searches are a little too much for an ordinary man in one day. The air pistol was the only 'dangerous' thing I had on me, and nobody found it where it lay along my belt.

The information I got was relatively small; the only thing that could be established was that the convoys had stopped for a day north of Kjevik and gone on the next night along the road to Arendal.

It was evident that the Germans had their eyes fixed on Oevrebö and were already fairly sure of their ground. We received a nice little piece of news one day by one of the regular messengers: 'A transmitter with the call-signs AKY, RFC, JDT, FPE has been located by D/F. Action is expected in the next few days!'

This information came from our German connections. Next day we got some more; our German friends had been called in and interrogated, along with practically all the employees of the *Hafenkapitän's* office. They were quite clearly suspected—and really with justification. Seven ships had gone to the bottom during the last month, including the tanker *Inger Johanne* just outside the entrance to Kristiansand. Things had gone so far that we sent out in the afternoon advance reports of fixed times of sailing; and a few hours later, when there was a south wind, the sound of dull reports came from the sea right up to Oevrebö.

Even the convoy's secret code signal had occasionally become known, so that England could call the convoy up and give it instructions—with the result that the Germans altered the code signal as soon as the ships had left harbour. But they made things hot for us in return. Thirty-seven Germans had thoroughly combed the ground north of the station, and had turned a number of farms upside down. A detachment of mountain troops had begun regularly to patrol the high rocky ground running up from Mosby and the country round; they had demanded the lease of one or two rooms at Homsteane school. Two officers and two N.C.O.s, on horseback, had been to the school to arrange this. They would not say what they were going to use these two rooms for; we formed our own opinion from everything else that was going on.

The only road which now appeared to be open from Oevrebö into Kristiansand was the main road. I say 'appeared to be' because this road was in reality the most dangerous. The police had begun to use two closed vans; outside they looked like ordinary commercial vans. One was a baker's van, the other belonged to a meat and fish dealer in the town. They shadowed all suspicious persons with these vans, and carried out an examination if the man had luggage of any size. . . . The road ran through the police camp at Stai, and there they were continually on the watch.

The Germans had calculated on our keeping note of the places where there were controls. They thought, therefore, that we should keep away from these and use the only road which was now 'free.' Unfortunately—the whole plan was sent to us in writing from our contact in the police camp, so the Germans made a bad miscalculation. On the few occasions when we now went to the town, we still used the Södal road, or went by road over the Brennaas. On both there were controls—the one as slack as the other.

But we had no reason for feeling ourselves on top. Every day in this last period things were on the verge of going wrong, and the whole thing was more than anything a gigantic game of chance, in which we staked all our pieces at once.

CHAPTER XXVIII

NOW *WE* GO TO ENGLAND

ONE day the cup was to run over. An urgent message came saying that the Germans had begun to set up a permanent D/F station inside the German camp close by. That was enough! During the last week we had not been able to obtain reports from our German friends; the investigations down in the port were doubtless being steadily intensified. In view of the conditions under which the station was now working, as well as the season which had begun with a good deal of bad weather which hindered air operations, it was decided to close the station and our activities in Sörland altogether. As the situation in Europe had developed, it could only be a question of how long the Germans would manage to hold out. With regard to Norway the question whether there would be fighting or not was naturally still unanswered.

Lasse was the first to go. He paid a lightning visit to the town, where he was able to meet his family at the house of some acquaintances. It was a big risk to take; but it went off all right in spite of controls both on the way in and on the way back. Then he was off to Oslo.

Jan and I remained a few days to pack. Some things were put into watertight tins and hidden in the woods round about; the essential part of the equipment was packed in cardboard boxes and got ready for despatch to Oslo by train. Gunnar Upsahl undertook to arrange for them to be sent off, and he did not fail us.

Jan took with him the whole of the meteorological equipment and a quantity of weapons. He nearly fell into the hands of a German patrol down among the rocks and also at Mosby station. He took the local to Grovane and went from there to Oslo by the Sörland railway in the company of our friend Ovesen. All went well.

I myself had to go into Kristiansand and arrange matters

with the fellows there, in case anything should happen after we had left. Our German friends were the greatest problem. They were now quite determined to steal the police boat and go across to England—the old plan which we had to some extent headed off. The plan was now if possible more crack-brained than before. In the first place the weather would make such a voyage impossible in a half-decked craft which was not built for a rough sea. Secondly, they would most certainly never get out of the harbour without being caught, as they had no idea of seamanship and knew nothing about boats of that type.

To us there was a far more important reason why they should not leave their post now. We reckoned on a continued contact between Claus and these two, based on a system of messengers eastward into Sweden. It was not impossible that we might later be obliged to return to the same district if the war, contrary to expectation, should drag on for a long time. Further, if these two cleared out now Claus would be compelled to go into hiding, as it was already fairly well known that the three had been on good terms. This would mean a most serious break in the whole system down in Kristiansand. If Claus did not clear out he would undoubtedly be arrested if the two Germans disappeared. If the Germans were arrested there would still be a possibility of keeping Claus as a liaison.

After some negotiations the Germans remained in their jobs and the contemplated voyage across the North Sea was indefinitely postponed. Claus too continued in his job. All this ought to have gone excellently, if other things had not cropped up immediately.

Back to Mosby, where the sack with all the most important stuff and the suitcase containing the American wireless transmitter had been placed in the cloak-room. On by the local to Grovane, where I jumped on to the ordinary night train to Oslo. Tveit was acting as guard. We came to Kongsberg, where we learned that there was a state of emergency at Hokksund. Nobody knew exactly what the reason was. Tveit made his own arrangements for the sack, while I took the suitcase containing the American transmitter and sat down in the corridor of a third-class carriage. The train was overcrowded as usual. In the corridor I had entered one flap-seat was missing, and here I stood the suit-case with the American transmitter on one end, laid my raincoat over it and sat on the top of it all.

'Hokksund!' The train ran slowly into the station; Germans everywhere, ordinary soldiers and police soldiers. No passengers might get out; the guard himself was not allowed to enter the station buildings. There was a rapid search of each carriage; samples were taken from people's luggage; generally speaking it looked as if the Germans were more interested in the appearance of the luggage which lay around on the different racks than in the people themselves.

Of course passports and tickets were examined, but as far as I could see no interest was taken in travel permits. To me, sitting on top of the American wireless transmitter, the situation seemed rather nerve-racking; but nobody was interested in the 'flap-seat' I was sitting on, only in my pass-port, which was in perfect order. That was all—for the time being—and the train was given permission to proceed.

In Oslo things were in pretty good order, at any rate as far as we were concerned. A number of arrests and raids had set people's imaginations working, and one could never tell for a moment what were facts and what were canards. People of all classes were in hiding, waiting for a chance of getting over into Sweden; the export organizations were working at high pressure—that is, those that were still intact. The atmosphere was far from pleasant.

In the course of a week all the stuff arrived from Mosby; Gunnar did an excellent job as usual. But the transport from the station to which the stuff was addressed was no longer quite a simple matter; once more the women did good service. The stuff was repacked, arms separately, wireless parts and transmitters separately, clothes and other things in a simpler way.

Again we played hide and seek through the streets of Oslo to get the things deposited in the various dumps outside the town. At Muren in Baerum, Larsen and his wife were again willing to receive anything of any kind, despite a recent raid on their farm. The Germans had turned everything upside down in the farmhouse and in the barn; little did their leader guess, when he stood on the top of a heap of bricks outside the police hut that under the bricks lay a whole load of things that might not see the light!

Kaare and Ingeborg Larsen did not work for us only. At regular intervals prisoners from Grini on outside work came in with their guards and got as much food, tobacco and other things as they wanted. Down at Bekkestua there was a Nazi with the same name, Kaare Larsen, and to be on the safe side N.S. sent pamphlets to them both! In this way Kaare and Ingeborg were among our best contacts outside Oslo.

We pushed ahead with the work in Oslo for a good fortnight, till everything was settled. Lasse was sent over into Sweden and arrived after a fairly exhausting journey. The conditions along the frontier were no longer so good; a fair amount of snow had fallen, and the guides on the different routes felt less comfortable on account of the tracks, which told their own story.

Jan and I were to go together. We had rather a tough journey. After a week we reached a place three hours from the actual frontier. The party consisted of four men, not counting the guide. But another party had started an hour earlier on the same route. It had come up against German patrols; two men had been shot, and the two others had been pursued a long way into Swedish territory.

The guide who met us and reported this refused to make the last part of the journey; it was hopeless to try to get through, as the Germans had set up machine-gun posts every hundred yards between the two lakes where we were to cross. Two hours from our goal, and we had to turn back! It was a bitter moment; but it was obvious that the guide knew what he was talking about. Back we went the same way, right back to Skarnes on the other side of the Glomma.

There were controls and guard-posts everywhere, and the motor drive from the bridge at Skarnes down to Eidsvoll will be forgotten by none who took part in it.

We set off again, and at last we were in Sweden—after having covered over a hundred miles in deep snow in four days, walking openly through Austmarka by night and day on a sparkling, crackling crust of snow—to cross at last that street cut through the countryside which marks the frontier.

The nightmare was over at last; at last one would be able to go about as one's real self, not skulk about like a gipsy or a hunted beast with no 'fixed abode.' Certainly I should still have one nut to crack in the shape of the detective-inspector in the Swedish magistrate's office, who declared that he had seen me once before under another name; but that side of the matter was pretty quickly cleared up. It must have been a cousin of mine who was incredibly like me and had been taken for my twin brother from childhood. The name was the same anyhow, and the other data agreed with what I was able to tell him, so inquiries by telephone of the police in Gothenburg produced nothing which contradicted my statements. Whether the detective-inspector was satisfied with the result is another matter. He was clapped into jail himself three weeks later, charged with espionage on behalf of a foreign Power!

We stayed in Stockholm for three weeks. Reports were to be written and a lot of work done in connection with future action at home. Lasse, Jan and I often sat studying developments at home since we had left Oslo. Messages streamed into the office in Stockholm which told us that conditions were becoming more and more difficult. At Stavanger one of our best agents had been arrested along with a number of his contacts.

They came at the same time—two telegrams, one from the Swedish Legation in Oslo and one from one of our contacts in the same place: 'Carl Sigurd Elligers shot in raid at 8 Nils Juelsgate 23rd. Ottomar Claus Otto arrested same place. Leif arrested Kristiansand.'

So it had happened. One of my best comrades, a friend from the days when we could hardly walk, from the life in forest and field as Scouts, from the years during the war, in which he had worked untiringly, better than most, for the Norwegian cause, for the land he so deeply loved. Once more, it was the best who made the sacrifice.

What had happened? Months were to pass before we

heard the details. Connections we had had in 1943, and had been compelled to break with in 1944, had continued to work for another organization. I do not want to go into details here; but it was the same old story of a file which the possessor was compelled to betray after torture. There was a man who at times had got passport photographs for us, and for some reason or other had decided to keep a copy for himself. He had also had communication by messenger with the Elligers twins in Oslo. In the file, which was now found by the Gestapo, was a piece of paper, and on it: 'O. C. Eilligers, 8 Nils Juelsgate, Oslo.' He had left the file in charge of another man; he himself got clear away.

From Stockholm we went on by air to London; Jan and I were still together. In London our ways parted; Jan met his fiancée, whom he had not seen for more than five years; they were married within a fortnight, and I had the honour of being best man three hours before I passed on to Canada.

Lasse came over a week later, only to acquire fresh knowledge in the branch in which he had now begun. Two months later he was dropped into Norway, and again did splendid work there till the liberation came. . . .

On May 8, 1945, the peace bells rang; for most it was a message of joy, for some of sorrow—they had lost. None of us will ever forget that day. We had won! Six long years of privation and misery were ended.

A short time afterwards I flew in over Norwegian mountains and along the Norwegian coast, bathed in summer sunshine. There lay the land we had fought for, free and lovelier than ever before; the land for which Norwegians throughout the centuries had sacrificed everything—it was again our own. That was our victory—but it was dearly bought.

We came together again—Rolf, Hjelm, Jan, Ottomar, Lasse and all the others who had given so much; connections, too, who had been sent to Germany or been held in Norwegian prisons, connections who had kept going all through those years. Only one of us was missing: Carl Sigurd Elligers, one of the thousands who had sacrificed all.

